China's Troubled Waters

How are China's ongoing sovereignty disputes in the East and South China Seas likely to evolve? Are relations across the Taiwan Strait poised to enter a new period of relaxation or tension? How are economic interdependence, domestic public opinion, and the deterrence role played by the US likely to affect China's relations with its counterparts in these disputes? Although territorial disputes have been the leading cause for interstate wars in the past, China has settled most of its land borders with its neighbors. Its maritime boundaries, however, have remained contentious. This book examines China's conduct in these maritime disputes in order to analyze Beijing's foreign policy intentions in general. Rather than studying Chinese motives in isolation, Steve Chan uses recent theoretical and empirical insights from international relations research to analyze China's management of its maritime disputes.

Steve Chan is College Professor of Distinction at the University of Colorado, Boulder. His most recent publications include *Enduring Rivalries in the Asia-Pacific* (Cambridge, 2013) and *Looking for Balance: China, the United States, and Power Balancing in East Asia* (Stanford, 2012).

China's Troubled Waters

Maritime Disputes in Theoretical Perspective

Steve Chan

University of Colorado, Boulder

CAMBRIDGE
UNIVERSITY PRESS

CAMBRIDGE
UNIVERSITY PRESS

University Printing House, Cambridge CB2 8BS, United Kingdom

One Liberty Plaza, 20th Floor, New York, NY 10006, USA

477 Williamstown Road, Port Melbourne, VIC 3207, Australia

314-321, 3rd Floor, Plot 3, Splendor Forum, Jasola District Centre, New Delhi - 110025, India

79 Anson Road, #06-04/06, Singapore 079906

Cambridge University Press is part of the University of Cambridge.

It furthers the University's mission by disseminating knowledge in the pursuit of education, learning and research at the highest international levels of excellence.

www.cambridge.org
Information on this title: www.cambridge.org/9781107573291

First published 2016
First paperback edition 2018

A catalogue record for this publication is available from the British Library

Library of Congress Cataloging in Publication data
Chan, Steve, author.
China's troubled waters : maritime disputes in theoretical
perspective / Steve Chan, University of Colorado, Boulder.
Cambridge, United Kingdom : Cambridge University Press, 2016.
LCCN 2015036044 | ISBN 9781107130562 (hardback)
LCSH: China – Boundaries. | Maritime boundaries – China. | China – Foreign
relations – Southeast Asia. | Southeast Asia – Foreign relations – China. | South
China Sea – International status. | South China Sea – Strategic aspects. | East
China Sea – International status. | East China Sea – Strategic aspects.
LCC KNQ2390 .C43 2016 | DDC 341.4/480951–dc23
LC record available at http://lccn.loc.gov/2015036044

ISBN 978-1-107-13056-2 Hardback
ISBN 978-1-107-57329-1 Paperback

Contents

Preface

China's unsettled maritime frontier has been in the news lately. Its disputes with Japan in the East China Sea and with several Southeast Asian countries in the South China Sea have caused occasional confrontations that threaten to destabilize their respective relations. In addition to these disputes, Taiwan's fate has been the subject of a long-standing controversy that has the potential of involving the United States in a military conflict with China. Almost all existing studies on these maritime disputes involving China have adopted an idiographic approach. In this approach, an analyst undertakes a qualitative study that focuses on the more unique or specific aspects of the situation or actor being studied. There is usually little interest in reaching beyond this case in order to either discern patterns from similar past episodes (whether those involving the same actor or others) or situate this case in a broader comparative context.

This book takes an opposite tack. It analyzes China's maritime disputes in the context of its own other border conflicts and that of cross-national patterns. It takes advantage of existing literatures following the nomothetic approach, which emphasizes attention to classes of events rather than specific episodes. This approach is interested in empirical generalizations. It does not need to be just based on statistical analyses and can involve, for example, comparative case studies pertaining to the same actor (at different times) or different ones (whether at the same or different times). There is an especially large body of quantitative research undertaken by international relations analysts who rely on standard data sets collected systematically over many years and for many countries. This research points to empirical patterns that are statistically compelling and highly relevant to policy considerations. As a result of this research, we now have a much better understanding about a number of topics, such as those processes and conditions affecting territorial settlement or escalation to war, the interactions of domestic politics and foreign relations, and the success or failure of attempts at extended deterrence.

I plan to introduce evidence from this research tradition in order to inform our understanding of China's maritime disputes, which have been typically studied without the benefit of drawing on this store of knowledge. At the same time, I hope to apply knowledge about the Chinese case to interrogate several popular theories of international relations, such as democratic peace and power transition. These intentions in turn mean that this book will not dwell on descriptive accounts or journalistic narratives of "who did what to whom." An emphasis on detailed or thick description is the hallmark of the idiographic approach of analysis, privileging the uniqueness of the actor or situation under analysis. As already indicated, I pursue the nomothetic approach, which emphasizes patterns of behavior and classes of phenomena, or empirical generalizations for members of an aggregate group. This approach is obviously contrary to the practice of "slow journalism" presenting descriptive narratives. The orientation and emphasis I have chosen here argue that the substantive, policy, and theoretical issues addressed in this book pertain to more than just China and its maritime disputes. They have broader implications for making causal attributions and policy inferences about other countries as well.

To illustrate implications for causal attributions, consider the problems posed by idiosyncrasy and irrelevance. The former arises when an alleged cause can produce different outcomes (such as when X can be followed by both Y and non-Y). The latter occurs when both the presence and absence of an alleged cause can produce the same outcome (that is, when both X and non-X can be followed by Y). Of course, sometimes a cause–effect relationship inferred from an isolated case at a particular time can be disconfirmed and even reversed when a larger sample is analyzed. In analyzing contested sovereignty involving China, one sometimes encounters these challenges to valid causal attribution.

Take, for example, three popular causal variables often cited in discourse on China's disputes with its neighbors: nationalism, democracy, and power shifts. Chinese nationalism is frequently mentioned as an important motivation behind this country's territorial disputes. Yet how can this constant factor account for variations in Beijing's behavior, such as its persistent pursuit of reunification with Taiwan *and* at the same time, its recognition of Mongolia's independence and concessions of large tracts of land to Moscow, land that was lost by the Qing dynasty to Czarist Russia? Chinese nationalism in and of itself also cannot account for how Beijing has reacted differently to popular sentiments in various episodes pertaining to China's maritime dispute with Japan in the East China Sea and in its discrepant management of two near-crises with Washington: the US bombing of the Chinese embassy in Belgrade in 1999 and the collision between a US spy plane and a Chinese fighter off Hainan Island in 2001 (Weiss 2014).

Democracy has also often been suggested as the key determinant of future Sino-American relations (e.g., Friedberg 2011). Although the democratic peace theory demonstrates that democracies do not fight each other, there is also good reason to expect that *ceteris paribus*, the larger a selectorate (Bueno de Mesquita *et al.* 2003), the smaller a leader's negotiation space to reach a foreign deal. More intense intra-elite competition and more influential public opinion (which often tends to be more nationalist than elite opinion) are likely to impede rather than enhance a government's (including China's) ability and willingness to compromise on salient foreign policy issues. Of course, Taiwan's democracy has also been routinely invoked as an important reason motivating US support for it. Yet this support has clearly predated Taiwan's democratization, and thus does not appear to be conditional upon this variable. In fact, US support has waned over time even as Taiwan has become more democratic.

As for power shifts, although many recent analyses have dwelled on China's relative gains in military and economic capabilities, and have inferred from this development that Beijing will therefore adopt a more assertive and even coercive foreign policy, the historical association between these variables has tended to point in the opposite direction. As Taylor Fravel (2008: 9) has remarked, "China has been much more willing to use force when its bargaining power has declined, not strengthened." Beijing's foreign policy was much more bellicose when it was weaker in the 1950s and 1960s, and it has become more conciliatory and cooperative when it has become stronger in the recent past. Moreover, when Beijing has resorted to force in the past, it has fought the strongest adversaries (e.g., the US, the USSR, India, Vietnam), but has often settled its border disputes with those neighbors who were much weaker than China and on terms generally more favorable to these weaker neighbors (e.g., Afghanistan, Burma, Laos, Nepal). Indeed, when China has enjoyed the strongest military advantage, such as in recovering its sovereignty over Hong Kong and Macao, it has taken time to negotiate a peaceful settlement rather than resorting to force to impose a unilateral resolution (Fravel 2008). Therefore, when the People's Republic has enjoyed greater relative power in a dispute, it has been less inclined to use force – a tendency that clearly contradicts the expectation of those who worry that a stronger China will be a more aggressive China. Extrapolating from his study of imperial China, Yuan-kang Wang (2011: 208) has suggested that a more powerful China will be more assertive and more inclined to pursue an offensive strategy. Naturally, Beijing's recent behavior does not exclude this possibility when China becomes even stronger in the future. Rather, the examples just presented remind us to be cautious in accepting mono-causal explanations, and to scrutinize the logic and evidence behind common assertions before accepting them.

As for this book's general implications for policy inference, consider the question of how one can discern a state's future intentions. Given its rising capabilities, foreign analysts and officials are naturally becoming more interested in learning about how Beijing will be disposed to use its capabilities. Historically, states have acted toward extant or aspiring hegemons not so much based on their assessments of these countries' power but rather based on their perceptions of these countries' intentions or motivations. Will these powerful countries apply their strength in a restrained and even benevolent way, or will they use it wantonly for selfish aggrandizement? This distinction between capabilities and intentions is critical for explaining why, contrary to the expectation of balance-of-power theorists, most major states (e.g., Britain, France, Japan, and even China in the 1970s and 1980s) had supported the stronger US during the Cold War against its weaker adversary, the USSR. Naturally, in order for a state to be seen as a threat to others, it must have both the requisite capabilities and intentions. It is, however, far more difficult to determine the latter than the former. Although discourse on international relations and on China is replete with distinctions between supposed revisionist and status-quo powers, satisfied and dissatisfied states, and defensively and offensively minded states, such inferences of intentions are only rarely substantiated by consistent logic or systematic evidence.

Beijing's conduct in its border disputes can be especially informative about its general foreign policy disposition, as territorial conflicts have historically been the most common reason for states to fight. If China pursues mutual accommodation in these conflicts even after its capabilities have improved, this behavior tends to communicate a peaceful disposition. Conversely, if it resorts to coercion, this behavior will point to an aggressive disposition. Beijing has concluded border agreements with most of its continental neighbors, but its maritime frontier remains unsettled. Jurisdictional disputes in the East and South China Seas have occasionally roiled its relations with Japan, Vietnam, and the Philippines. Even though relations across the Taiwan Strait have improved significantly in recent years, this case of contested sovereignty presents the most likely situation for a large armed conflict and one that could potentially involve the United States. Studying China's conduct in these maritime disputes is therefore pertinent to a practical concern for conflict mitigation in addition to providing an analytic leverage to gauge Beijing's foreign policy intentions in general. I am specifically interested in those conditions that are likely to affect the persistence, escalation, or settlement of China's maritime disputes, which constitute the dependent variable of this analysis if you will. At the same time, China's behavior in these disputes sheds light on a larger question. It serves as a window to study Beijing's general disposition in conducting its foreign relations, and this book is therefore not *just* about its maritime disputes.

Declining to treat China as *sui generis*, I argue in this book that we can look to general theories of international relations, cross-national patterns of behavior, and historical parallels to advance our understanding of the Chinese case. For instance, if we treat the dispute over Taiwan's future as a secessionist movement seeking self-determination, how often have such efforts succeeded historically? And if we consider Taiwan's disputed status as a matter of geostrategic concern from Beijing's perspective, what can we learn from comparable cases such as Cuba for the US and Cyprus for Turkey? Can we draw any lessons from past episodes of both escalation and settlement (e.g., the Falklands/Malvinas War, contested sovereignty over the Svalbard archipelago) about the prospects for ending China's maritime disputes in the East and South China Seas? Because the US plays a critical role in protecting Taiwan and others involved in disputes with China, what can international relations research tell us about those conditions that can contribute to or detract from a successful attempt at extended deterrence? Similarly, can we gain any insights from those theoretical perspectives that seek to link domestic politics to international conduct, and economic interactions to political cooperation?

Generally speaking, the dynamics and incentives illuminated by perspectives such as those just mentioned suggest that Beijing is likely to bide its time and refrain from resorting to violence in order to impose a settlement in its maritime disputes. Its current and most likely posture for the immediate future can be best described as "reactive assertiveness" (International Crisis Group 2013 at www.crisis.group.org/~/media/Files/asia/north-east-asia/245-dangerous-waters-China-japan-relations-on-the-rocks.pdf; Li 2011, 2012 has used "non-confrontational assertiveness" to describe this general posture). It is disposed to postpone the resolution of its disputes and continue normal relations with its counterparts, but will push back forcefully if in its view its counterparts have sought to alter the status quo unilaterally. Significantly, this characterization puts Beijing in the role of a defender that seeks to deter unwanted initiatives from others, not a role that it is customarily assigned to in much of the current discourse, which depicts it as a revisionist challenger to the existing international order.

My interpretation and prognosis recognize that China is gaining increasing military and economic capabilities. This ongoing change will obviously give it more influence in the Asia Pacific. Significantly and contrary to conventional wisdom, a stronger and thus more confident China is likely to be less inclined to use force. This proposition is in line with Fravel's (2008) conclusion from his study of China's dispute behavior, suggesting that regime insecurity and weakening bargaining position have inclined Beijing to use force in the past. International relations research has shown territorial disputes and sovereignty contests to be the most common cause motivating militarized interstate disputes, whose increasing incidence is often a precursor to war. This research also shows that increasing commercial ties tend to dampen interstate conflict. China's peaceful settlement of most of its territorial disputes, the rising levels of economic interdependence among the disputing countries, and Beijing's general disposition to wait for conditions to mature rather than forcing issues right away should augur for continuing peace and stability in the region. There will of course be occasions when tensions will rise and tempers flare. But it is questionable that a rising China will necessarily threaten its neighbors and destabilize the region.

Naturally, this view contradicts the expectations of offensive realism and power-transition theory, both of which predict that a rising China will be expansionist and a source of instability in interstate relations. Indeed, the logic of my argument suggests that so long as Beijing expects to sustain its upward power trajectory, it will likely continue to act as a conservative power motivated largely by a desire to preserve its gains. It will be content to set aside its quarrels for the time being, or will even be disposed to compromise in ways that tend to favor its weaker counterparts. Conversely, a China in trouble or disarray – one whose growth begins to sag and whose leaders are besieged by popular discontent – is likely to be more risk-prone in trying to prevent or reverse its perceived losses. Such a China will be more insecure and more bellicose. This expectation conforms generally to the prediction of prospect theory based on the pioneering work of Nobel laureate Daniel Kahneman and Amos Tversky (1979, 2000). This work has shown that people experiencing a setback are inclined to take risks seeking to reverse their loss whereas those who have made recent gains tend to eschew risk-taking.

1 Embedding China's maritime disputes in generic IR research

When the US president telephoned, he was told that his call has come too late. It is now impossible to recall the military forces on their way to invade the islands. This situation has come about because, as the voice at the other end of the telephone line explains, protracted negotiations have been unproductive. This counterpart leader feels that his country has been "strung along" for years by delaying and evasive tactics. Various concessions to woo the islanders have evidently failed to change their mind. Now his government has lost patience. It hopes and expects the US to adopt a neutral position in the impending military showdown. In planning their invasion project, this leader and his colleagues have calculated that they would achieve an easy and quick victory and that their opponent would concede rather than resist. These beliefs turn out to be mistaken. The US decides not to stay on the sideline but instead intervenes on behalf of their opponent, who fights back to evict the invading force after considerable bloodshed. This outcome on the battlefield, however, does not resolve the underlying dispute about sovereignty. It continues to fester and to cause recurrent political tension and military strain.

These words are not about an imaginary scenario intended to conjure up what could possibly come to pass if the impasse across the Taiwan Strait were to come to blows. They describe what actually happened in the 1982 war between Argentina and Britain over the Falklands/Malvinas. This war occurred even though neither side had wished for it – indeed, Buenos Aires and London would have much preferred a negotiated settlement, even a face-saving one, to a military confrontation. The contested islands had but a small population, few resources (although rumors abound that the surrounding seas hold large oil reserves), and little strategic value. In the words of the poet Jorge Luis Borges, this war over a small, barren, wind-swept archipelago in a far corner of the world reminds one of two bald men fighting over a comb (Ellyatt 2013).

Yet Argentina and Britain did go to war. Moreover, despite intense US efforts to mediate a settlement between its two allies, war happened nonetheless. Although the islanders (the Kelpers, whose number was about 2,500 in 2013 but only about 1,800 in 1982) have declared their wish to continue as a British Overseas Territory in a March 2013 referendum, the status of this contested territory is still very much in limbo as Argentina, supported by its South American neighbors, has refused to accept the current state of affairs. Even though Britain had prevailed in the 1982 war, it finds itself in a situation that is hardly sustainable in the long run, politically, militarily, and economically (notwithstanding possible royalties from oil exploration and production in the surrounding seas – a prospect that will face considerable practical and legal difficulties in the face of Argentine opposition). Because of their geographic location (being barely 300 miles away from Argentina), the future of the Falklands/Malvinas is inevitably tied more to Argentina's economy than Britain's and these islands are within closer range of the former country's military force. In contrast, Britain suffers from the disadvantage of being located 8,000 miles away.

Although it is common to characterize interstate conflicts as a zero-sum game, the situation involving the Falklands/Malvinas is more accurately described as negative sum. There are no winners, as all concerned parties have borne heavier costs without additional benefits after the 1982 war. Even for the Kelpers, whose right to self-determination was supposed to have been London's reason for going to war, a negotiated accommodation with Buenos Aires would have surely improved some important aspects of their lives, such as those relating to travel, communication, and commerce. The deadlock on clashing sovereignty claims has a significant opportunity cost, in terms of not only imposing heavier defense burdens and transaction costs for the disputants (money that could have gone to other worthwhile purposes) but also the foregone benefits of peaceful interstate relations such as those that could have been gotten from profitable exploitation of the ocean's resources. Political risks and legal uncertainties tend to frighten away business investments with promising socio-economic returns.

The Falklands/Malvinas conflict and other maritime disputes have much to teach us about China's ongoing relations with Taiwan and its other sovereignty claims in the East and South China Seas, claims that are being contested by several of its neighbors that are formal or tacit US allies. I am interested in introducing a broader comparative context to inform inquiries about these disputes as most extant analyses have tended to focus on the more specific and even idiosyncratic aspects pertaining to Beijing's pronouncements, decisions, and moves. They have therefore generally missed an opportunity to learn from historical parallels or precedents offered by other countries' experiences. These studies have also by and large bypassed a large and cumulative body of empirical evidence developed by quantitative research of past episodes of militarized interstate disputes (MIDs) or research based on comparative case studies, especially variables that have played a significant role in the occurrence, persistence, and termination of enduring rivalries.

In writing this book, I intend to draw on these research approaches and to benefit from various strands of international relations (IR) theorizing such as bargaining theory and extended deterrence. By offering the pertinent cross-national evidence and generic explanations, I hope to broaden the study of China's foreign relations beyond the domain of country specialists, and to situate this study as a part of international relations inquiry in general. Reciprocally, I hope that the latter inquiry can be enriched by insights from China's perspective and experience. In advancing this agenda, I obviously believe in the value of empirical generalizations, the importance of *not* treating China as *sui generis*, and the analytic priority of trying common (i.e., generic) explanations before appealing to particularistic ones (i.e., before appealing to case-specific or idiosyncratic factors) – notwithstanding personal assets in language proficiency, research contacts, and life experience in undertaking the idiographic approach.

Bargaining as a general perspective

Misperception and miscalculation certainly contributed to the escalation of the Falklands/Malvinas conflict (e.g., Lebow 1985). I contend in this book, however, that the tragedy of this conflict and others like it is more deeply embedded in the nature of the situation that confronts the leaders of the disputing countries. I therefore apply a rationalist perspective which asks what people with common sense would have generally done if they found themselves in similar circumstances. This rationalist perspective does not assume that people are infallible in their judgments, but rather takes as its starting premise that people are strategic in the sense that they try to formulate their policy and adjust their action in anticipation of how others are likely to react to their behavior. We thus need to first of all identify and grasp those structural conditions that shape the incumbent officials' perceptions and calculations. Only after we have gained a more sound understanding of the influence of the pertinent structural conditions can we begin to explain their policy choices and to recommend strategies intended to defuse or resolve their disputes.

As in the case of the Falklands/Malvinas, China's ongoing maritime disputes involve to varying extent the issues of contested sovereignty, competing regime legitimacy and popularity, complicated historical legacies, and an aroused sense of past grievances and popular appeals to national solidarity and ethnic identity. Freedom of navigation, ocean resources, geostrategic rivalry, and the dynamics of alliance politics are also engaged. In 1982, budgetary stringencies, economic hardship, and fractious domestic politics (e.g., the miners' strike in Britain, the military junta's brutal suppression of leftists in Argentina) characterized the decision context on both sides of the Atlantic. Today's Asia Pacific faces a somewhat different situation even though the reverberations from increasingly pluralistic politics (if not necessarily democratization in China) and deep global recession (2008–12) have had their own not inconsequential effects. There was in 1982 a widely shared perception that Britain was in decline and anxious to trim its military commitments outside of its obligations to the North Atlantic Treaty Organization (NATO). Today it is almost impossible to discuss China's maritime disputes without an obligatory reference to regional power shifts resulting from "China's rise" (e.g., Raine and Le Miere 2013). In both situations, Washington has been *the* critical third party, one that has the wherewithal to affect the bilateral balance of capabilities and incentives between the direct contestants.

I apply the general theory of bargaining to study China's maritime disputes. In broad terms, this theory is about how states try to communicate with each other in their efforts to reach a mutually acceptable deal (e.g., Fearon 1995, 1997). Various obstacles, such as deliberate misrepresentation and private information, stand in the way of concluding this settlement (for important emendation to this generalization, see Kirshner 2000; Slantchev 2010). States therefore sometimes find themselves fighting a war which they would have preferred to avoid. Bargaining theory calls attention to the challenges of undertaking effective communication whether the intended audience is foreign or domestic. They are relevant to attempts to persuade foreigners about one's intentions and capabilities such as in demonstrating one's resolve to stand firm and to fight if pushed too far. They also involve efforts to reassure foreigners about one's limited objectives and one's commitment and capacity to carry out the terms of a deal if a bargain is struck (foreigners are unlikely to waste their political capital if they believe that one is unable to deliver on a negotiated deal – that is, if one cannot overcome domestic opposition to a negotiated deal). The intense US domestic debate on whether to ratify the nuclear deal negotiated by President Barack Obama with Iran (a deal that has also involved five other major states as negotiation partners) highlights this latter concern.

Officials may also feign doubts and weaknesses in order to extract more generous concessions from foreigners in negotiating the terms of a settlement or, alternatively, in order to abet foreigners' complacency and overconfidence so that they can be exploited by a strategic surprise. The latter consideration in turn presents a dilemma: should a state communicate its resolve by undertaking highly visible and credible actions which, however, can also have the effect of tipping off the other side about its intention to escalate and therefore inviting this counterpart to undertake counteraction to prepare for a possible showdown? That is, there is a trade-off between demonstrating one's resolve to deter a counterpart and forfeiting the advantage of strategic surprise should this deterrence fail and a war have to be fought. Efforts to enhance one's deterrence credibility during the pre-war period can diminish one's capabilities in fighting a subsequent war should deterrence fail. Bratislav Slantchev (2010) points to China's intervention in the Korean War as an illustration.

As just mentioned, bargaining and signaling do not "stop at the water's edge." The metaphor of two-level games (Putnam 1988; Evans *et al.* 1993) suggests that incumbent officials must negotiate not only with their foreign counterparts, but also with their own domestic constituents (including the political opposition) so that whatever deal is reached with foreigners will have the necessary domestic support or at least the acquiescence of important stakeholders. Therefore, bargaining theory encompasses efforts to reassure, mobilize, or otherwise communicate to domestic audiences. Former US Secretary of Labor John Dunlop is said to have remarked that every bilateral deal requires three agreements, one across the table and one on each side of the table (Putnam 1988: 433).

Because democracies obviously have more veto groups that can block a deal with a foreign adversary, their negotiators will be more constrained in making concessions to the latter (they will have a smaller win set or bargaining space to negotiate with their foreign counterpart). Conversely, because authoritarian leaders will have more control over the policy process and are less likely to face a divided government, they face less domestic opposition and have more room to negotiate. This latter consideration in turn implies that they are less able to argue that their hands are tied by their domestic constituents, and they are therefore less able to use this argument credibly to resist foreign demands for concession and are more likely to be "pushed around" to make concessions. A corollary of this inference is that autocracies will have an easier time in trying to reach a deal with a foreign adversary than democracies and that democratization can actually make it more difficult for countries caught in disputes to reach an accord. The more authoritarian former Soviet republics, namely Kazakhstan and Tajikistan, were able to reach border accords with Beijing more quickly and with less fuss than the less authoritarian Kyrgyzstan (Chung 2004: 138). India's democratic institutions and vocal political opposition have often caused problems for government officials who might have preferred a softer line in negotiating with China in these countries' border dispute (Chung 2004: 151).

Interstate and intrastate communication in bargaining situations can involve both verbal and nonverbal means. Public declarations and military displays offer ways for a government to signal its resolve. This resolve can be communicated by other means such as economic sanctions, nuclear tests, regime-sponsored mass protests, and even deliberate shocks administered to financial markets. Naturally, politicians do not just engage in such disclosures, they also often try to disguise their intentions, hide their country's capabilities, and mislead both their domestic constituents and foreign allies (not to mention their adversaries). Or they can choose to be intentionally vague, declining to be locked into a predetermined position. Finally, they can be purposefully inconsistent, conveying different messages to different audiences in different forums and on different occasions (e.g., through official statements, private reassurances, tacit acknowledgments, informal accommodation, and messages delivered by intermediaries). Bargaining theory thus pertains to both formal negotiations and tacit exchanges. It opens the analytic door to various other theories – such as power transition, democratic peace, and diversionary war – to inform us, for example, about how the shifting power balances among states, rising tides of economic interdependence and nationalism, and evolving elite solidarity and regime popularity can facilitate or constrain officials' efforts to reach a negotiated settlement.

Such a settlement, as already noted, requires ratification in the sense of support, approval, or at least indifference by important veto groups both at home and abroad (Cunningham 2011; Tsebelis 2002). The relevant "abroad" includes multiple states with a direct or indirect stake. Thus, for example, the reunification of Germany took a multilateral deal involving not just the two German sides and their respective domestic constituencies, but also the US, the USSR, France, Britain, and Poland (among others) and their respective internally negotiated pacts (Stent 1999). With respect to China's various maritime disputes, the US clearly looms large as a significant other. Its role in these disputes has been prominently featured whether in the discourse on pivotal deterrence or that on extended deterrence (e.g., Crawford 2003; Huth 1988a), topics that I will discuss in more detail later.

Just as my analytic style and approach tend to depart from the mainstream of scholarship on China's foreign relations, my substantive conclusions also differ from those reached by perhaps most other colleagues. In my judgment, the impression conveyed by most current analyses, especially those published in the more popular media, tends to be too pessimistic and even alarmist. Predictions of impending armed clashes, even a large military conflict between the US and China, appear to be too dire. They overlook ongoing trends, such as increasing economic inter-dependence and political de-alignment, which offset the effects of terri-torial disputes and competitive rivalry. One may even argue that precisely because relations among Asia Pacific countries have reached a more stable and peaceful situation, they should feel less restrained to quarrel loudly because they realize that the risk of a run-away escalation has now been greatly reduced. This logic would argue analogously that because democracies rarely, if ever, go to war against one another, these countries should be more disposed to enter into disputes of lower intensity because compared to their authoritarian counterparts, they can be more assured that such quarrels would not affect their fundamental friendship and that their disagreements would be resolved long before reaching the point at which blows are exchanged. Conversely, when states find themselves in a dangerous hair-trigger situation, their leaders should be more cautious so that their actions will not produce an unwanted confrontation or escalation.

This line of reasoning illustrates my earlier point about people being strategic and being capable of planning their moves in anticipation of others' reaction. The example introduced above also provides an unusual interpretation that disagrees with conventional wisdom. In the analyses that follow, I offer other inferences and conjectures, such as those about the prospects of US military intervention in the Taiwan Strait, the danger of China's resort to armed forces in its maritime disputes, and the prob-able effects of democratization on Beijing's foreign policy. These infer-ences and conjectures often offer unorthodox propositions. These propositions could of course turn out to be wrong. Whether they do, or do not, is an empirical matter – to be settled by history's verdict. Falsifiable prediction provides one (albeit an important) criterion for judging the validity of our analysis. Being explicit rather than vague in stating one's propositions is an analytic virtue, and even if a proposition is contradicted by subsequent events it is helpful for advancing our knowl-edge. What the readers of this book will not encounter is an "echo chamber" that repeats much of the received wisdom featured in many extant studies of China's foreign relations. What is sometimes taken as a matter of fact reflects rather constructed reality and common interpreta-tion shared by members of particular communities. An unnamed Wall Street pundit has been quoted saying, "I get scared when everyone gets to one side of the boat." Irving Janis (1982) has coined the phrase "group-think" to describe the tendency for people, even very smart ones, to jump on the conveyor belt of conventional and consensual thinking.

What about cognitive and affective factors?

Rationalist explanations attend to the common structure of decision making faced by all incumbent officials regardless of their national origin. This perspective introduces generic considerations – rather than turning to cognitive and affective factors that influence the views and motivations of particular leaders, organizations, or cultures – as the first order of business for empirical inquiry. This analytic disposition suggests that we should consider common structural properties in attempting to understand decision choices before resorting to those variables pertaining to lower levels of analysis.

Certainly, motivated biases and just plain ignorance have contributed to distrust and miscalculation in interstate disputes. It is, however, usually difficult for analysts to make such causal attributions when they lack good access to classified archives disclosing the pertinent officials' actual perceptions and true reasoning (retrospective memoirs and even contemporaneous documents may suffer from well-known validity problems due to their authors' natural desire to bolster their political position and protect their reputation). We know that officials often disguise their real intentions and issue statements that later turn out to be false or misleading. I argue in this book that in many situations, one does not necessarily have to invoke perceptual or judgmental errors (or for that matter, divergent cultural dispositions) in order to explain the occurrence or escalation of interstate disputes. In advancing this argument, I do not mean to suggest that these variables are irrelevant or unimportant. Rather, their analytic purchase should be judged by the extent to which they are able to address that which has not yet been accounted for by generic rationalist explanations. One should consider the more general or commonly shared factors in proposing explanations before introducing others that are less so.

This analytic posture raises the possibility that dispute impasse and conflict recurrence may be due to common, even understandable, reasons that are inherent in the nature of interstate relations. As in the game of poker, deliberate misrepresentation (i.e., deception intended for the very purpose of inducing misperception and causing misjudgment) and imperfect information (in the sense that one lacks access to observe a foreign counterpart's decision processes) are an integral part of the nature of interstate interactions (what is the point of playing poker if bluffing is not allowed or if the players can see others' "hole cards"?). As Mark Twain reportedly quipped, "what makes a horse race is a difference of opinion." The same goes for poker games and interstate disputes – and as I will argue later, these differences of opinion are not necessarily a result of psychological biases or cultural misunderstanding. It is also pertinent to note that as the reference to horse races (or other such comparable situations, for example stock transactions and sports matches such as the games of the National Football League; Kirshner 2000) suggests, a difference of opinion can exist even when complete information is publicly available to all the participating actors.

War is a costly business. The belligerent countries expend money, lives, time, and political goodwill on their fight, resources that could have otherwise been used for other purposes. War is also a risky proposition because it can end badly for these countries, sometimes ending in their military defeat and foreign occupation. The leaders of the vanquished can suffer not only the loss of their political power but also their personal demise (e.g., Adolf Hitler, Benito Mussolini, Hideo Tojo, and Saddam Hussein). If the leaders of the opposing sides had reached an agreement to settle their dispute peacefully, they would have spared themselves the costs and risks associated with fighting a war. They could not reach such an agreement because they did not have 20/20 foresight about how a military conflict would eventually turn out. What factors then stand in the way of their ability to anticipate this outcome? Even though leaders realize that wars are inefficient in the sense just described, they still often decide to fight instead of coming to a negotiated settlement. This phenomenon presents the central analytic puzzle that scholars of bargaining theory try to explain (Blainey 1973; Fearon 1995; Gartzke 1999; Wagner 2000).

As the proverbial saying goes, it takes (at least) two to tango. To state the obvious, the persistence of China's maritime disputes with the other claimants is a result of their discordant expectations. When the parties continue to carry on and even escalate their dispute, they evidently believe that their behavior will gain for them a better deal than their counterpart is currently willing to accept in a negotiated settlement. When they choose war to settle their differences, both belligerents must believe that they hold a stronger hand than they are given credit for by their opponent (Fearon 1995). A resort to arms thus becomes a way for both sides to communicate their greater resolve or stronger capabilities that in their view should entitle them to a more favorable settlement (they use military displays and actual fighting to do the "talking" for them just as poker players rely on their betting to communicate or represent the strength of their hand). Typically in such situations, the costlier and riskier the signals to a sender (costs whether in terms of tangible resources or intangible reputation, and risks in the sense of Schelling's 1966 advice of following policies that deliberately leave something to chance), the more likely that this sender is sincere and not bluffing (even though he/she can still be wrong). This is so because insincere actors (i.e., those who are just pretending) would not have accepted the high costs and great risks that a sincere actor is willing to take on in order to demonstrate his/her seriousness. The fact that the contestants evidently disagree about the terms of a possible settlement does not necessarily imply that cognitive and affective distortions are responsible for this disagreement. This disagreement can also stem more fundamentally from the inherent structure of their relationship. Both contestants cannot be correct in their discrepant anticipation of how a protracted dispute or military confrontation (or horse race) will turn out, and in that sense there must be miscalculation by at least one and perhaps even both sides.

It also stands to reason that when a dispute results in a standoff and negotiation is at an impasse, the parties are likely to have different expectations about what the future holds. If both sides had shared the same expectation of the future, they could and would have settled on the basis of that common anticipation, thereby sparing themselves the costs of a gridlock in the meantime. In other words, one strong plausible reason for holding out is if one believes that the prevailing trends and also one's own ongoing efforts can make a difference in changing the future in one's favor – or more accurately, in demonstrating or enhancing one's bargaining position to a greater extent than the other side is currently willing to acknowledge and concede. Again, both sides cannot be right even though they can both be wrong in continuing a deadlock – unless of course delaying a deal into the future will somehow make both sides better off (which of course begs the question of what is preventing them from reaching this deal now).

Playing for time may make sense if the costs of accepting and ratifying an agreement are expected to abate in the future. These prospective costs very much include calculations about domestic partisan politics (such as anticipated hostile popular reaction to reaching an accommodation with a foreign adversary and criticisms from domestic lobby groups, opposition parties, and dissident elite segments). Thus, for example, several US presidents were said to have professed a readiness to initiate supposedly controversial policies, such as ending a foreign war (e.g., Vietnam, Afghanistan) or conciliating with an adversary (e.g., China, Cuba), after having secured for themselves a second term in office. Significantly, this formulation points to a potential principal–agent problem: the chief negotiator (e.g., the president) and the country he/she is representing may not have identical interests, so that the chief negotiator may postpone or veto a foreign deal even if it may be politically feasible and in the country's objective interest (Putnam 1988). Another important implication of this perspective is that officials may put off reaching a deal if they expect that their foreign counterpart's next administration will be more accommodative (Wolford 2007). Conversely, if hardliners are waiting in the wings to succeed this counterpart's current administration, they should be more willing to reach a deal now rather than waiting until later. As a general proposition, whether incumbent politicians are politically secure has a bearing on their propensity to compromise with or confront their foreign counterparts in an ongoing dispute (Huth and Allee 2002). Politically insecure leaders are generally more constrained from making concessions to their foreign counterparts in order to reach a deal, and they are more tempted to resort to tactics aimed at using foreign crises to boost their domestic popularity (as shown by the escalation of the Falklands/Malvinas dispute).

That the various parties to China's maritime disputes have not yet come to an agreement to settle could be due to another plausible reason: deadlock or delay can simply be due to a lack of any attractive policy option at the present and a concomitant unwillingness to make a hard choice among all the unpalatable options available. With severe resource constraints, domestic discord, and distraction from other more pressing issues of higher priority, playing for time – "talking simply for the sake of talking" or what Lawrence Freedman (1988: 30–33) describes simply as "prevarication" – is not an unnatural response, as exemplified by Britain's negotiation with Argentina about the status of the Falklands/Malvinas before the 1982 war (Freedman and Gamba-Stonehouse 1991). Similarly, strategic ambiguity, as shown in Washington's policy for the Taiwan Strait, can be an attempt to make a virtue out of necessity when one wants to avoid expending political capital on a divisive bureaucratic or partisan debate and publicizing such domestic division for foreigners to listen in. Deliberate vagueness in some aspects of this US policy predated 1979, when Washington switched its diplomatic recognition from Taipei to Beijing. Throughout the 1954–55 offshore crises, the US remained purposefully ambiguous about whether it would defend Quemoy and Matsu (Chang and He 1993; Wang 2002; Zhang 1998: 210–224). As another example of "playing for time," Beijing was willing to shelve its dispute with Tokyo over the Senkaku/Diaoyu Islands until it perceived the Japanese side to have violated a tacit understanding not to disturb the status quo (in part prompted by Tokyo Governor Ishihara Shintaro's campaign to purchase these disputed islands from their private owners, a situation that in turn illustrates how domestic political opposition might attempt to influence an incumbent government's policy agenda and shape its choices).

These illustrations suggest that a difference of opinion held by the parties to a dispute does not have to be due to biases in perception or judgment (although such factors need not be ruled out). Indeed, to the extent that these contestants have had extensive experience in dealing with each other and also have a common culture and shared history (as exemplified by relations on the Korean Peninsula and across the Taiwan Strait and, to a lesser extent, in relations between India and Pakistan and between Israel and its Arab neighbors), they should *ceteris paribus* be less prone to commit such errors than officials from countries that have had far less contact and familiarity with each other such as Chad and Denmark or Bolivia and Cambodia (Chan 2013). Contesting neighbors should be the *least* likely to commit misperception or misjudgment. Learning theory suggests that after repeated confrontations, they should be in the best position to gauge each other's intentions and capabilities, just like two seasoned poker players who have had many prior encounters. Who should be in a better position to understand Pyongyang than those in Seoul, and vice versa? The same goes for Beijing and Taipei.

Indeed, in view of my previous reference to officials' occasional resort to deliberate misrepresentation (i.e., to lying), it is not unnatural for them to pretend misunderstanding even when they understand each other perfectly well. As an example, it would seem preferable to blame the furor over Washington's issuance of a visiting visa to Taiwan President Lee Teng-hui on diplomatic misunderstanding, bureaucratic snafu, congressional pressure, or anything else other than a deliberate decision to renege on a promise to the contrary given to Beijing's officials just a few days prior to this decision (Garver 1997). To cite another example from recent events, it is more convenient to explain Hong Kong authorities' decision to allow Edward Snowden to leave for Moscow as some kind of mishandling or misunderstanding of the US request to extradite him than to acknowledge that this decision was a deliberate effort to obstruct and embarrass Washington in its efforts to prosecute this individual who has leaked information about secret surveillance programs conducted by the US government.

In light of this discussion, I am more inclined to interpret the distrust shown by Beijing's leaders toward Taiwan's Lee Teng-hui and Chen Shui-bian (and vice versa) as stemming from the bargaining situation characterizing their relationship than as a product of mutual or one-sided misperception (e.g., Bush 2005). Their reciprocal skepticisms are natural and to be expected given the circumstances they find themselves in. For instance, what is there to prevent future Chinese leaders from disregarding Beijing's current promises to Taipei after the latter's government renounces its claim to sovereignty? Similarly, one need not introduce culture to explain Beijing's suspicions about Washington's motives with respect to Taiwan (e.g., Zhang 1998), as the US had also questioned similar Soviet aid to the nearby island Cuba. Beijing's objection to Washington's arms sales to Taipei should not be too difficult to comprehend if one recalls that Washington had not reacted with equanimity to Soviet military assistance to Havana – after the US had orchestrated the Bay of Pigs invasion of the island. A cultural explanation offers little additional analytic value when a geostrategic interpretation can already account for both cases (e.g., Wachman 2007).

As mentioned previously, national leaders may be unwilling to conclude a foreign deal even when they personally prefer it because they face or anticipate strong objections from powerful domestic interest groups. And even when they favor such a deal privately, they may feign doubts in order to squeeze further concessions from their opposite number (just as in the case of a poker player who may deliberately misrepresent his/her hand in order to extract the maximum amount of payoff from others). Finally, leaders may put a public spin on a foreign deal and deliberately omit key aspects of this bargain from public knowledge – such as the *quid pro quo* involved in the withdrawal of Soviet missiles from Cuba, with Washington pledging to also remove US missiles from Turkey and not to invade Cuba again (Allison and Zelikow 1999). I will elaborate on these remarks further in later discussion, suggesting that situational explanations should be tried first before resorting to motivational explanations. The motivational factors are often inherent in the situational or structural conditions. It is inherently more difficult to decipher others' intentions which, just like their capabilities, are also subject to change in the future (in part in response to one's own current behavior). This is why officials often dismiss their counterparts' "cheap talk" and insist on tangible evidence of credible commitment from these counterparts.

Attending to cross-national patterns

Renowned international relations scholar James Rosenau often counseled his students to start their inquiry by asking "what is this an instance of?" (Anand 2011). His advice recommends situating one's topic of analysis in a general empirical and theoretical context, thereby enabling one to gain analytic and policy relevance beyond the particular case or actor being studied. I will follow this advice, starting from the premise that China can be studied as a "regular" state like any other in international relations analyses. In so doing, I choose to focus on what it shares in common with other countries (such as the decision logics presented by the rationalist perspective) rather than what sets it apart. I ask how much generic formulations of interstate conduct can advance our understanding without having to appeal to China's supposed uniqueness or resorting to the more idiosyncratic aspects of its decision processes. I believe that the general theories and broad empirical patterns offered by international relations research can teach us much about individual cases such as China's maritime disputes.

Naturally, an event or situation can belong concurrently to several analytic categories (i.e., it can be an instance of several classes of phenomena). Thus, China's maritime disputes can be considered instances of contested sovereignty over disputed territory and as such, they can be informed by empirical patterns concerning territorial conflicts in general. These disputes also represent instances of extended deterrence (Huth 1988a) to the extent that a third party such as the US is involved in checking China's assertiveness. As instances of protracted impasse, they exemplify negotiation failures. Rationalist explanations (Fearon 1995) provide a generic account for such failures and even the occurrence of war despite its known inefficiency. Finally, China's maritime disputes highlight the interactions of domestic politics and foreign relations, and they can be analyzed as instances of "two-level games" (Putnam 1988). As already indicated, I will analyze Beijing and its counterparts' behaviors in the general context of bargaining interactions (e.g. Weiss 2012).

The various strands of theoretical and empirical research just mentioned are usually overlooked in commentaries on China's territorial disputes. I argue that this research can provide important and even counterintuitive insights on this topic. For example, quantitative studies based on systematically collected data on territorial disputes are useful in calling attention to those conditions that escalate these contests to outright war and subsequently spread it to engulf third parties. Alliance politics, armament competition, and recurrent militarized crises have typically played an important role in the dynamics of escalation (e.g., Vasquez 2009). Given this stylized fact, we can ask whether these ingredients for a combustible brew have increased or decreased in China's current territorial disputes.

As another example, officials can try to communicate their country's commitment to defend an ally either by publicizing clear, consistent statements that engage their reputation, or by making visible, costly allocation of tangible resources to defend this ally ("tying hands" and "sinking costs" as described by Fearon 1997). This perspective in turn directs our attention to analyzing how the US, evidently the most important ally for most countries involved in maritime disputes with China, has acted in recent years in view of these injunctions for credible (extended) deterrence. Has it "talked the talk" and "walked the walk"? With respect to the dynamics of two-level games and the distinction between cheap talk and credible commitment, what are foreign audiences likely to conclude from the Pentagon's declared intention to "pivot to Asia" and the recent and ongoing debate about the "fiscal cliff" and "budgetary sequestration" in Washington?

As a final example, territorial disputes are more likely to enflame popular emotions and arouse nationalism than other kinds of interstate controversies. As such, they are more easily manipulated, even hijacked, by politicians for domestic partisan reasons, such as when foreign crises and confrontations are used by officials to distract citizens from their domestic problems as suggested by the diversionary theory of war (Tir 2010). There is also an obverse side to this possibility of politicians manufacturing or exploiting foreign tension for domestic partisan reasons. As a country's political process becomes more pluralistic, its leaders are more likely to compete for public support or at least to attend to public opinion which is often more bellicose and nationalistic than elite attitudes. This development can in turn become a more serious constraint on politicians, discouraging them from making the necessary compromises with their foreign counterparts in order to break a deadlock. Certainly, dovish leaders have been known to pay a heavy political price and even with their lives (e.g., Anwar Sadat, Yitzhak Rabin) for their conciliatory policies (Colaresi 2004).

The general phenomenon of democratization, elite fragmentation and competition, or just a trend toward more pluralistic politics tends to limit the domestic win set (which in Putnam's 1988 terminology means the range of politically feasible terms for a negotiated deal, given the prevailing distribution of interests and influence of domestic constituents) for concluding a foreign deal, a development that in turn suggests a less sanguine view of the peaceful disposition of those countries in the midst of political transition than is typically portrayed by the "democratic peace" literature (Mansfield and Snyder 2005). Thus, contrary to some commentaries (e.g., Friedberg 2011), a more democratic China does not necessarily mean a more accommodating China in its international relations. At least according to the so-called accountability model that tries to explain the democratic peace phenomenon (Huth and Allee 2002), democratic leaders, especially those who are politically insecure (such as when they face tough re-election challenges), tend to be less conciliatory and more belligerent in their foreign disputes.

Parenthetically, there may be an important distinction between politically insecure leaders and politically insecure regimes. When an authoritarian regime with strong leaders faces domestic economic difficulties or separatist insurgencies, its response to this situation could very well be a greater inclination to seek accommodation on its border disputes. China's past behavior is congruent with this pattern (Fravel 2008). In contrast, democratic leaders facing a strong domestic opposition (in this case, the regime itself is not threatened but the incumbent officials are unpopular and thus likely to be rejected by the voters) may be expected to adopt a hard-line policy and even escalate territorial conflicts.

This line of reasoning implies that by credibly restricting the Kuomintang's (KMT) bargaining space to strike a deal with Beijing, Taiwan's Democratic Progressive Party (DPP) actually enhances a "pan blue" (that is, a Kuomintang-led) government's leverage to demand concessions from Beijing – while at the same time, limiting the extent to which this administration is prepared to make concessions to Beijing due to its potential vulnerability to a domestic political backlash. Intriguingly, this same logic would suggest that Beijing has a vested interest in Ma Ying-jeou's popularity and likewise, Taipei has a similar interest in Xi Jinping consolidating a strong position in Chinese domestic politics because *ceteris paribus*, such conditions expand a counterpart's win set, thereby increasing this chief executive's bargaining space to make concessions and thus reducing the danger of his/her "involuntary defection" (the risk that this chief executive is unable to deliver on a deal already negotiated with a foreign counterpart because strong domestic opposition prevents its ratification). The so-called Sunflower Movement in Taiwan in 2014 illustrates such an instance whereby a politically unpopular Ma Ying-jeou was unable to overcome domestic opposition to a pact he had negotiated with Beijing for free trade in the service sector. This inability to "deliver" on a negotiated pact in turn damages an incumbent politician's credibility and undermines foreigners' willingness to enter into further negotiations with him/her in the future.

According to this logic, politically strong and popular leaders are more credible and are in a better position to negotiate and ratify deals with foreign counterparts. As a thought experiment, would any of China's current leaders have the political stature and influence to undertake what Mao Tse-tung did in launching the initiative and concluding the agreement to open Sino-American relations in 1971–72? As for "involuntary defection," the example of the US Senate's refusal to join the League of Nations comes to mind. But even when legislative approval is eventually given to a treaty (such as the deals pertaining to the Panama Canal and the Strategic Arms Reduction), the substance and process of domestic political discourse leading up to this outcome (disclosing, for example, strong objections from key congressional leaders) can discourage future attempts by both sides to seek another accord, because this information would make the leader of the ratifying country more wary of repeating the same experience and because foreign leaders may infer from the same information that their counterpart is in a weak domestic position to negotiate and conclude a settlement.

On a more ominous note, domestic politics on both sides of the Atlantic Ocean exacerbated the Falklands/Malvinas conflict. The tragedy of this conflict is of course that Argentina and Britain went to war in 1982 even though their officials had previously wanted to settle their dispute and avoid a fight. Once armed hostilities had broken out, however, domestic politics made it near nigh impossible for officials on both sides to back down rather than to face further escalation. Having won a military victory and retaken these islands, London is now saddled with an expensive defense commitment that it had preferred not to take on before the war (Freedman 1988). Its pyrrhic victory does not resolve its dispute with Buenos Aires, a dispute that will become increasingly costly for Britain to sustain militarily, politically, and financially in the long term. Although the 1982 military campaign turned out to be politically popular and boosted Margaret Thatcher's domestic standing, it is not nearly as clear whether Britain's long-term interests have been advanced by it. To the extent that Britain's domestic lobbies and partisan competition had tilted the conduct of diplomacy and popular discourse leading up to the war (e. g., Gamba 1987), one is again reminded that partisan politics does *not* necessarily stop at the "water's edge" of foreign relations and that political representatives who are their people's agents may have incentives that differ from their principals. The domestic unpopularity stemming from the Argentine generals' mismanagement of the economy and their brutal suppression of leftists also contributed to their motivation to invade the archipelago (for the sake of mobilizing public opinion to rally to their support).

Other people may suggest different analytic categories to which China's maritime disputes may belong. They may also disagree with my analytic placement of the cases and my characterization of the relevant categories. For instance, the official Japanese position is that there is *not* a dispute between Tokyo and Beijing over the Senkaku/Diaoyu Islands. In an interview with CNN, former Japanese Prime Minister Yoshihiko Noda argued that this issue involves "only a question of ownership emanat[ing] within Japan." He was quoted saying, "The Senkaku Islands are an inherent part of Japanese terri-tory, historically as well as under international law, so there's no territorial claim issue between the two countries ... Right now, it is the ownership issue – whether the individual owns these islands, or the Tokyo metropolitan government or the state. And I think we have to clearly and solidly explain these stances to the Chinese side" (Whiteman 2013). In light of this official position, when former

Japanese Prime Minister Yukio Hatoyama acknowledged the existence of a dispute while visiting China in January 2013, his remarks were controversial back home. Japanese Defense Minister Itsunori Onodera stated publicly that upon hearing Hatoyama's acknowledgment, "the word of [sic] 'traitor' arose in my mind" (Yuan 2013).

As another example, Manila tried to clarify Washington's commitment under their mutual defense treaty during its confrontation with Beijing over the Scarborough Shoal/Huangyan Island in May 2012. US officials, however, refrained from either confirming or denying whether Washington is bound by its treaty obligation (e.g., Simon 2012). Even though the terms of this treaty include a reference to an armed attack on "the island territories under [either party's] jurisdiction in the Pacific or on its armed forces, public vessels, or aircraft in the Pacific," unnamed people were reported to have "come to conclude [that the US] security cover applies to only acts of aggression by a foreign military entity on the main Philippine islands" (Samaniego 2012). Thus, there is some vagueness about whether extended deterrence by the US is applicable in this case and possibly others (Manila and Washington have entered into an Enhanced Defense Cooperation Agreement since then). With respect to relations across the Taiwan Strait, strategic ambiguity has been described as the US policy (Tucker 2005). This policy declines to formally commit the US one way or the other should a war break out between China and Taiwan. Indeed, whether the two sides across the Taiwan Strait are parties to interstate relations or participants in an unfinished civil war points to the very crux of the controversy regarding their legal and political status – despite efforts by both sides to engage in creative ambiguity to finesse this fundamental issue.

Therefore, possible disagreements about "what X is an instance of" are hardly trivial. As later discussion will try to show, these disagreements are in themselves highly informative about competing attempts by the parties involved to frame issues, set agendas, and gain bargaining leverage. As a quick illustration, the US would naturally like to present its role as an impartial intermediary engaged in "pivotal deterrence" (Crawford 2003) in the Taiwan Strait – that is, to present its policy objective as seeking to deter *both* Beijing and Taipei from upsetting the status quo by non-peaceful means. It is, however, not unnatural for Beijing to interpret this US policy to preserve the status quo as having both the intent and effect of perpetuating Taiwan's *de facto* separation from China. Beijing is more likely to see the US policy as an attempt at extended deterrence rather than pivotal deterrence (which is sometimes also described as dual deterrence aimed at discouraging both Beijing and Taipei from unilaterally changing the status quo).

As another example of competitive efforts to frame discourse and manage public relations, self-determination was the key theme played up by the British in the Falklands/Malvinas War, and emphasized by Western supporters for Taiwan's independence and for the right for Kosovo, Bosnia, Slovenia, and Croatia to secede from Yugoslavia. In the 2014 controversy about a referendum held to determine whether the people of Crimea should break away from Ukraine and join Russia, the same Western countries chose to emphasize instead the sovereignty and territorial integrity of Ukraine, pointing to Ukraine's constitution and the right of *all* of its people (not just those residing in Crimea) to have a voice in deciding Crimea's fate. The latter arguments of course reflect Beijing's position with respect to Taiwan.

To return to the topic of aggregating cases into particular classes of phenomena, I am certainly aware that the labeling of analytic categories and the placement of individual cases in these categories can be controversial. That I have included Taiwan, the Senkaku/Diaoyu Islands, and China's maritime disputes in the South China Sea in the same analytic category called "maritime disputes" can be expected to encounter objections. Not the least of such challenges is likely to be voiced by Beijing, which views its relations with Taiwan as an internal (i.e., intrastate) matter and its disputes about the status of islands in the East and South China Seas as involving its external (i.e., interstate) relations. An overwhelming majority of other states, including the US, have basically accepted this position. They have accorded diplomatic recognition to Beijing as the sole legitimate representative of China, and they have also acknowledged Beijing's position that Taiwan is a part of China. Therefore, there is a basis for arguing that most other states will view China's treatment of the Taiwan issue as a special case, one that is distinct from and one that is therefore not necessarily indicative of its foreign policy disposition in general (e.g.,Kang 2007).

My seeming aggregation of "apples" and "oranges," however, reflects an alternative rationale, one that attends more to interpretive logic than legal status. To the extent that nearly all states in fact view the Taiwan issue as China's domestic matter and thus as qualitatively different from China's other maritime disputes, this consensus implies that Beijing would be likely to face fewer adverse international repercussions if it were to undertake various coercive moves – including a resort to military invasion – in the former case than in the latter ones. *Ceteris paribus*, if Beijing eschews coercive steps under this more permissive circumstance, this self-restraint could in turn be informative about its unwillingness to undertake similar coercive moves under less permissive circumstances, such as those involving its disputes in the East and South China Seas. That the Taiwan issue is far more salient in Chinese domestic politics than the other maritime disputes again lends itself to the same interpretive logic. If China is willing to compromise on the former, one may infer that it will be similarly disposed or even more so inclined in the latter cases. The basic underlying logic is of course that Taiwan represents the "most likely" case over which Beijing is willing to risk a setback in its general reputation for peacefulness and even a war that could destabilize its external relations and upset its domestic development plans. According to this logic, if it eschews violence in this "most likely" case, a resort to arms is even less probable in the other cases, *ceteris paribus*.

Biases in history remembered

Historical memories – such as the so-called lessons of Munich and Vietnam – shape officials' perceptions of policy situations and influence their responses to these situations (e.g., Khong 1992; May 1973). Scholars also often invoke historical parallels and precedents in their research. Like other people, they are not immune from hindsight bias (Fischhoff and Beyth 1975), a tendency to exaggerate the certainty of historical outcomes after they learn how events have actually turned out. There is therefore the danger of seeing historical developments in a more deterministic and less stochastic way than warranted (Lebow 2010). Moreover, like people in general, scholars are often drawn to remember and study those situations that are dramatic, recent, or familiar to them (the so-called retrievability or recall bias, Tversky and Kahneman 1974) and, conversely, to overlook others that are less so. They are also susceptible to the tendency to invoke situational attributions when explaining their own country's or an ally's questionable and even objectionable behavior but to make motivational attributions when explaining similar behavior by an adversary (Mercer 1996). That is, they are inclined to explain unpopular or undesirable conduct by themselves or someone close by appealing to compelling circumstances ("my hands are tied"), but to interpret similar behavior by a disliked other as evidence of its aggressive disposition or shady character ("inherent bad faith").

As a consequence, one often uses alternative logic to explain similar behavior by different countries, depending on one's affinity to them. To illustrate, US–Cuba relations and China–Taiwan relations are at least comparable in geostrategic terms. As a counterfactual experiment, how would most American analysts interpret China's behavior toward Taiwan if Beijing were to replicate US actions in the Bay of Pigs invasion and its blockade of Cuba in October 1962? Would they be inclined to accept Beijing's reasoning in such a situation if it were to invoke justifications similar to those given by Washington with respect to Cuba? As another source of cognitive and affective bias, some historical analogies come to mind more easily than others because they may be politically more convenient or congenial to one's self-image. Thus, as another example, are the two sides across the Taiwan Strait to be considered participants in interstate relations or parties to an unfinished civil war and if the latter, is their relationship comparable to the fight between the Union and Confederacy in 1861–65? The right to secede and the legitimacy of foreign intervention tend to be treated very differently in these cases and others such as Vietnam, Korea, Germany, the former Yugoslavia, and most recently, the controversy over Crimea's status involving Ukraine, Russia, and the West.

For reasons similar to those given above, students of current disputes in the South and East China Seas do not typically assign these quarrels to the same general class of phenomena that includes other comparable cases such as the Beagle Channel settlement between Argentina and Chile, the 1920 Svalbard Treaty that recognized Norway's qualified sovereignty in that maritime episode (Khanna and Gilman 2012), or for that matter, US relations with its neighbors in the Caribbean and Gulf of Mexico. Similarly, Western analysts of relations across the Taiwan Strait do not generally frame their analyses in terms of secessionist movements seeking to gain political independence (Heraclides 1990; Young 1997), and rarely consider possible precedents or parallels from episodes that are more distant in time or personal familiarity (or those more prone to engender cognitive or affective dissonance), such as Norway's separation from Sweden, the American Civil War, and the breakup of the USSR, Yugoslavia, Czechoslovakia, Singapore's union with Malaysia, or, from an earlier era, Gran Colombia and the Austro-Hungarian Empire. They almost never ask whether there may be lessons to be drawn from these historical cases as well as others such as those involving Biafra, Bangladesh, Eritrea, and Ireland, representing both peaceful and violent episodes producing secessionist successes as well as failures. For those secessionist movements involving civil wars, what conditions affect the prospects of durable peace in their aftermath (Mason *et al.* 2011; Tir 2005a, 2005b)? Legal or physical partition does not necessarily mean that a conflict has ended (e.g., Cyprus, Kashmir, Ulster, and Palestine).

Most people tend to also dwell on just a particular set of cases or outcomes – in the parlance of social scientists, to select on a dependent variable – such as when they decide to focus on disputes that are featured in current news headlines, especially those that appear to augur heightened interstate tension. As a consequence, they miss the opportunity to ask, for instance, why Beijing evidently adopted a generally conciliatory policy in settling nearly all of its land borders while appearing to be more assertive in its current maritime disputes. Beijing conceded much larger tracks of land to Czarist Russia in the 1800s when it settled its borders with Moscow but is currently embroiled in a dispute with Japan over small uninhabited islands whose controversial status also dates back to the period of China's historical weakness and humiliation at the hands of imperialists. (Japan argues that it acquired the Senkaku/Diaoyu Islands as *terra nullius* before the 1895 Treaty of Shimonoseki forcing China to cede Taiwan to it, whereas China points to the Potsdam Declaration and Cairo Declaration stipulating that Japan must give up territories it had gained by military conquest). Similarly, what could have accounted for China's different attitudes toward the juridical independence of Mongolia and Taiwan? The former's territory is much larger, representing one sixth of the area of contemporary US (about as large as Texas, New Mexico, Colorado, and Arizona taken together, or an area roughly equivalent to Britain, Ireland, France, Spain, Portugal, Switzerland, and the Benelux countries combined; Sanders 1987: 1). Ironically, while claiming to represent the Republic of China, Taiwan's maps for many years showed Mongolia to be part of China even though Beijing had recognized that country's independence as early as 1949 (the US did not establish diplomatic ties with Mongolia until 1987; previously when Taiwan represented China in the United Nations, it vetoed Mongolia's admission until 1961).

Both the Chinese Nationalists and Communists were inclined to compromise on Mongolia's independence and Soviet influence in that country in order to pursue more important goals such as to counterbalance the puppet regime Manchukuo created by the Japanese during the Sino-Japanese war and subsequently, the control of Manchuria during the Chinese Civil War. The Kuomintang government recognized Mongolia's independence in 1945 as part of a deal to ensure Moscow's neutrality in the latter conflict and as a consequence of the Yalta Accord, to get the USSR to fight Japan in the waning days of World War II. In 1949–50, the newly formed Communist government again subordinated the Mongolia issue in negotiating the Sino-Soviet Treaty and used it as a bargaining chip to gain Soviet concessions in northeast China, restoring China's sovereignty over the Changchun Railroad and the ports of Lushun and Dalian (Liu 2006; Shen and Li 2011). Thus, as shown by Fravel (2008) on other occasions, China has quite often shown flexibility in compromising on its territorial disputes and pursuing settlements in order to achieve higher goals (in the Chinese Communist parlance, to focus attention on the "main contradiction" or the most important and pressing problem of the moment).

For example, Chi-kin Lo (1989) has shown that Beijing's policies toward its counterparts in the South China Sea disputes have been motivated by the larger geostrategic picture, specifically its relations with the USSR and the US during the 1970s and 1980s. Another example was provided by Chien-peng Chung (2004: 38–41) who reports that Beijing's leaders had side-stepped the dispute with Japan over the Senkaku/Diaoyu Islands in the late 1970s, when they were more interested in concluding a peace and friendship treaty with Tokyo professing a joint "anti-hegemony" (meaning anti-Soviet) position.

This discussion points to various biases inherent in an approach that singles out a particular actor or case for attention, and treats it in isolation from other comparable actors or situations. It thus makes an argument in favor of nomothetic as opposed to idiosyncratic analysis. China is often treated in a separate analytic category by itself, and its conduct is not compared to that of other countries. As a result, we often attribute to the current government in Beijing special and even unique qualities, and overlook its possible similarities with others (including earlier Chinese governments). As another illustration in addition to the example given above concerning the policies adopted by the Chinese Communists and Nationalists toward Mongolia, the nine-dash line propagated by Beijing to stake out its claim in the South China Sea was actually first introduced by the Kuomintang in 1947 when it still ruled the mainland (in the form of an eleven-dash line, with two of the dashes demarking the Gulf of Tonkin, deleted subsequently by the Communists, Hayton 2014: 58–59). The logic of comparative social inquiry calls for substituting the proper names of our cases with the names of the pertinent variables for explaining an empirical phenomenon (Przeworski and Teune 1970).

As mentioned earlier, there is still another analytic tendency that deserves to be highlighted. Scholars are more inclined to study the occurrence of dramatic, even sensational, events than to attend to the non-occurrence of the expected. In the parlance of research design, they tend to select on the dependent variable (focusing just on those occasions when X has happened and not when it has failed to happen). Unlike Sherlock Holmes, most of us do not ponder about those cases when "the dog did not bark." Non-events are typically absent in our analyses and always excluded from the standard data sets (which, for example, have not thus far reported a Chinese invasion of Taiwan). Such omission means that one does not obtain sufficient variation in the dependent variable being studied. If one just looks at China's current maritime disputes without also considering its previous border settlements with its other neighbors (when acrimonies did not occur or when disputes have ended), one may end up with the mistaken impression that Beijing has always followed an uncompromising approach in such disagreements.

Selecting on the dependent variable often involves another important analytic issue, one that has been described as selection bias. Recognition of this bias stems from the realization that people are strategic; they choose to enter – or not to enter – into certain encounters or relationships based on their anticipation of how these episodes will turn out. When they eschew involvement, history records their decisions as non-events. By recording only those occasions when people decide to engage each other, history presents a biased sample that excludes those encounters that could have happened but did not.

To illustrate the analytic importance of this selection bias, consider the fact that most attempts at economic sanction have failed to achieve their declared purpose (Hufbauer et al. 1990; Pape 1997). Does this phenomenon mean that sanctions are ineffective? Not necessarily – because such a conclusion does not take into account those unobserved cases when the potential targets of sanction agreed to make the necessary concessions before sanctions had to be actually imposed (that is, their concessions had made the imposition of a sanction unnecessary; Drezner 1999). As a consequence of this consideration of sanction threats succeeding preemptively, those historical episodes recording when sanctions did occur tend to represent the more difficult cases for this policy to succeed (hence, a biased sample), cases for which the targets (e.g., North Korea, Iran, Cuba, Russia, and China) must have been more determined to resist (because the less resolved targets would have already "selected" themselves out of these encounters). A valid assessment of the efficacy of sanctions would have to include those occasions when an unpublicized threat of undertaking them has had the desired effect, thus nullifying the need to actually implement them. Of course, as a practical matter it is impossible to include in one's analysis a universe of all potential sanction situations – or more generally for the purpose of our discussion, to identify all cases where bluffs have not been called or when states have decided not to start a confrontation because of a preexisting deterrence threat.

Naturally, leaders also sometimes decide to "select" themselves into particular encounters. Just as when they choose inaction or non-involvement, these decisions can be meaningful – especially when they seem to be counterintuitive. For instance, why would Beijing and Washington, depicted in some accounts as inevitable adversaries, want to enter into an intense economic relationship as shown by the two countries' heavy trade, investment, and loan exchanges (Chan 2012d)? Adversaries are not supposed to enter into such exchanges because they can contribute to the other side's military strength and increase one's own vulnerability to a political holdup. As another example, Beijing backed down in several previous confrontations after Washington threatened to intervene on Taiwan's behalf. In view of this experience, what does the selection logic imply if Beijing were to mount another challenge? Similarly, having observed the results of Chen Shui-bian's initiatives promoting Taiwan's independence, what inferences can one draw if another leading politician from the Democratic Progressive Party were to adopt a similar policy stance in the future?

I will pursue such questions in more detail later. For now, I would just mention that much of the literature on deterrence hinges on the idea of reputation – which assumes interdependency between events and actors (what X does or does not do today will influence how Y will behave toward it tomorrow). But is there any empirical support for this reputation effect (e.g., Mercer 1996)? Or can knowledge about the other side's prior behavior turn out to be even self-invalidating (Mercer 2013)? For instance, knowing that the other party (whether in a poker game or interstate confrontation) has bluffed before, should I expect that he/she will repeat this behavior next time (e.g., Sartori 2005) – or should I instead suspect that his/her prior (called) bluff was a deliberate advertisement designed to set me up for entrapment the next time (such as when repeated Arab military exercises were used as a ruse to disguise Egypt and Syria's true intention to subsequently attack Israel in October 1973)? Having conceded in a previous dispute, should I expect the other side to concede again – or to be less inclined to yield again the next time (as the Russians apparently felt about German intimidation in July 1914)? If I care about my reputation for firmness and reliability, shouldn't my counterpart also care about his or hers – especially if this counterpart has backed down previously and has thus suffered an embarrassing setback?

People try to learn from the past and use this information to deliberate their future choices. If not self-invalidating, perhaps this phenomenon implies that history should show a self-correcting tendency (if I know you have bluffed before, and you know that I know, and I know that you know I know, and so on and so forth). If true, this tendency means that events reflecting people's decisions should *not* exhibit serial dependency – so that, for example, the idea that one needs to fight or stand firm for the sake of protecting one's general reputation (e.g., the admonition that appeasement this time will invite further aggression in the future, the fear of falling dominoes, etc.) is unwarranted. Paul Huth (1988a: 81) shows that a state's past behavior presents an ambiguous indication of its future behavior: past weakness appears to undermine a defender's deterrence credibility but past firmness does not necessarily contribute to this credibility. Moreover, a defender's past behavior toward *other* challengers does not offer a good basis for making inferences about how it will respond to a *current* challenger. Indeed, shouldn't one expect a country with a strong record of having resisted others' challenges in the past to be more inclined to take advantage of this reputation and to therefore be tempted to bluff more often (e.g., to pretend that it will fight again in order to gain concessions on the cheap)? Only those with a weak reputation will have to invest more effort to convince others that they are serious *this time*.

Returning to the question posed earlier, knowing that the US has sent credible signals to intervene in the Taiwan Strait in previous crises and having failed to intimidate Taiwan in these prior encounters, what must have changed in the minds of Beijing's leaders if they were to start another armed confrontation? Should we conclude that they must have become more optimistic – or more desperate – based on the information that has become available to them in the interim?

Anticipating the book's substantive conclusions

In contrast to many extant studies of China's maritime disputes and especially its relations with Taiwan, I see bilateral and regional ties in the Asia Pacific moving generally in the direction of greater stability and mutual accommodation. This view does not imply that contentious relations will disappear and disputes will be resolved quickly. It does suggest a generally favorable tendency whereby contested sovereignty will be kept in check so that it will not jeopardize the current political and economic ties binding the disputants. The parties may not be able to reach a definitive settlement in the near future, but their disagreements are also unlikely to erupt into war. Dampening and shelving these disagreements while continuing to maintain and even strengthen the other aspects of bilateral and multilateral relations is the most likely development for the immediate future. Although the issues standing in the way of a negotiated settlement may appear intractable, the longer-term prospects for resolving these disputes are reasonably promising.

This promise hinges on the emergence of what Robert Keohane and Joseph Nye (1977) described as a world of complex interdependence characterized by dense and deep transnational networks of stakeholders with cross-cutting interests. Even in the case of historically tense relations across the Taiwan Strait, a new relationship "premised on high-level contact, trust, and reduced level of force" (Gilley 2010: 50) has taken shape. The evolution of this relationship tends to vindicate the liberal position that "a broad integration of domestic interests will pacify relations between states far more than a militarized balance of power" (Gilley 2010: 60). Similarly, despite recent news on Sino-Japanese acrimonies, these countries' relationship has generally shown more accommodation than confrontation in recent years (e.g., Hagstrom 2012; Jerden and Hagstrom 2012). Prognoses based on realists' core expectations have often turned out to be too pessimistic. One fundamental fact stands out in this respect: China's foreign policy was much more bellicose in the first few decades after 1949 when it was much weaker, but this bellicosity has declined even while it has become much stronger in recent years. Thus, the temporal correlation between China's bellicosity and its capability is in the opposite direction to realists' prediction.

In the following chapters, I will present my rationale for being generally more sanguine than most other commentators on China's maritime disputes. This rationale incorporates multiple considerations. I mention just three of them here. First, contrary to the impression given by some accounts, China has actually been a rather "average" country in its management of territorial disputes. It has not been more inclined to use force or less prepared to compromise compared to other countries involved in such disputes (Fravel 2008: 40–41). It has been rather patient and inclined to shelve these disputes unless it believes that the other side is trying to change the status quo such as evidenced by Jawaharlal Nehru's "forward policy," Chen Shui-bian's "referendum politics," and, most recently, Shintaro Ishihara's campaign to purchase the disputed Senkaku/Diaoyu Islands.

Significantly, this pattern of Chinese behavior contradicts the tenet of offensive realism (Mearsheimer 2001), contending that states would push to expand their power as much as their capabilities would enable them – that is, until and unless they are stopped by other states' countervailing power. In China's recent history of territorial disputes, Beijing has actually pulled back and refrained from seizing large chunks of disputed territory after defeating its opponents in military actions, such as India and Vietnam. This pattern suggests a defensive, reactive, and even status-quo orientation rather than an offensive motivation (e.g., Fravel 2007a, 2007b). China's actual historical conduct appears to suggest an insistence that other parties must first recognize the principle of its sovereignty claims, and having achieved this recognition, Beijing has actually been quite willing to compromise and even accept terms of a settlement that are generally more favorable to its counterparts.

This observation is supported by Chien-peng Chung (2004, 171), who argues that Beijing has actually demanded few border concessions in its territorial conflicts; it has been willing to settle these disputes on reasonable terms if its counterpart is willing to acknowledge that a border problem exists and that this problem reflects past injustice. Beijing's demand for the other side to accept the latter conditions, however, presents a serious challenge of credible commitment. This is so because acceptance of these conditions would make China's counterpart vulnerable to a possible subsequent defection by Beijing. That is, once this counterpart admits to a border problem and acknowledges past injustices, its claims would be severely undermined if Beijing were to use such an admission as a bargaining lever to gain concessions.

Second and related to the above discussion, a more secure and powerful China has been historically less disposed to initiate military action. This tendency is seemingly counterintuitive and contradicts much of the recent literature that argues that Beijing's capability gains will incline it to become more assertive and even aggressive in its foreign policy. In the past, Beijing's resort to force has in fact tended to be associated with its domestic weakness or declining bargaining position. Thus, as a general proposition, "a stronger China might be less prone to using force" (Fravel 2008: 314). This proposition makes sense in view of the central tenet of prospect theory (Kahneman and Tversky 1979, 2000), which claims that people tend to accept greater risks in order to forestall a setback or recover from a loss whereas they tend to behave conservatively in the domain of gain (i.e., when they have improved or expect to improve their relative position).

Significantly and emphasizing the idea of strategic anticipation (Copeland 1996), this observation contradicts the power-transition theory's expectation. States that are making relative gains and expect a benign future to bring additional gains from cooperation would behave conservatively (they would rather not rock the boat because a continuation of present trends is likely to bring them further gains), and they are more inclined to postpone or compromise on territorial conflicts from a position of bargaining strength. It is not in their interest to destabilize the status quo and thereby to jeopardize their ongoing and anticipated gains. Conversely, those states that are suffering from a relative decline or expect a future rupture of relations are more disposed to take risky actions. They do so in order to reverse their recent or impending losses. That states, and people in general, are forward looking is important even though this observation may seem obvious. This observation calls attention to the phenomenon that when making decisions, people try to anticipate and take into their consideration the possible ramifications of their own and others' actions.

Third, people's awareness that their behavior can affect future relations in turn suggests that their perceptions of their interests and even their identity are not fixed. Interests and identities can evolve as a result of increased exchanges and interactions – and vice versa, producing a positive reinforcement between the two. This idea was propagated quite some time ago by Karl Deutsch and his associates (1957) in writing about the formation of the North Atlantic security community. Richard Merritt (1966) also wrote about the emergence of a common American identity even before the Declaration of Independence. In the current context, these studies point to a third reason for relative optimism. Public attitudes on Taiwan have shown some signs conducive to national reconciliation. A 2013 poll conducted jointly by Taiwan Competitiveness Forum, a private think tank, and the Apollo Survey and Research Company reports an overwhelming majority (90.4%) of respondents identifying themselves as Chinese in ethnicity (Kuomintang 2013). This identity can coexist with a strong Taiwanese identity. It also does not preclude dramatic swings in election outcomes, such as when the voters provided Ma Ying-jeou with a decisive re-election victory in 2012 and then an over-whelming rejection of his party's candidates two years later in mayoral elections.

Increasing economic exchanges and social interactions across the Taiwan Strait (as well as between China and the other claimant states in the East and South China Sea disputes) have tended to restrain the danger of military escalation. The survey cited above also reports Taiwanese people's views on the prospective benefits of increasing eco-nomic interdependence and the concomitant danger implied by the ongoing power shifts between the two sides of the Taiwan Strait. It discloses that 52.5% of the respondents regarded China's development as an opportunity for Taiwan to take advantage of, compared to 18.7% who considered this development to constitute a threat to the island, and 14.9% who thought that Taiwan should proactively take part in China's development (Kuomintang 2013). These figures speak to the central point of contention between classical liberal views about the promises of economic cooperation and traditional realist fears about the danger of unfavorable power shifts, and they indicate how far things have changed since the days of military confrontation across the Taiwan Strait.

Returning to the idea of selection logic, recent news about maritime disputes involving China and others (such as between Taiwan and the Philippines) actually implies a greater confidence in the pertinent coun-tries' ability to manage conflicts and more mutual awareness on their part. Although not framed explicitly in terms of the selection logic, Brantly Womack's (2011: 375) astute remark corresponds with this view: "To put it simply, there is no threshold of military superiority that would make it beneficial for China to establish its control over all the Spratlys at the cost of strategic hostility with Southeast Asia. Therefore, ironically, all parties can persist in their contention without fear of a major international con-flict since the costs of decisive victory exceeds the benefits even for the strongest contender, and the prospect of oil wealth makes each anxious to expand claims and reluctant to yield."

As the "game" is currently structured, a failure to take tangible actions to challenge others' claims means to forfeit one's standing in a dispute. Thus, this situation necessitates and encourages the claimant states to participate in highly publicized contests. Moreover, selection logic implies that the weaker Southeast Asian countries' decisions to challenge China's sovereignty claims actually indicate their relative confidence that the latter will be restrained from escalating their conflict. As a thought experiment, what inferences would one draw if Mexico or Venezuela were to confront the US navy over some disputed islands in the Gulf of Mexico? The logic presented here argues that these countries must have been reasonably confident that they would not be subjected to the full force of US retaliation.

Naturally, propositions such as this one should be subjected to empirical verification. History is the ultimate arbiter of competing opinions (Ray and Russett 1996), and falsifiable prediction provides an important albeit hardly exclusive basis for judging the relative merit of alternative approaches or perspectives (one may make accurate predictions that are based on faulty reasoning, and similar predictions may actually be based on different logic and evidence). Moreover, some cases can deviate from a general pattern, so that, for example, China acted offensively and opportunistically when it attacked the South Vietnamese in 1974 to take over the Paracels entirely (this case therefore contradicts the characterization of Beijing's strategic posture as reactive assertiveness).

Do situations evolve in the general direction expected by an analysis, and produce outcomes that are generally in accord with its expectations? Given the probabilistic nature of these expectations or predictions, isolated cases of disconfirmation may be disappointing but not devastating. But when predictive failures persist and happen in many instances and forms, the damage done to an analysis or perspective is far more serious. Likewise, when an analysis or perspective fails to pass easy tests (i.e., when it turns out to be inadequate in circumstances where it should have performed especially well) or when history actually contradicts its central claims, its credibility is more severely strained. Thus, for example, critics of realism call attention to major anomalies (from realism's perspective) to discredit it, pointing to various occurrences of the unexpected and nonoccurrence of the expected (again, from realism's perspective) such as the USSR's voluntary dissolution, Germany and Japan's decision not to arm themselves with nuclear weapons, the formation of the European Union with its supranational institutions, the reunification of Germany supported by its former enemies in World Wars I and II, and the failure of the other major states to form a countervailing coalition against US preponderance. These are momentous developments in recent history that cut to the very core of realism with respect to its claims about the primacy of anarchy, self-help, states, and policies seeking to balance against the most powerful state.

The rest of the book

The remainder of the book unfolds in the following sequence. Chapter 2 presents brief reviews of international relations research following the nomothetic approach pertinent to several topics of interest, such as democratic peace, economic interdependence, militarized interstate disputes, and polarity and polarization. Based on large and systematically collected historical data, this scholarship has produced some persistent empirical patterns. Several patterns are sufficiently robust to represent "stylized facts" (such as that associating territorial contests with the occurrence and recurrence of militarized interstate disputes). They point to the "central tendencies" in interstate interactions, and thus offer a set of initial baseline expectations for thinking about China's foreign relations in general and its territorial disputes more specifically.

Chapter 3 turns to an attempt to explain bargaining failures, such as the impasse that has characterized relations across the Taiwan Strait. It draws particularly from James Fearon's (1995) insights that seek to explain why wars happen even though the belligerents have a shared interest to avoid this costly undertaking. His seminal article points to several seemingly intractable factors that hamper efforts to reach a negotiated settlement. Deliberate misrepresentation to disguise one's capabilities and intentions, and the inaccessibility of a counterpart's decision processes, are inherent in the structure of these bargaining situations. A reciprocal deficit in trust is another impediment to reaching an agreement because the disputants cannot be confident that a deal struck today will be honored tomorrow. Some issues such as those dealing with tariffs and currency exchange rates are by their nature more easily addressed in terms of quantitative obligations to be discharged by the parties to an agreement. Compliance to such an agreement should also be more easily monitored and enforced than others with more subjective or intangible terms. According to the theory of collective action (Olson 1965), "narrower" issues tend to engage the attention and mobilize the actions of only a small set of special interests rather than a broad spectrum of the electorate. In contrast, symbolic issues such as those pertaining to national sovereignty and regime legitimacy are inherently less subject to division (i.e., to being quantified and partitioned) and they are also more politically charged. By their very nature, such issues involving greater political salience or controversy are more difficult to resolve than the less politicized ones.

Chapter 4 expands on the abstraction of bilateral bargaining games. It takes up the topics of pivotal deterrence and extended deterrence (e.g., Crawford 2003; Huth 1988a). This discussion introduces the US as the critical third party in China's maritime disputes. Washington's role has been variously described as a defender of the status quo seeking to discourage all sides to a dispute from unilateral assertion, or as a counter-vailing force to discourage Chinese aggression. In either case, the bargaining game becomes more complicated and interesting, now that there are at least three parties involved. The dynamics of alliance politics becomes relevant. Whether as a formal ally or tacit partner to one or more of the parties challenging China's sovereignty claims, or as an impartial defender of the status quo, how can Washington communicate to the pertinent parties its credibility? Or should it?

US officials are evidently aware of the danger of moral hazard, referring to the perverse tendency for a declared policy to produce behavior that it is supposed to discourage in the first place. Perceptions of Washington's support and protection may incline its formal or informal allies to escalate their dispute with Beijing in the hope of leveraging and committing the US to their own cause. Indeed, when caught in a lopsided dispute with a much stronger adversary, the weaker side's most obvious strategy is to avoid being caught in a bilateral contest and to offset its inherent disadvantage by internationalizing the conflict. Washington therefore faces the challenge of navigating between the Scylla of supporting its allies and the Charybdis of entrapment by them (Snyder 1997). How are Beijing and Taipei likely to interpret signals coming from Washington? Drawing inferences from selection logic, this chapter will discuss the danger of a Sino-American confrontation over the Taiwan Strait.

Chapter 5 further expands the analytic terrain by bringing into the picture domestic groups in the context of two-level games. A critical factor in the evolution of the Falklands/Malvinas conflict is the acceptance and assertion by Britain that this dispute hinged on the central issue of the islanders' right to self-determination (something that it did not insist on while negotiating with Beijing over Hong Kong's repatriation; moreover, when pressed, only 24% of respondents in a British poll supported a policy to be determined by the Kelpers' wishes alone – compared to 72% who wanted to take into account the interests of Britain as a whole; Freedman 1988: 100). Once the issue was framed as a matter of the islanders' right to self-determination and once the islanders' representatives joined the talks as a third party (and thus exercised veto power over any negotiation progress; Freedman and Gamba-Stonehouse 1991: 10; Kinney 1989: 46–52), London had in effect forfeited the initiative to the Kelpers who did not have any wish to live under Argentina's jurisdiction – and who still do not, as shown by their overwhelming vote in the March 2013 referendum in favor of remaining as a British Overseas Territory (before the war Buenos Aires and London had tried to finesse their deadlock by negotiating over the fine distinction between the Kelpers' "rights" versus their "interests;" e.g., Gamba 1987: 155).

The Kelpers' incentives are easy to understand. They wished to receive the benefits of economic assistance from and trading with Argentina without the associated political costs of living under its rule. Prior to the 1982 war, they had tried to extract economic benefits from Buenos Aires without, however, yielding to its political demands. In the meantime, London also agreed to Buenos Aires's economic courtship of the Kelpers but was reluctant to put pressure on the latter to accept Argentine sovereignty. It was moreover unwilling to expend on military measures to deter an Argentine attempt to seize the islands (Lebow 1985; Lippincot and Treverton 1988). It sought to buy time by protracted negotiations with Buenos Aires, "talking just for the sake of talking." Argentina naturally felt that it had been "strung along." Richard Ned Lebow (1985: 104) described the Argentines' sense of frustration: "They came increasingly to believe, and not without reason that they were behaving like the proverbial donkey, tricked into pulling the cart by a carrot on a stick dangled before him." Facing serious domestic political unpopularity, the Argentine generals finally concluded that in view of Britain's evident unwillingness to commit to the islands' defense, a quick successful military invasion would achieve a *fait accompli* that London would not try to reverse. In the end, leaders in both Argentina and Britain chose to fight rather than disengage because they agreed on one thing: they could not otherwise sustain their respective domestic political position. War happened despite both sides' wish to settle rather than fight and despite US efforts to mediate. The main driver for escalation came more from a domestic than a foreign source.

Taiwan's political economy features a much more heterogeneous set of interests and incentives than depicted above for the Kelpers. By and large, the island's large financial institutions are internationally oriented and have favored economic opening abroad (Kastner 2009). Many of Taiwan's manufacturers, even medium-sized firms, have diversified their operations to China and have acquired an important stake in sales to the mainland market. Even for those firms that have not physically moved their operations to China, many have become deeply integrated in cross-border production chains. Compared to these commercial interests, farmers, small labor-intensive producers, and companies catering to domestic services have faced competitive pressures from the mainland. Chapter 5 investigates how these evolving economic interests, civilian transactions (e.g., tourism, cultural exchanges), and public opinion are likely to affect bargaining across the Taiwan Strait. From the study of domestic institutions in mature democracies (Tsebelis 2002), we know that the larger the number of veto groups and the farther apart their respective preferences, the greater the difficulty of moving from policy stasis to a new consensus. The power of these groups and their preferences, however, are not fixed but are subject to change due to changing circumstances and political entrepreneurship.

Turning to the East and South China Sea disputes, Chapter 6 further expands the analytic landscape by considering multilateral relations for which the theory of collective action is pertinent (Olson 1965). It is well known that Vietnam and the Philippines want to see more active involvement by the ASEAN (Association of Southeast Asian Nations) as an organization, thereby multilateralizing their disputes with China. They are supported in this approach by Washington. In contrast, Beijing has thus far stressed its preference for bilateral talks – understandably so since its bargaining leverage can be enhanced in such one-on-one negotiations. In order to forestall a united coalition against China, Beijing is likely to focus on the weakest link in any coalition that may be formed against it and to encourage this country's defection by making timely concessions. Those contesting China's sovereignty claims have, conversely, the choice of making separate deals with Beijing or sticking to united action. Collective action by China's counterparts in Southeast Asia is complicated by the fact that these countries are also involved in their own territorial disputes, such as between Malaysia and the Philippines, or other kinds of competition.

In the terminology of coalition politics, the Southeast Asian countries have offsetting incentives that tempt them to shirk, hide, free ride, or appease Beijing (Schroeder 1994). The first one to break ranks and negotiate a separate deal with Beijing is likely to receive the best terms, whereas the last holdout is likely to be left in the cold. Thus, timing seems to be important. This view points to the contesting parties' mixed motives so that all those involved would want to be the first one to strike a deal and none of them would want to be the last. This tendency could of course engender a self-fulfilling momentum to reach bilateral accords with China. At the same time, the prospect of reaching a multilateral deal is hampered by the difficulties of organizing collective action among those contesting Beijing's sovereignty claims, including those difficulties attributable to other claimants' information asymmetries and divergences in their domestic political calendars.

There is also a corollary to the above remarks. The state that is most adamant and vigorous in resisting China's claims is likely to pay the heaviest price as it will attract Beijing's hostility and retaliation, while the benefits of its resistance may actually redound to the other claimant states. The general logic presented by this observation should be familiar to those who have tried to explain the failure of a countervailing coalition to form against US global hegemony: the state that makes the first move in this direction is most likely to end up focusing Washington's wrath on itself and runs the risk of being "picked off" before a countervailing coalition has a chance to consolidate (Brooks and Wohlforth 2008).

Finally, the presence of multiple maritime disputes – such as Japan's other disagreements with South Korea and Russia over the Dokdo/Takeshima and Southern Kuril/Northern Territories, respectively – suggests that moves made in one case can affect the others. As in the case of some Southeast Asian countries with their own territorial disputes, this phenomenon presents an interesting empirical and theoretical question: which factors – such as geographic proximity, cultural affinity, historical animosity, commercial ties, shared democracy, or common alliance ties (with the US) – appear to be more influential in a state's decision to give greater priority to some disputes than others? Different theories (e.g., democratic peace, balance of power, economic interdependence) make different predictions about which disputes the pertinent states will contest more vigorously and which ones they will prefer to set aside for the time being.

Finally, studies on civil wars invite a parallel inquiry about bargaining over maritime disputes. It pertains to the issue of a state's reputation when it is involved in several disputes at the same time. Why do some incumbent governments accommodate separatist groups but others fight them? One hypothesis that has been advanced and that has received some empirical support contends that these decisions incorporate anticipation of other secessionists who may be encouraged by the governments' concessions (Walter 2003, 2006). In other words, this reasoning argues that governments (rightly or wrongly) invest in their reputation; they choose to fight rather than accommodate when they want to discourage other possible separatist challenges in the future. Does a similar reasoning apply to states when they are involved in several concurrent foreign disputes? Does this simultaneous involvement encourage their intransigence or does it have the opposite effect of inducing them to settle some disputes so that they can concentrate on others?

In Chapter 7, I summarize my arguments. The 1982 war fought by Argentina and Britain shows that there is always a risk of unwanted escalation. Moreover, reaching territorial settlements requires overcoming formidable domestic and foreign obstacles standing in their way. Yet as attested by the boundary agreements that China has already reached with almost all its land neighbors, such accords are far from improbable. Comparing the security and peacefulness of China's land borders today with the situation prevailing in the first three or so decades of the People's Republic's existence, there is reason for optimism that the general trend has been favorable to settling its remaining territorial contests. Rising economic interdependence in particular tends to restrain China's current maritime disputes from destabilizing bilateral and regional relations. Therefore, the glass is more half full than half empty.

Additionally, if Beijing refrains from using its stronger capabilities to impose a settlement of its maritime disputes and instead accommodates other claimant states in reaching compromises with them, this behavior communicates a peaceful disposition in conducting its foreign relations in general. The reverse also holds. To the extent that Beijing applies its increasing power for self-aggrandizement, this behavior signals aggressive intentions. As argued previously, how Beijing intends to use its increasing power presents a more demanding and important question than the prognosis that it is likely to further improve its relative power. How Chinese intentions are likely to be influenced by Chinese capabilities cuts to the very core of debates about Chinese foreign policy, and international relations theorizing in general. This book's tentative conclusion questions and reverses the expectations of offensive realism and power-transition theory. Contrary to these theories' expectations, it suggests that China's capability improvements tend to moderate its intentions. This proposition, based on the study of just one country (albeit one that is becoming increasingly powerful), demonstrates that country-specific analyses and theoretical generalizations are not inherently incompatible enterprises.

This said, one should also consider historical precedents. What should be the benchmark for assessing whether China's behavior indicates an expansionist ambition or a modest agenda? One parallel comes naturally to mind: how did Washington behave during its period of rapid ascendance in the late 1800s and early 1900s? What policy agenda did it pursue in the Caribbean and the Gulf of Mexico and, more broadly, in the Western Hemisphere and even the Pacific? How does conduct such as its proclamation of the Monroe Doctrine, its confrontation with London in the Venezuelan boundary dispute, its invasion of Cuba in the Spanish-American War, its annexation of Guam, the Philippines, and the Hawaii archipelago, and the construction of the Panama Canal compare with Beijing's current and recent behavior? The overwhelming consensus of international relations scholars has been that the US was a status-quo power, and this attribution helps them to explain why war was avoided when it overtook Britain as the world's dominant power. They also tend to agree that today's China is a revisionist power. Many of these analysts share the premises of offensive realism and power-transition theory, but appear to want things both ways, shuttling their analytic logic and conclusion depending on the proper names of the cases being studied rather than these countries' actual conduct.

2 Territorial conflicts
Mitigating and aggravating circumstances

Territorial disputes are the most likely cause for interstate conflict. When accompanied by armament races and alliance dynamics, they often escalate to war which in turn threatens to engulf other states beyond the direct contestants (Vasquez 2009). China has settled most of its land borders (Fravel 2008), a development that should augur more stable and peaceful relations with its neighbors. Beijing's maritime frontiers, however, have become more contentious with recent news highlighting competing sovereignty claims in both the East China Sea and the South China Sea. Some Chinese officials have reportedly characterized these disagreements as impinging on China's "core interests," thus elevating them to a level of importance traditionally associated with defending China's proclaimed sovereignty and maintaining its territorial integrity such as with respect to Taiwan and Tibet. Understandably, these statements tend to arouse foreign concerns about a more assertive, even belligerent, China in pursuing its claims.

It would be useful to put such concerns in the context of China's own past behavior and that of states in general. When examined in this light, China appears to be a rather "normal" state; that is, its conduct has generally followed the statistical norm for all states. Taylor Fravel (2008: 41) reports that Beijing compromised in 88% of its disputes when it is considered a challenger in such disputes, compared to a benchmark figure of 79% for all similarly situated states. Although the differences between these two figures is not statistically significant at the 0.05 level of confidence, the direction of this difference points to Beijing being more conciliatory than the cross-national average. While also not presenting a statistically significant difference, Beijing has threatened the use of force less often than the cross-national average. Beijing has made such military threat in 38% of its territorial disputes, but the average for all other states is 45%. Of China's twenty-three territorial disputes, Beijing has pursued compromise in seventeen of them (Fravel 2008: 54). Most of its remaining disputes involve contested jurisdiction over islands or islets (with the demarcation of the Sino-Indian boundary being the one major unsettled land border).

Naturally, there are mitigating and aggravating factors that influence baseline dispositions such as illustrated by those figures just mentioned. Geography is one such factor. Due to the "stopping power of water" (Mearsheimer 2001), China was for many years much less able to assert and protect its maritime claims in comparison to its disputed land borders. This situation, however, has been changing recently as Beijing acquires more military capabilities and becomes the largest trading partner for most of the other countries involved in these maritime disputes. These disputes gain attention not only because China is now more powerful militarily and economically, but also because the US is a formal or tacit ally of those countries contesting China's claims. The specter of rising tension producing a wide conflagration has even led some pundits writing for popular press to invoke events leading to World War I as a parallel (e.g., Tharoor 2013).

In this chapter, I review several pertinent strands of literature from quantitative analyses of international relations. These analyses have drawn on large, systematically collected data from history, and have shown some strong empirical patterns. These patterns can be taken to indicate central tendencies in the particular behavioral domain in question, and can thus offer baseline expectations when we try to predict how a particular country such as China is likely to behave in a specific situation. Rather than treating China as a special case, this analytic stance starts with the assumption that it is comparable to other countries. This does not mean that its behavior will be "average." It is possible for its behavior to depart from the average. But will China's behavior be significantly different from that of its peers after one adjusts, as one typically does in quantitative analyses, for the putative influence of generic factors, such as the nature of a country's political system, its economic size and physical location, its status as a major or minor power, and the relative military balance, ideological affinity, and strength of economic ties characterizing its relations with pertinent others? And if China is different, what is the direction and size of this difference?

A few examples may be helpful. Considering China's economic size, does it over- or under-spend on its defense budget compared to other countries? After adjusting for its number of contiguous neighbors, does it have a disproportionately large number of territorial disputes? And, relative to its level of development, does it have a comparatively open or closed economy as measured by the amount of foreign trade and direct investment in relation to its gross domestic product? Does it turn out to be a "normal" country in these comparisons, or an outlier? The results of such cross-national comparisons will likely suggest that China has not spent particularly heavily on its military or engaged in a disproportionately large number of territorial disputes during its period of rapid ascent, and has had in recent years a more open economy than many of its peers. Except for Japan and Germany (the two major defeated belligerents in World War II), when compared to the other countries that are typically classified as "major states" (the US, the USSR/Russia, Britain, France, even India), China has undertaken fewer military interventions abroad and fought fewer foreign wars since 1945.

Some of the variables mentioned above refer to a country's attributes, such as whether its political system is democratic or authoritarian and whether it is located in a crowded neighborhood with many contiguous states. Other variables refer to a country's behavior, such as its proclivity to spend on the military, enter into territorial disputes, and open its economy to foreign trade and investment. These two kinds of variables point to the general difference between what a state has versus what it does. They also correspond approximately to what have been called "opportunity" and "willingness" (Most and Starr 1989). The nature of a country's political system and its relative military strength may expand or limit the menu of policy options available for its leaders to choose from ("opportunity"), whereas its economic interests, elite competition, and ideological impulses may give it the incentives ("willingness") to make certain choices. Of course, sometimes the same variable may be relevant to both concepts, such as when relative military strength can both provide a country's leaders the wherewithal to fight a war and encourage their motivation to do so. Nevertheless, the general difference between attributes and behavior and between opportunity and willingness should be reasonably clear.

But why is this distinction pertinent to thinking about China's maritime disputes? Power-transition theory (e.g., Organski 1958; Organski and Kugler 1980), for example, argues that a war between two leading states becomes more probable when a latecomer gains relative power *and* when it has revisionist motivations. These are individually necessary and jointly sufficient conditions to produce the predicted outcome. Much of the current discourse on China's rise attends to recent power shifts favoring Beijing without, however, trying to discern how its incentives (or intentions) may have changed. The connection that ties changing capabilities to changing motivations is not always clear. Why should one expect a state with rising capabilities to become more aggressive rather than more satisfied? Why would it want to upend the existing international order that has facilitated its rise rather than to preserve it so that this rising country can continue its upward trajectory? Would it be reasonable to expect the opposite tendency: namely, a declining but still stronger country is the one that has both the necessary capability and the motivation to launch a preventive war – to attack a latecomer in order to arrest or reverse the declining hegemon's weakening position while it still enjoys an advantage?

To introduce another example to highlight the difference between what a country has versus what it does, consider Aaron Friedberg's (1993/94) much-cited prediction that Asia was ripe for rivalry. Friedberg calls attention to various factors that encourage the formation or intensification of interstate competition, such as the Asian countries' heterogeneous cultures, their unequal levels of economic development, and their different systems of government, in addition to their relatively low levels of participation in international organizations and of economic interdependence compared to the European countries. Variables such as the first three describe countries' attributes and as such, they are typically relatively static and difficult for officials to manipulate (it is not easy to change a country's culture, economic development, government system, or, for that matter, its geographic location). The latter two factors mentioned refer to behavioral variables and as such, they are more within the power of officials to affect and alter. It is one thing to call on China to democratize because empirical research has shown that democracies rarely, if ever, fight each other. It is another thing to suggest that increased participation in international forums and expansion of foreign commerce can contribute to the abatement of interstate conflict. Past research has shown that the influence of democracy on the propensity of politically relevant pairs of countries to get involved in militarized interstate disputes is greater than the influence of the other two variables, the amount of bilateral trade and the number of joint memberships in intergovernmental organizations (e.g., Russett and Oneal 2001). Democratization entails an arduous process involving institutional reforms and changes in civic cultures. By comparison, expanding foreign trade and joining multilateral organizations are easier for officials to undertake, and these actions can bear the desired fruit on conflict abatement more quickly. In other words, they have a more immediate and practical relevance when considering approaches to reduce militarized interstate disputes, even though long-standing and fully developed democracies rarely find themselves in such disputes in the first place.

Territorial contests

Dispute over land has been by far the most common issue engendering interstate conflict (Vasquez 1993, 2009). This is one of the strongest empirical generalizations to come from quantitative international relations research. The reasons for this phenomenon are not difficult to understand. Physical contiguity conduces interaction opportunity. Neighbors come into more frequent contact than those that are located far from each other. Neighboring countries are more likely to fight each other for the same reasons that most homicides are committed by acquaintances rather than strangers. In both cases, close contact provides the opportunity for engagement of both the positive and negative kind.

There is a second related reason for neighbors and acquaintances to quarrel. Close contact and frequent interaction suggest that the parties involved have a greater stake in their relationship; they are likely to have more competing as well as shared interests. Neighboring countries are natural candidates for commercial partnership and defense collaboration against a common security threat given their physical proximity and cultural affinity. But because their borders intersect, they also have something valuable – land – to quarrel about. Historically, territorial conquest has been sought to increase national power and wealth. Thus understandably, those sharing a common frontier also have the greatest reason to fear each other's expansionist ambitions. For reasons of both "opportunity" *and* "willingness" (Most and Starr 1989), neighboring countries are more likely than distant ones to have intense relations, whether conflictive or cooperative.

These remarks lead directly to the following implication: some states should have more territorial disputes than others. *Ceteris paribus*, those states with a larger number of neighbors should have more opportunity to get into territorial disputes. Empirical evidence shows that this is indeed the case. The incidence of a country's involvement in wars and militarized disputes tends to be correlated with the number of its neighbors (Starr and Most 1976, 1978). How does this empirical generalization bear on China and its territorial disputes?

China has the largest number of neighbors in the world. In contrast, the US has just two contiguous neighbors to its north and south, and two oceans flank it on the east and west coasts. In contrast, other major powers such as Germany, Russia, and China have many more neighbors. Moreover, geographic location matters. The US is located in the Western Hemisphere where it has not faced any peer competitor since London conceded regional hegemony to Washington in the late 1800s (Friedberg 1988). The last time that a European power could have tried to block the US from ascending to regional hegemony and to challenge its territorial integrity was during the American Civil War, and London decided against intervening on behalf of the Confederacy (Little 2007). In contrast to the US, Germany and China are centrally located in Europe and Asia respectively. They have shared borders with several other major powers or are located within close distance to them (e.g., Russia,

France, Britain, Japan, and India). Their respective geographic situations therefore suggest different security environments which should in turn indicate different baseline expectations for their relative disputatiousness and comparative odds of getting into fights or being invaded.

To the extent that oceans provide a defense barrier against a possible invasion as suggested by John Mearsheimer's (2001) idea of the "stopping power of water," we should again expect insular countries, such as Britain and Japan, to face a more benign security environment than continental ones (e.g., Germany, France, Spain, Russia, and China). Some scholars (e.g., Levy and Thompson 2005, 2010) have argued that maritime states are inherently less threatening to their neighbors than continental powers because they lack the large number of infantry soldiers needed to invade and conquer others (presumably, fellow European states rather than overseas colonies). Whether maritime powers such as Athens (during the Peloponnesian War), Venice (in the early modern era), and the Netherlands, Britain, and Japan (in more recent times of colonialism and imperialism) have presented less of an existential threat to other peoples is an empirical question. Moreover, the extent to which a country is strictly a maritime or continental power is subject to debate because some (e.g., imperial France and Spain, and contemporary US) have possessed both large land-based and naval capabilities.

Given the protection afforded by the Atlantic and Pacific Oceans, the US enjoys a security environment more similar to the insular states than the continental ones. Because other states have fewer "opportunities" to conquer insular states and because these states have fewer "opportunities" to get into territorial disputes with others, island nations should be less "willing" to spend large amounts of money on their defense establishments. When they do spend relatively large sums for military purposes and when they do find themselves in frequent territorial (or colonial) disputes in faraway places, this phenomenon should be highly informative because it tends to contradict the baseline expectation just sketched. This information points to a more offensive than defensive disposition – it reflects a greater "willingness" to engage in disputes notwithstanding more limited "opportunity." One indication of a country's tendency to fight such "conflicts of choice" is whether most of its wars are waged on its home territory or close to its borders rather than in distant lands.

Physical contiguity implies geographic proximity, but the obverse is not necessarily true. Taiwan is located close to China but it is not connected to the mainland by land. *Ceteris paribus*, proximity is correlated with a country's ability to project its power. Kenneth Boulding's (1962) well-known "loss of power gradient" argues that the farther a country has to extend its capabilities from its home base, the weaker will be the effects of its capabilities on a local situation. This ability to project one's capabilities abroad is subject to even more severe erosion when it has to overcome sea barriers. John Mearsheimer's (2001) observation about the "stopping power of water" sharpens the distinction between contiguity and proximity. The Taiwan Strait has served as a critical barrier, shielding Taiwan from China's military power. Had it not been for this geographic fact, the island's security situation would have been much more dire (analogously, Cuba would have been even more vulnerable to US pressure). Even greater oceanic distance impairs China's ability to assert and protect its territorial claims in the South China Sea.

By the same logic, a conflict in the Taiwan Strait would diminish the large advantages enjoyed by US air and naval forces because it is located much closer to China than the US. Again, the analogy presented by the Cuban Missile Crisis comes to mind; the US commanded not only superior strategic forces in that episode but also a great advantage in conventional assets stemming in part from the island's proximity to its home base. This situation was reversed in several crises during the 1960s involving Berlin, located inside East Germany where the USSR had enjoyed a conventional and geographic advantage.

To a greater or lesser extent, the "stopping power of water" pertains to maritime situations in general. Compared to territorial competition between contiguous states, maritime disputes should have a lower potential to escalate to a large-scale military conflict because the core center for most states' populations and industries is not located on those islands being contested (such as the Falklands/Malvinas for Britain and Senkaku/Diaoyu for Japan, even though Britain and Japan are themselves island nations). The generally peripheral status of these contested islands in turn implies that maritime contests often impinge more on symbolic or intangible values than material or security considerations. Because most states have historically lacked the requisite naval or air capabilities to sustain their maritime contests (the necessary investment for such capabilities tends to be expensive and lumpy, with only a handful among the most powerful countries being able to afford it), this limitation on their "opportunity" to wage war often works in tandem with their less intense motivation (or "willingness" in the terminology of Most and Starr 1989) to engage in such conflicts to the extent that the islands being contested are either sparsely populated (or even uninhabited) or perceived to lack strategic importance.

This remark does not deny that countries have gone to war over islands that have few inhabitants and little perceived strategic value, and that are separated by large stretches of ocean from their home base (there were in 1982 only 1,800 Kelpers living on the Falklands/Malvinas, located about 8,000 miles from Britain – considerations that would suggest the much greater influence exercised by domestic politics in producing this war). Rather, my observation above tries to distinguish most maritime disputes from the typical situation characterizing land disputes involving substantial and even large populations living in a contested area (e.g., in Bosnia, Kashmir, Palestine, and, during an earlier era, Sudetenland, and Alsace and Lorraine). The resulting difficulties such as the need to settle or resettle displaced peoples are often among the major obstacles hampering a negotiated deal in these land disputes, even though such difficulties are not necessarily absent in attempts to partition some islands (e.g., Cyprus, Timor, Sri Lanka, and Hispaniola).

Naturally, the perceived political or strategic importance of the islands being contested is a matter of degree (rather than a dichotomous question of "either/or"). It stands to reason that states care more about developments on those islands closer to their home base, even when the legal status of these islands is not in dispute, than others that are located farther away. It is hardly surprising that events involving Sri Lanka, Ireland, Cyprus, Timor, and Hispaniola and Cuba would attract attention from New Delhi, London, Ankara, Canberra, and Washington respectively, as these islands' internal stability and external alignment can easily spill across borders if for no other reason than their geographic proximity. Such contagion effect can be transmitted by refugee exodus (e.g., Haitians arriving on the shores of Miami) and ethnic or religious tension (e.g., Cyprus, North Ireland). Thus, even when stripped of the nationalist emotions typically associated with debates on separatist demands, it is natural for Taiwan to loom very large in Beijing's policy agenda. Britain's saga with the Irish independence movement and the numerous episodes of US military intervention in and occupation of Cuba, Haiti, and the Dominican Republic suggest that Beijing's concerns with respect to Taiwan are hardly exceptional. Indeed, as an "unsinkable aircraft carrier" (in Douglas MacArthur's words), the island of Taiwan controlled by a foreign enemy would be as concerning to Beijing as Cuba would be for Washington (as shown in part by the Cuban Missile Crisis). Others, such as Ankara and Djakarta, have also threatened to use or have actually used military force in similar geostrategic circumstances (i.e., in Cyprus and East Timor).

Thus, again, quite aside from the issue of nationalism and domestic politics, geostrategic considerations alone in Taiwan's case are consequential for Beijing (Wachman 2007) just as they are for other similarly situated states. This remark illustrates what I had in mind when I said that one need not necessarily introduce individual leaders' perceptions, the idiosyncrasies of national decision processes, and particular regime characteristics or cultural dispositions to explain that which structural conditions would do. For example, democratic countries appear to have been no more indifferent to their island neighbors' external alignment or internal conditions, no more inclined to accept changes in these neighbors' juridical status, and no more disposed to refrain from coercive behavior toward these neighbors than their authoritarian counterparts (such as Turkey's invasion of Cyprus after a *coup d'état* by Greek Cypriots aimed at political union or *enosis* with Greece). At least as a starting point for one's analysis, one need not invoke a different explanation for Beijing's conduct toward Taiwan than the one used for Washington's (or Ankara or Djakarta's) conduct toward its nearby island neighbors (and even more distant ones like Grenada that hardly posed a geostrategic threat to anyone).

The pertinent structural conditions should provide a baseline for common expectations. One would want to introduce the more idiosyncratic variables only after these common expectations have been shown to be analytically disappointing to the extent that the pertinent states' behavior turns out to be highly heterogeneous. Such does not appear to be the case, for example, with respect to the major powers' willingness to submit to binding international arbitration or to refrain from actions threatening the freedom of shipping. Just as Beijing has declined to accept the intervention or judgment of international organizations in its maritime disputes (as requested by the Philippines), Washington has refused to acknowledge the latter's authority (such as when Nicaragua complained about the US mining of its harbors). The US blockade of Cuba in 1962 and China's missile tests in Taiwan's vicinity in 1995–96 show that both can resort to military coercion jeopardizing international shipping. Such general similarities suggest that both countries' conduct stems from common structural factors rather than the particulars of their political system or culture.

As just touched upon, maritime disputes are different from territorial disputes on land in another respect. Because the former involve contests over open sea, they inevitably impinge on other countries' concerns about the freedom of navigation. Thus, maritime disputes are by their very nature more likely to be or to become multilateral affairs in comparison to territorial disputes on land. This multilateral aspect complicates maritime disputes especially if a great deal of commercial shipping travels through the contested area. It has been estimated that about one third of the world's trade and one half of its oil and gas transports pass through the South China Sea (Simon 2012), thus increasing this area's importance beyond the direct disputants.

The obverse implication of these remarks is that when major powers, as either interested parties or direct claimants, become voluntarily or involuntarily disengaged, such fortuitous circumstances can contribute to the resolution of a previously entangled contest. Germany's defeat in World War I, Russia's ensuing civil war, and the withdrawal of US commercial interests presented a confluence of events that had the effect of advancing Norway's cause in claiming the Svalbard archipelago. Oslo benefited from this timing and the availability of a congenial forum, the Paris peace conference, to secure the 1920 treaty confirming its sovereignty (Finne 1977 cited in Purser 2013; Singh 1980), one that turned this archipelago and the seas around it into a demilitarized zone and the world's first international free economic zone. Although Oslo has legal sovereignty, the citizens of this treaty's other signatory states can visit Svalbard without visas and are guaranteed the right to explore its resources without discrimination. In addition to renouncing militarization of the area, Oslo agreed to limit its authority to collect taxes and has restricted the use of this revenue to only fund services on the archipelago.

From the case of Svalbard archipelago, one can also discern where historical parallels can break down. An important structural difference between it and the current situation in the South China Sea is obviously that Norway is *not* China. Being a small and relatively weak country, Norway's larger and more powerful neighbors can more afford to accede to its sovereignty claim. The additional resources from the archipelago are unlikely to shift significantly the bilateral and multilateral balances of power among the concerned parties (e.g., Sweden, Germany, Britain, Russia/the USSR, and the US in addition to Norway). Norway, in other words, is not in a position to expand its power to such an extent as to become a threat to its neighbors. Its relative weakness in turn suggests that it can be trusted to carry out its pledge of demilitarizing the area and according open and equal access to all of the treaty's signatories. Being small and relatively weak therefore has its advantages, and this condition facilitated settlement in this case. Moreover and as already mentioned, Germany and Russia/the USSR were sidelined because of the former's defeat in World War I and the latter's ensuing civil war. Sweden's claim was undermined by Britain's opposition as Stockholm was perceived by London to have been sympathetic to Germany in the Great War.

In contrast to and quite separate from other states' assessments of Beijing's current and future intentions (i.e., their perceptions of Beijing's motivations or its "willingness"), China's very size and growing capacity (economic and military) contribute to the impasse in the South China Sea disputes (i.e., the "opportunities" conferred upon Beijing by its size, location, and perceived capabilities). Concessions made to

Beijing would bring additional scale to gain, that is, introducing further and cumulative advantages to China in the future, a country which for structural reasons alone is already too big for its neighbors' comfort and which has already been on a sharply upward trajectory of national growth in recent years. Yet at the same time, it is not as overwhelmingly powerful as the US is in the Western Hemisphere, especially in the Caribbean and the Gulf of Mexico. China thus occupies an intermediate position – it is neither a small power like Norway that can be accommodated without compromising the regional balance of power, nor a regional hegemon like the US that is simply unstoppable. From a realist perspective, balancing Norway is unnecessary and balancing the US is impossible. For China, balancing is both necessary and possible.

What has just been said about the South China Sea disputes pertains to an even greater extent to Taiwan's reunification with China, as this combination would add even more to China's already considerable power stock no matter how one wishes to define it. Whether or not Norway is inherently more trustworthy than China, it obviously lacks the capability to defy the collective wishes of its larger neighbors that also have a stake in the disposition of the Svalbard archipelago. Simply because it is bigger and more powerful, China will have a much tougher time to reassure the other interested states that it can be trusted to fulfill the terms of an agreement if one should be reached. This problem of credible commitment is equally pertinent in Beijing's efforts to seek a settlement with Taiwan, and this topic will be taken up in more detail later. For now, the general point is that a country in China's position faces a challenging job in trying to reassure its neighbors lest they join a countervailing coalition against it (Germany and Russia have historically also been in a comparable position).

Lest I be misunderstood, the preceding remark about structural conditions should not be construed to mean that these conditions are everything or even the most important thing, only that they can and should provide the beginning point for proceeding with an analysis. If structural conditions are so constraining that they deny the possibility of any policy choice, human agency is removed from the picture and we all become prisoners of the circumstances we find ourselves in. Human agency is of course important because this is after all what policy analysis is all about (e.g., how one can develop effective ways to credibly reassure others). Rather, my remark about structural conditions is intended to serve as a warning against the tendency, mentioned earlier, for people to resort to and shuttle between different interpretive logics. They typically adopt circumstantial explanations (or justifications) when analyzing their own undesirable or unpopular behavior while giving dispositional explanations to account for similar behavior by others (e.g., US action toward Cuba compared to Chinese action toward Taiwan). They reverse, however, these tendencies when the behavior in question is viewed positively. In such cases, people tend to use dispositional explanations when it comes to their own positive behavior (i.e., to explain such behavior in terms of their benign intentions and inherent goodwill) but to attribute similar behavior by others to their circumstances (e.g., to interpret their positive behavior as the result of involuntary concessions forced upon them by their dire circumstances rather than being due to their free volition). Thus, for example, an adversary's arms reduction is apt to be seen as a temporary aberration caused by its economic distress but similar behavior by oneself is likely to be presented as a sign of one's peaceful disposition.

Returning to China's maritime disputes, rumors have suggested the presence of substantial mineral deposits in the East and South China Seas. If interstate disputes were to be confined to just competing claims over material resources such as fisheries and energy deposits (i.e., if they were to be somehow separated from the more emotionally charged issues concerning state sovereignty, regime legitimacy, or historical animosity), they should be more amenable to a negotiated settlement. Democracies are less likely to get into intense conflicts, and one reason for this phenomenon appears to be that they have largely removed territorial contests as a contentious issue in their relations (Gibler 2007, 2014; Gibler and Tir 2010; Park and Colaresi 2014) – a phenomenon that in turn points to the possibility of reversed causality, namely, settled borders tend to promote democracy and encourage peace among democratic countries. Having settled their borders, democracies are less likely to become engaged in territorial disputes (which present the most common cause for militarized interstate disputes and war). They also consequently have less reason to spend large sums of money on their armed forces, and to develop a centralized bureaucracy for the purpose of defending their frontiers (McDonald 2009). Moreover, to the extent that democracies do get into disputes, their disagreements tend to be over economic issues, often those involving fishing quotas and maritime boundaries. The latter issues are of course also present in China's maritime disputes. Democratic contestants, however, have generally managed to keep such disputes from becoming overly politicized and thus to prevent military escalation (Mitchell and Prins 1999).

In contrast to disputes confined to just material resources, those that involve competing claims over intangibles such as regime legitimacy, ethnic identity, or sectarian allegiance tend to be much more intractable. Rationalist explanations of bargaining failures offer one plausible reason for this difference, pointing to the relative divisibility of the good being contested (Fearon 1995). Disputes involving land, minerals, fisheries, and money are in principle more easily settled because these resources can be more readily divided and their allocation can be more effectively monitored and enforced by the competing claimants. Historically, inter-state contests over territories that are valued for economic reasons appear to have been *negatively* related to military escalation (Huth 1996: 112–113). Such disputes typically involve lower levels of conflict, and are more amenable to management and resolution. Compromises are more likely if disputes are over access to or control of natural resources of economic value (Huth 1996: 153). In contrast, by their very nature, national sover-eignty and regime legitimacy involve exclusive claims over more intangi-ble or symbolic substance. Statistical evidence from past episodes of territorial disputes tends to support this generalization: fatal military confrontations are more likely to stem from land disputes valued primar-ily for ethnic reasons than those valued for economic or even military reasons (Huth 1996; Huth and Allee 2002; Tir 2005a). In view of this distinction, it becomes more understandable that in its effort to defuse its dispute with Beijing, Manila has sought to separate rival sovereignty claims in the South China Sea from the issue of joint resource exploration in the contested area.

In light of this discussion, the importance attached to and the contro-versies surrounding the "one-China consensus" also become more understandable. Beijing has insisted on an agreement on the "one-China consensus" as the basis for any talks with Taipei (even though it has tacitly acquiesced to allowing each side to interpret freely the meaning of "one China"). It has professed a willingness to negotiate with Taipei about any issue so long as this negotiation is based on the principle of "one China." Those who favor Taiwan's independence have resisted this idea, and have argued that acceptance of this principle would be tantamount to conceding the island's sovereignty at the outset of any negotiation. I will discuss this idea further in Chapter 3.

In practice, disputes about territory (or resources in general) and dis-putes about sovereignty are often intertwined, defying attempts to resolve them such as through joint custody or a leaseback option (the latter represented a failed proposal for continued British administration of the Falklands/Malvinas under Argentine sovereignty; Kinney 1989: 57–60). When territorial disputes become embedded in the mobilization of group legitimacy and enshrined in non-negotiable principles (such as a people's right to self-determination, religious autonomy, or historical entitlement) – as exemplified by the controversies surrounding the status of Jerusalem, Kashmir, Kosovo, and Ulster (Goddard 2006) – the divisibility of con-tested land becomes problematic and its resolution elusive.

This said, states have also been known to settle their territorial disputes when domestic and foreign conditions are aligned to promote this outcome. When faced with international pressure or duress, they have sometimes chosen to settle some of their disputes in order to give more attention and effort to others. In seeming contradiction to my earlier hypothesis, the replacement of an old discredited regime by its democratic successor can in some cases facilitate a settlement. These factors appear to have played a role in Argentina's initial decision to compromise with Chile on the three disputed islands located in the Beagle Channel, and the subsequent consolidation of their peaceful relations after the fall of military regimes in both countries (Mani 2011). As remarked earlier, foreign and civil wars involving the other claimant states had also produced a window of opportunity for the confirmation of Norway's sovereignty over Svalbard after Germany and Russia were sidelined and Sweden's bargaining position was weakened.

This discussion points to a fundamental difference between the controversy involving Taiwan on the one hand and China's sovereignty claims over the East and South China Sea islands on the other hand. The 23 million inhabitants of Taiwan and the island's political processes present an additional critical political dimension that is absent in China's other disputes as the latter disputes pertain to islands or islets with little or no human settlement. At the same time, national reunification (with Taiwan) has been an avowed and long-standing goal of Beijing's leaders, with widespread popular support on the mainland. Although Beijing advances its claims in the East and South China Seas on historical grounds, it has not had physical control of some of the disputed islands in recent memory. In contrast, the Kuomintang government – a government that had in fact ruled China and claimed to represent it (a claim backed by the US during 1949–79) – did exercise effective control of Taiwan after World War II. Thus, Beijing's argument that attempts to foster Taiwan independence represent a secessionist movement has some traction whereas this same idea does not apply to its East and South China Sea claims for the obvious reason that most of the islands or islets in question have been uninhabited. Beijing's stake in resolving Taiwan's status is much more consequential for its reputation (with respect to both its domestic and foreign audiences) and could set a possible precedent involving China's other outlying territories such as Tibet and Xinjiang. This line of reasoning suggests that China's sovereignty claims pertaining to Taiwan and to the East and South China Seas are dissimilar in important respects even though Beijing has supposedly indicated that they all engage China's "core interests."

Significantly also, if one views Taiwan's bid for independence as a secessionist move – as indicated by most countries' diplomatic recognition of the Beijing government as the sole legal representative of China and their acknowledgment that Taiwan is a part of China – cross-national historical evidence suggests that the odds are against its success. Most countries have sided with an incumbent government in its confrontation with secessionist movements and unless this incumbent government has been seriously weakened by internal turmoil or foreign defeat, it has usually been able to defeat demands to secede (Heraclides 1990; Mason et al. 2011). Naturally, during the Chinese Civil War, it was the Communists who were the rebels and the Nationalists (i.e., the Kuomintang) who were in control of the government – until they were defeated and withdrew to their last refuge on Taiwan.

Beijing has sought bilateral talks to settle its maritime disagreements, and it has shunned involvement by international organizations. This position is understandable in that China would clearly enjoy a stronger bargaining position when matched against each of the other parties in these disputes separately in comparison to a situation whereby a third party also becomes involved. In adopting this position, Beijing's preference is no different from the traditional practice of US statecraft in East Asia, where Washington has pursued a hub-and-spokes approach to managing its bilateral alliances (Cha 1999; Hemmer and Katzenstein 2002). That is, the US has entered into separate bilateral defense treaties with its junior partners in Asia without promoting formal alliance ties among the latter countries. Hence, in contrast to Western Europe, East Asia does not have a multilateral defense organization like NATO.

In insisting that relations across the Taiwan Strait are China's domestic matter, Beijing is wary of accepting mediation by third parties as it once did with respect to the US role in the Chinese Civil War during the 1940s. Yet, from the perspective of two-level games, the involvement of foreign mediators, including international organizations, can sometimes help to soften domestic opposition in China's weaker counterparts to reaching a settlement. It would be politically easier and more palatable for the latter to accept a deal that is presented as the outcome of international arbitration, adjudication, or mediation rather than being seen as making direct concessions to Beijing's stronger coercive power (Simmons 2002). The Vatican's role in settling the Beagle Channel dispute between Chile and Argentina is pertinent even though the balance of power between these two contestants was not characterized by the same degree of asymmetry as in the case of China's relations with its dispute counterparts (including Taiwan). This mediation by an impartial third party provided a face-saving way for Buenos Aires to compromise on an issue on which it had previously been unwilling to yield given its domestic politics.

The above discussion suggests that China's dispute involving Taiwan is in some important respects more challenging than those involving the East and South China Sea islands. Beijing has evidently a stronger commitment to its cause in the former than the latter cases. But by the same reasoning, if relations across the Taiwan Strait show promising signs of détente and accommodation, one would have more reason to be optimistic about the prospects of settling the East and South China Sea disputes peacefully. Similarly, Beijing's management of the latter disputes may portend its approach to cross-Strait relations. A more assertive or even bellicose stance with respect to the East and South China Sea disputes could have a demonstration effect. Surely, Beijing's leaders are aware that Taipei (as well as others such as the US) will be observing China's behavior in these other disputes in an effort to discern its possible intentions in handling cross-Strait relations. Similarly, how China behaves in its dispute with Japan over the Senkaku/Diaoyu Islands will be watched by the other parties in the South China Sea disputes for possible hints about how China will conduct itself in these latter disputes (taking into account, however, the unsettled debate on reputation effects as discussed elsewhere in this book). China's various maritime disputes can thus be connected in this sense, with developments in one arena potentially presaging or affecting the direction of events in another arena. A historical parallel comes to mind in Argentina's concerns about the linkage between the Falklands/Malvinas and Beagle Channel disputes (Freedman and Gamba-Stonehouse 1991: 6–7); specifically, Buenos Aires was worried about possible collusion between Britain and Chile to threaten its overall position in the South Atlantic and Antarctica.

Such linkage effects have usually been highlighted in descriptions of the diffusion process whereby a local bilateral conflict develops into a wider regional, even global, conflagration such as World War I. Yet, this diffusion can also work in a reverse way, operating to spread and encourage détente and accommodation. Mikhail Gorbachev's retrenchment policies set off such a chain reaction that culminated in the termination of the Cold War. They triggered a domino effect that toppled communist rule in Eastern and Central Europe, and enabled Germany's reunification at a speed and in a peaceful manner that no one had quite anticipated (Stent 1999). In Asia, Moscow withdrew its troops from Afghanistan and ended its support for Hanoi, actions that in turn provided the necessary conditions for a Sino-Russian rapprochement and derivatively, the restoration of normal relations between Beijing and Hanoi and between Hanoi and Phnom Penh. These events remind us that cascade effects can operate to promote either tension or détente. Moreover, notwithstanding serious impediments standing in the way of resolving China's maritime disputes, there are also opposing trends that offset the effects of these impediments and that help to render these disputes less dire and hopeless than they are sometimes portrayed.

Concurrent processes: armaments, alliances, and economic interdependence

To analyze the danger of conflict occurrence, escalation, and contagion, one may ask whether the pertinent processes are facilitated or hampered by other prior or concurrent conditions. As mentioned earlier, quantitative research on the life cycles of past conflicts presents some strong statistical evidence pointing to the influence of several antecedent or concomitant factors. Territorial disputes are at the very top of factors contributing to the onset of interstate conflict (Vasquez 2009). These disputes tend to be the root cause for enduring rivalries between neighbors (Tir and Diehl 2002; Vasquez and Leskiw 2001). They are much more likely to invite repeated confrontations than non-territorial issues, and they are more likely to escalate to militarized interstate disputes (Hensel 1994, 1998; Vasquez and Henehan 2010). This strong statistical association explains why Western Europe and North America have achieved enduring peace, and why China's settlement of most of its land borders with its neighbors is encouraging for East Asia's peace and stability. This association between territorial settlement and peaceful interstate relations also underscores the importance of Germany's recognition of its post-1945 border with Poland, Britain's acceptance of the US proposed arbitration to settle the boundary dispute between Venezuela and British Guiana in 1895, and the African states' pledge of the inviolability of their borders inherited from the colonial era. These decisions or practices legitimize the acceptance and preservation of existing boundaries, and thus help to defuse or avoid territorial disputes.

The examples just mentioned remind one of the influence of historical legacies and of those significant others who have participated in these legacies. Various colonial powers, leading regional states, and the victors of World War II played an obvious and determinative role in deciding territorial demarcations in their wake. Taiwan's current status is of course inseparable from Harry Truman's decision to impose the US Seventh Fleet in the Taiwan Strait shortly after the outbreak of the Korean War, thereby preventing the Chinese Communists from invading the island and completing the defeat of their Nationalist (or Kuomintang) nemesis in the Chinese Civil War. Washington also had a role in the current Sino-Japanese dispute over the Senkaku/Diaoyu Islands. It administered these islands after World War II, and turned them over to Tokyo after it had agreed to Okinawa's reversion to Japanese jurisdiction. The US included them in the territorial definition of those islands to be returned to Japan, even while professing that this action did not prejudice their eventual legal status (Blanchard 2000: 120). Washington has sought to distinguish territories under Japan's sovereignty from territories under Japan's administration, a subtlety that lacks credibility in Beijing's eyes.

In a survey of the accumulated empirical evidence on interstate conflict dynamics, John Vasquez (2009) tied territorial disputes to the pathway that such conflicts generally follow when they escalate in intensity and spread to engulf multiple states. An intense and enduring rivalry between states is typically accompanied by efforts on the part of both sides to seek allies, build up their armed forces, and face off each other repeatedly in militarized confrontations. These variables – alliance formation, armament competition, and recurrent militarized disputes – tend to feed on each other, thereby producing a general dynamic that sustains and heightens tension. Territorial disputes are a fourth variable in this complex of factors abetting the escalation and diffusion of interstate conflict. Each of these variables contributes directly to the danger of war, and also indirectly to this danger by encouraging those behaviors indicated by the other three variables. These variables therefore have a compound effect on the evolution of an initial bilateral dispute to become a multilateral conflagration.

Paul Senese and John Vasquez (2008: 197) have reported the pertinent statistics based on these variables' historical associations in past wars. When two states have a militarized interstate dispute (MID) over a piece of contested territory, they have a 0.165 chance of going to war within the next five years. When both contestants have foreign allies, this probability increases to 0.486. When these states' contentious relations have involved them in repeated militarized confrontations, the danger of a war breaking out rises further to 0.692. If one adds the presence of armament competition to this combination of factors, this probability reaches 0.921. Thus, when all four factors in this constellation are present, the risk of war occurring becomes very high. Historical evidence suggests that its chance of occurrence within the next five years is better than nine out of ten.

One can interpret the above information in a way that is analogous to the known contributors to diseases or physical ailments such as diabetes, lung cancer, and high blood pressure. For instance, the risk of suffering a heart attack goes up when a person is obese, smokes cigarettes, eats fatty food, and has a genetic predisposition and a personal or family history of such episodes. With the presence of each such condition, the risk of cardiac attack rises. Each condition has an additive effect on this risk which is therefore cumulative. Some of these conditions also have a compound effect as they contribute to the danger of heart disease indirectly by reinforcing each other's deleterious effect. Such statistical information is of course useful in telling us about how the removal of each contributing condition will reduce the overall risk profile. Some such conditions, like genetic inheritance, are beyond the control of a patient or physician (just as states do not have much choice over their geographic location), but others are more easily altered. By analogous logic, we can gain a better perspective about the odds favoring the maintenance of peaceful interstate relations by examining the extent to which those variables reported by Senese and Vasquez (2008) are present or absent in the disputants' dyadic relationship and in the relations prevailing among their respective associates. With each subtraction of the effects of these variables, the danger of war declines.

That China has settled most of its land borders should therefore lower its overall chance of getting into a militarized interstate dispute over territory. Although military expenditures have gone up for China and many of its neighbors in absolute terms, their respective defense burden (the share of their national economy allocated to defense spending) has not risen significantly over time (Chan 2012a, 2013). Moreover, we have thus far not seen evidence of unfolding armament races as reflected by large, reciprocal and serial increases in military spending by those countries involved in maritime disputes. Furthermore, instead of the rigid, exclusive alignment patterns prevalent during the Cold War, Asia Pacific states have now forged more open and multilateral ties. There has been a general process of de-alignment and a concomitant process of deepening commercial ties among these countries. Intraregional trade and cross-border investments have taken off since the days of the Cold War. Finally, although there have been recurrent confrontations on the high seas, these episodes have generally involved Chinese civilian vessels and coast guard patrols. The disputing countries, including China, have exercised tacit restraint in generally avoiding the deployment of military forces in their physical encounters.

To further pursue the medical analogy introduced above, one can reduce the risk of heart attack by offsetting actions such as regular exercise and healthy diet. Two recent and ongoing trends are significant. First, Asia Pacific countries have opened their economies and have become one another's important trade and investment partners. There has been a general tide of rising economic interdependence, and China has assumed a central position in this increasingly dense and intense network of commerce that has penetrated and interlocked nearly all countries in the region (with North Korea being the clear exception to the norm). China has become the largest trade and investment partner for practically all the major contestants involved in its maritime claims, including Japan, Vietnam, and Taiwan. States with significant commercial and financial ties have been known to go to war, as in the case of the European belligerents in World War I. We also know, however, that these economic relationships have tended to be one of the strongest forces promoting interstate peace. The risk of militarized interstate disputes between two states tends to be negatively correlated with the extent to which they have extensive trade, and states that have high levels of economic development, open economies, large overseas financial involvements, and active trade and heavy investment abroad are generally more peaceful in their external relations (e.g., Gartzke 2007; Gartzke and Weisiger 2014; Russett and Oneal 2001). Increasing economic interdependence and an emphasis by nearly all the region's governing elites (again with North Korea as the lone exception) on economic growth as the overriding national priority suggest that important forces are at work to restrain China's maritime disputes from getting out of hand (Chan 2012a; Solingen 2007). The processes of economic opening and interdependence have created powerful domestic stakeholders in furthering these processes, thereby in effect fostering and consolidating a cross-national coalition of interest groups that would oppose the rise of interstate tension and, worse, the outbreak of military conflict. These groups are self-motivated to restrain bellicosity because interstate tension and conflict would obviously jeopardize their agenda of promoting domestic development and sustaining economic openness.

At least one study on East Asia's island disputes has concluded that economic interdependence has acted as a powerful brake that has checked the danger of escalation (Koo 2009). Although these disputes have not been resolved and have in fact continued to trouble bilateral relations, the countries involved have also exercised strong reciprocal restraint due to their growing economic stake in mutually beneficial commerce. Indeed, one can expect that as East Asia's economies become more open and involved in international commerce, a deadlock (or the persistence of "no agreement") on the current island disputes will become more and more objectionable to those who have an interest in maintaining and even expanding cross-national trade and investment (as tension from these disputes can upset profitable commerce). Put alternatively, a political economy dominated by internationalist groups will foster a larger win set for reaching foreign deals than one that is dominated by isolationists who are less likely to be as keen on reaching such deals (Chung 2004).

Second, tight alignment patterns in states' external relations to form two competing blocs have historically encouraged the escalation and contagion of conflicts. This tendency of bipolarization is likely to engender a process of "chain-ganging" (Christensen and Snyder 1990), whereby an initially bilateral conflict between two minor powers (or between a minor power and a major one) spreads to other states through the dynamics of alliance politics. If left alone, such bilateral conflicts are likely to be managed by the contestants and if they fight, their military clashes are likely to be contained and concluded quickly. The expectation held by one or both sides of these local conflicts that allies may intervene to help their cause abets their incentive to escalate and prolong a conflict, especially for the weaker side in these disputes (Chan 2012b). When patrons or sponsors of those minor powers get involved, what was originally a localized dispute becomes multilateral. This process of diffusion engulfing more and more states is transmitted through alliance ties, especially when these ties, as just noted, align states in two antagonistic camps as was the case on the eve of World War I (Thompson 2003). The idea of "entrapment" describes the risk that a major power may be dragged into an unwanted conflict by an associate or client. This major power faces the moral hazard that its alliance commitments may embolden its ally to initiate or escalate a conflict, thereby undermining the purpose of deterrence that such commitments were intended to serve in the first place.

The alignment pattern of Asia Pacific countries reflected a bipolarization during the Cold War years, with a communist bloc and an anti-communist bloc led by Moscow and Washington respectively. In recent years, however, this pattern has broken down so that, for example, China has established strong ties with its former adversaries (e.g., the US, Japan, South Korea, and Taiwan). This process of political de-alignment has developed in tandem with the rising economic relations noted above. Moreover, in contrast to the past, there are now important avenues and forums for bilateral and multilateral dialogues. The Association of Southeast Asian Nations is but the most prominent example of intergovernmental organizations which have engaged China as well as Japan, South Korea, Australia, and the US, among others, in multilateral diplomacy. These intergovernmental organizations and other *ad hoc* groups (e.g., the Six-Party Talks to discuss North Korea's nuclear program) provide institutions for the participating countries to coordinate their actions and expectations. States' joint membership in intergovernmental organizations tends to dampen militarized interstate disputes by promoting norms of confidence building and peaceful resolution of disputes. Naturally, a state's decision to join and remain in these organizations is in itself a sign of its predisposition to accept and participate in multilateral diplomacy. In contrast, when states insist on going their own way, they are likely to boycott or withdraw from such organizations (e.g., the League of Nations for the USSR, the US, Germany, and Japan).

What about democracy and power transition?

I am agnostic, even skeptical, about the effects that two other macro conditions or processes have on interstate relations, especially in regard to their impact on China's maritime disputes. The first one pertains to the phenomenon of democratic peace, and the other to power shifts in inter-state balance. There is a huge literature on the former topic which, in essence, suggests that democracies rarely, if ever, go to war against one another. The empirical evidence supporting this proposition is robust but the explanations advanced to interpret this phenomenon have not been entirely persuasive (Chan 2012c). For instance, prior territorial settle-ment or congruent national interests could have contributed largely to the observed relationship between democracy and peace (Farber and Gowa 1997; Gibler 2007). Moreover, the putative causal mechanisms – such as democracies' political institutions and civic culture – have not often had the hypothesized effects in restraining an inclination to go to war when one undertakes in-depth case studies or examines institutional variations across countries (e.g., Chan and Safran 2006; Howell and Pevehouse 2007; Reiter and Tillman 2002; Rosato 2003; Owen 1997). For instance, legislative oversight, electoral sanction, and popular pacifism were not much in evidence in stopping the US and British invasion of Iraq (Kaufman 2004, 2005), a war of choice rather than necessity (Mearsheimer and Walt 2003). Although major democracies have not fought each other in large wars, they have also not refrained from covert action aimed at destabilizing or overthrowing those democratically elected governments that they dislike (such as Mosaddegh's Iran and Allende's Chile; Kegley and Hermann 1995, 1996). Reversing the causal logic suggested by the democratic peace theory, politicians have also not shied away from justifying their decisions to wage foreign war in the name of spreading democracy (Meernik 1996; Peceny 1999).

   Three important considerations are often overlooked in popular and even scholarly discourse on the phenomenon of democratic peace. First, although the evidence is strong that *established* democracies do not fight one another, countries with mixed regime characteristics are not neces-sarily more peaceful when they are undergoing the process of becoming more democratic (Mansfield and Snyder 2005). It appears that these transitioning countries are more likely to become involved in foreign conflicts. Second, although evidence is strong in pointing to an absence (or near absence) of large-scale combat between two established democracies (the so-called dyadic version of this theory), empirical sup-port for the proposition that democracies in general are less likely to fight other states regardless of the latter's political character (the so-called monadic version of this theory) is much more flimsy. Mixed dyads – pairing a democracy with an autocracy – are in fact most likely to become involved in interstate conflict. Third and related to the above observation, authoritarian governments are also generally able to maintain peace in their relations (Peceny et al. 2002). Therefore, shared regime character-istics – rather than their specific democratic or authoritarian orientation – tend to have a pacifying effect.

Furthermore, recent research shows that some types of authoritarian regimes are also subject to domestic constraints, and those with institu-tionalized party rule – such as China – are at least as peaceful as the established democracies (Weeks 2008, 2012). Therefore, whether China becomes more democratic is not the only or even the most important factor in maintaining its peaceful relations with other states. If anything, more pluralistic politics, increased leadership fragmentation, and greater sensitivity to public opinion are likely to encourage rather than discourage Beijing's bellicosity. Parenthetically, regime character does not appear to be a major factor in determining how separatist demands have been met historically. We have had violent responses from the more democratic systems (e.g., the US Civil War, Ireland's independence from Britain) as well as peaceful resolutions (e.g., Norway and Sweden, Slovakia and the Czech Republic). Similarly, the more authoritarian systems have had a mixed record in these experiences (e.g., the USSR's peaceful dissolution, the war of Bangladeshi independence).

Statistics on the outcomes of civil wars offer some clues about relations across the Taiwan Strait. The Chinese Civil War, as remarked earlier, started with the Communists in the role of rebels or insurgents and the Nationalists (or the Kuomintang) in charge of the incumbent govern-ment. Since the Nationalists' defeat on the mainland, the Beijing govern-ment has regarded Taiwan, which is currently under Kuomintang rule, as a renegade province. Many conflicts classified as civil wars have involved short episodes of coups d'état. In the remaining cases, foreigners are more likely to support the incumbent government rather than the rebels (who are often fighting for secession or autonomy), notwithstanding much publicized recent episodes of Western intervention in Kosovo, Libya, and Syria (Heraclides 1990). In terms of the outcomes of these contests, governments enjoy an edge of about 1.35 to 1 in prevailing over the rebels (Cunningham et al. 2009: 588).

Barbara Walter (2003: 137) reports that the most intractable civil wars during 1940–96 were not fought over ideological or ethnic divisions.

Rather, the most intractable ones were fought over territory, that is, over the issues of secession and self-determination. The belligerents in these territorial civil wars were 20% less likely to enter into peace negotiations and even when these negotiations were undertaken, they were less likely to produce a peace settlement. Walter (2003: 137) observes that "in only 17 percent of the cases in which a government faces rebels who sought independence or greater regional autonomy did the government agree to accommodate the rebels in any way." Moreover, although democratic governments are more inclined to undertake reforms to accommodate the rebels' demands, "higher levels of democracy appeared to have little effect on a government's willingness to offer full independence" (Walter 2003: 148). Compared to authoritarian governments, democracies are equally unwilling to grant full independence to secessionists.

Significantly, even when a secession movement succeeds, peace and stability in the post-partition period cannot be assumed (although secessions necessarily mean partitions, not all partitions or territorial transfers involve secessions – this distinction, as indicated earlier, sets relations across the Taiwan Strait apart from China's sovereignty claims over those contested islands in the East and South China Seas). In fact, militarized crises and violent confrontations recur in the aftermath of most partitions (e.g., Sambanis 2000; Tir 2003, 2005a). Thus, partition does not usually put an end to armed conflict. Understandably, even when they are successful, violent processes of secession are likely to be followed by further violence. Conversely, in those cases where territories are transferred as a result of overwhelming military victory or peaceful negotiation, the post-transfer situation is more likely to avoid further violent challenges (sometimes both of these processes can be present, albeit sequentially, as in the settlement of Germany's post-1945 borders). A negotiated settlement (e.g., Singapore's divorce from Malaysia) or an utter defeat for the separatists (e.g., the Confederacy in the US Civil War) also tend to be associated with lasting peace, whereas a protracted impasse involving foreign intervention (e.g., across the Taiwan Strait, on the Korean Peninsula, the contesting halves of Vietnam) is more likely to engender repeated clashes.

Contrary to some popular views about the effects of regime orientation on conflict propensity, whether Beijing is or will be a democracy does not appear in itself to be a critical factor, as remarked upon earlier in the context of a general proposition about how incumbent governments usually respond to demands to secede. Related to this proposition, pertinent statistical analysis indicates that whether a regime is democratic does not affect the probability of peaceful transfer of territory (Gibler and Tir 2010). The causal arrow appears instead to point in the other direction:

namely, peaceful border settlement enhances the prospect for democracy. The latter tendency is effectuated through two mechanisms. Peaceful border settlement reduces the tendencies for militarization and centralization that typically characterize a state caught in a territorial dispute, tendencies that are inimical to the development and consolidation of democracy. Moreover, this settlement lowers the danger of a state being targeted by another in a militarized interstate dispute stemming from their territorial disagreement.

Power shifts are also often mentioned in most analyses about China's foreign relations (e.g., Mearsheimer 2006). It is, however, not always clear how China's recent ascendance is supposed to affect these relations. There is often a disconnection between the evidence introduced to show China's relative gains in national capabilities and its expected external conduct, although the implied proposition is often that a stronger country, presumably any country, will also be a more assertive one. This proposition appears to contradict the general tendency shown in Beijing's past behavior whereby domestic disarray and foreign vulnerability have actually been associated with a more bellicose posture, whereas when Beijing senses that it is in a relatively strong bargaining position, it has been more inclined to compromise (e.g., Christensen 1996; Fravel 2008, 2011). As a general hypothesis relating power to ambition, one should consider how countries other than China have behaved historically when they make relative power gains (such as when the US became a unipolar power after the USSR's collapse). One should also entertain the opposite expectation that states facing relative decline are more inclined to take risks in order to avert their ongoing or impending losses (such as Germany's decision to launch a preventive war in 1914; Copeland 2000; Levy 1987, 2008; Ripsman and Levy 2007). Power shifts are constantly happening, if only because of a counterpart's poorer performance (such as when the US and China both improved their relative positions in the wake of the USSR's demise).

Much of the discussion on power shifts or power transition in the context of China's recent experience tends to be based on questionable historical and theoretical arguments (Chan 2008). Evidently, both those states with rising and others with falling power have found themselves at war. As John Vasquez (2009: 331) has remarked, "the issue of boundaries, not the issue of relative power, is what will determine the probability of war for most states." As for the question of how power shifts have historically affected the settlement of territorial disputes and separatist movements, it appears that states weakened by external war or internal decay are more likely to be compelled by their circumstances to make concessions (e.g., the breakup of the USSR, the Austro-Hungarian

Empire, and the former Yugoslavia). One may infer from this tendency that Taiwan's opportunity to gain independence was greater when China was relatively weak (paradoxically, during those earlier years both Taiwan and the US were insisting that the government in Taipei actually represented China), but this window is closing with China's recent rise.

Power-transition theory obviously points to changes in a bilateral balance of power that has become more equalized even if a lagging country has not yet caught up to or overtaken an existing leading country. One obviously pertinent theoretical question is whether the closing gap between Chinese and American capabilities is supposed to be conducive to peace and stability. For realists who typically emphasize the importance of balanced power and bipolarity in promoting this general outcome (e.g., Mearsheimer 2001; Waltz 1979), one would have expected that a reduction in the imbalance between Chinese and American capabilities should have this salutary effect. This is, however, not the general impression conveyed by most American realists, even those who aver that states balance against preponderant power and that their balancing behavior contributes to peace, stability, or the defeat of hegemonies. Whether Asia Pacific relations are becoming more bipolarized in the sense of the pertinent states selecting themselves into two opposing camps headed by Beijing and Washington respectively (e.g., Ross 1999, 2004) is an empirical question, although I rather doubt that this movement toward a tighter and more exclusive alignment pattern is happening. I tend to instead see Asia Pacific relations moving toward what have been variously described as multilateral, open, or soft regionalism, and complex interdependence (Ciorciari 2010; Goh 2007/08; Shambaugh 2004/05; Keohane and Nye 1977). Asia Pacific countries would prefer not having to choose between the US and China, thereby committing themselves to unilateral and exclusive dependency relationships.

Naturally, even if for the sake of argument one were to reach the conclusion that Asia Pacific, or just East Asia, now represents or is becoming a bipolar region, one would want to ask why this situation should matter for its prospects for peace or stability. What specific causal mechanisms are at work for this situation of bipolarity or process of bipolarization to affect these prospects? As should be evident from my earlier comments, I see the main regional tendency to be depolarization. This tendency is in turn likely to increase interaction opportunities among different states by breaking down the barriers that separate them, and it will also increase officials' decision uncertainty in trying to anticipate who will support whom and the relative strength of the contesting coalitions should there be a military showdown (e.g., Bueno de Mesquita 1981a, 1981b; Deutsch and Singer 1969; Singer and Small 1968). More interaction opportunity and greater decision uncertainty are in my view the main causal mechanisms as a result of which depolarization is likely to bring about more peaceful and stable regional relations (Chan 2013). Greater interaction opportunity should help to erode adversarial identifications dividing in- and out-groups, and greater decision uncertainty should introduce more caution in policy processes. Both of these developments should therefore contribute to international peace and stability.

3 Trust, reassurance, and credible commitment

There is a Chinese adage: "listen to his words; watch his deeds." People's statements can be informative but these declarations can also just be "cheap talk" and even deliberately designed to deceive and mislead. Therefore, it is necessary to observe people's conduct to determine whether their professed intentions should be taken seriously.

How can one determine the trustworthiness of another person or country (Kydd 2005)? The standard answer from realists is of course to never trust anyone. They argue that one can never take for granted a counterpart's future intentions. If so, this means that we will always have to assume the worst of people. There is also no way for those who want to to communicate their good faith and cooperative intent to others. These friendly gestures will be dismissed by others if realists are correct. Worse still, these gestures may be taken as a sign of weakness, thereby producing the counterproductive effect of encouraging one's counterpart to become more assertive or recalcitrant.

It is questionable whether the world works in the manner of the zero-sum games that have often been used as a metaphor to depict international relations. As Robert Axelrod has noted, many people are used to thinking about these relations as analogous to contests such as football and chess, competitions that produce only one winner. "But the world is rarely like that. In a vast range of situations mutual cooperation can be better for *both* sides than mutual defection. The key to doing well lies not in overcoming others, but in eliciting their cooperation" (Axelrod 1984: 189–190; emphasis in original). This being the case, officials are faced with the challenge of how to avoid fostering or engaging in zero-sum games and hopefully to transform them into positive-sum games.

The rationalist perspective acknowledges that it is difficult for states to reassure one another, and thus to elicit others' cooperation. Cooperation depends on trust. Trust is less important when one's counterpart can be counted on to behave in the desired manner because this behavior will advance its own interests. The other side's trustworthiness becomes a greater concern when one wants to know whether it can be depended on to behave in this way even when it is not in its interest to do so (or at least not if this interest is defined myopically). Will it be an opportunist that will take advantage of changes in circumstances? Concerns about trust gain salience because of uncertainties about future circumstances and about how the other actor will perceive its interests (and thus its future intentions). The importance of this concept derives from the facts not only that cooperation usually requires reciprocal trust, but also that misplaced trust can be quite costly (such as when one believes mistakenly that another country is peacefully inclined when it actually harbors aggressive intentions – a wolf in sheep's skin). Naturally, there is also the danger of "false positive" – believing another country is hostile and behaving in such a way that one's actions produce a self-fulfilling prophecy (i.e., one's behavior elicits hostility from the other side, thus vindicating one's prior belief). In this event, reciprocal hostility perpetuates a deadlock and both sides suffer the opportunity costs of foregone cooperation.

Whereas it is relatively easy to determine the relative capabilities of the parties engaged in a contest and also the ongoing trends affecting their respective capabilities, it is much more difficult to discern their future intentions. It is, however, intentions rather than capabilities that tend to be the more decisive variable in interstate relations. Thus, whether other countries decide to balance against the US, China, or the USSR/Russia is dependent not so much on their assessments of these states' power but rather on their judgments about how each country would use its power (will it be used with restraint and benevolently, or recklessly for self-aggrandizement?). States tend to balance against threat, a concept that requires taking into account not only another state's capacity to do harm but also its perceived intention to do so (e.g., Walt 1987). Were decisions on foreign alignment to be based only on states' assessments of one another's relative capabilities, the other major states' decisions to join the (more powerful) US in opposition to the (much weaker) USSR during the Cold War would be inexplicable. Therefore, the extent to which another state, especially a very strong one, can be trusted with power is an overriding concern for officials.

Why distrust impedes negotiated settlements

Trust boils down to a question of why one should believe the other side. It pertains to one's beliefs about the other side's sincerity and reliability. Does the other side mean what it says? Is it likely to keep its promises – and execute its threats when the pertinent conditions come to pass? Sometimes, states use beguiling or deceptive ploys, pretending to be friendly when they actually have hostile intentions. Sometimes, they agree to deals on which they renege subsequently (as will be noted later, however, this defection can be voluntary or involuntary). An inability to distinguish those that are trustworthy from others that are not impairs states' willingness to reach a negotiated deal that could spare them the costs of fighting or the costs associated with enduring an impasse. Their efforts are hampered by the difficulties they encounter in trying to determine their counterpart's true resolve, and by their uncertainties about whether the other side will honor the terms of a settlement in the future. The idea of trust (Kydd 2005) captures concerns about both states' disposition to misrepresent and their inability to make credible commitment to refrain from future defection (Fearon 1995), concerns that were introduced in Chapter 1. As explained there, the rationalist perspective on conflict takes on the puzzle of why states end up fighting even though they would have been better off if they had been able to reach a negotiated settlement. It points to the problems caused by the tendency to misrepresent and the difficulty of making credible commitment as serious obstacles blocking possible settlements. Moreover, the indivisibility of some issues being contested also impedes settlements. (These issues can pertain to perceived benefits to be derived from fighting a war that are indirect to the conflict itself, such as establishing a belligerent's international reputation, deriving domestic partisan gains; Kirshner 2000.)

States can bargain by means of private negotiations or public displays. They can communicate their bargaining moves by making promises and issuing threats. These communications can be tacit or explicit, and they can be conveyed by words or deeds. In this chapter, I take on the topic of how states try to reassure each other, demonstrating their sincerity and reliability (that they really mean what they say, or that others should not pay attention to what they say but should instead watch what they do – behavior showing that they can really be counted on to keep their promises). In the next chapter, I will turn to states' deterrence efforts, which also involve communications, albeit ones intended to warn others about the dire consequences of transgression and to discourage them from undertaking an action. (In deterrence situations, states want to show that they are not bluffing; that is, their threats are genuine and will be implemented should the other side engage in the undesired behavior.)

As I will discuss in Chapter 5, bargaining involves not just communications across interstate boundaries; it also pertains to deliberate or inadvertent signals coming from or intended for one's domestic constituents. The metaphor of two-level games (Putnam 1988) points to the phenomenon whereby officials are simultaneously engaged in both foreign and domestic boards of bargaining. Moreover, there are still other parties (state as well as non-state ones) that attend to these communications.

Thus, for example, the pertinent Southeast Asian states will watch China's management of the Senkaku/Diaoyu dispute for clues about Beijing's possible behavior toward them in the South China Sea disagreements. In addition, financial markets will pay attention to how political developments can positively or negatively affect corporate profits, interest rates, trade flows, and investment barriers, among other market-moving variables.

The presence of multiple audiences both complicates and facilitates communications. Officials often try to convey different messages to different audiences. For example, they want to emphasize their patriotic credentials when competing for partisan support, often engaging in efforts to outbid their domestic political opponents in resisting or challenging real or contrived foreign adversaries. At the same time, the same officials often want to reassure their foreign counterparts and financial markets that they are not about to cause political turbulence. Their words and deeds can therefore send mixed signals, and these mixed (even contradictory) signals can in turn produce confusion, skepticism, and even distrust that in turn hamper bargaining efforts to seek a settlement. Yet, the presence of multiple audiences also restrains officials from the temptation to misrepresent (or lie). They cannot, for example, bluff war without at the same time causing panic in the financial markets. Thus, the prospect of unsettling these markets and undermining business confidence encourages officials to be honest – that is, not to fake resolve or manufacture international tension for domestic partisan gain.

How can one discern trustworthiness?

It is difficult to tell whether another actor is sincere because the insincere ones will try to mimic the sincere ones' behavior. Thus, for example, someone who bluffs in a poker game will try his/her best to pretend that he/she should be taken seriously. Lebow (1981: 105) uses "masking effect" to describe the resulting difficulty in separating the sincere from the insincere type (since their behavior tends to be identical and this observed behavior is likely to be compatible with how either type can be expected to behave).

There is another side to this situation, one described by international relations analysts as information asymmetry. I know that I have no intention of attacking you, but you don't have the same information about my intention as I do. My predicament then is how to communicate to you my peaceful intention without having you dismiss this communication as "empty talk" or even worse, as an attempt at deception. How can I get you to take my reassurance seriously?

Several kinds of evidence can be helpful in distinguishing sincere actors from insincere ones. When a person behaves contrary to his/her immediate interest, this conduct gives a clue about this person's dependability or trustworthiness. The observer infers a person's immediate interest from seemingly compelling circumstances. So, for example, when a person continues to pay rent even though he/she has been unemployed for a long time, one infers from this behavior that this person takes contractual obligations seriously. Analogously, it is one thing for a country to be a fair-weather debtor that pays off its loans when its economy is doing well. It is quite a different matter, however, when this country continues to do so even in the midst of a sharp recession and when instituting severe self-imposed austerity programs. Similarly, it is easy for a country to profess its allegiance to free trade when it has a trade surplus, but when it continues to resist protectionist measures during economic hard times, its commitment to free trade becomes more credible. As yet another example, a government that takes its citizens' civil liberties seriously even during periods of national emergency is obviously more sincere than a counterpart that restricts or retracts these freedoms in comparable situations. As a final illustration from Sino-American relations, Washington may pledge to Beijing that it intends to reduce its arms sales to Taipei, but in a close election, the president (George H. Bush) may reverse this commitment and decide to export jet fighters to Taiwan apparently motivated primarily by domestic considerations. These illustrations suggest that a person or state's true character is more likely to be revealed in stressful circumstances when the temptation to cheat or defect is the greatest. Do one's words and deeds still correspond in these circumstances?

In addition to such "stress tests," one may be in a better position to infer another's trustworthiness or sincerity by observing this actor's behavior in highly permissive circumstances. These are circumstances in which the person or state in question can act with great discretion and perhaps even impunity without having to worry about others pushing back (such as when one can reasonably discount the possibility of powerful foreign countries taking strong counteractions). Does this actor behave in an untrustworthy manner when it faces little danger of suffering serious repercussions from its action? In such instances, circumstances do not dictate behavior, which is likely to instead reflect the actor's volition. Accordingly, whether the US invasion of Iraq is truly a "war of choice" (as opposed to a "war of necessity;" e.g., Mearsheimer and Walt 2003) bears on this question. Other examples come to mind. Does one take advantage of a defenseless or incapacitated person (such as stealing from someone who is seriously sick or inebriated)? Does one cheat when a teacher is not around to monitor a test and when other students are cheating? Does one attack a country or suppress a people that can neither put up an effective self-defense nor expect others to defend it? In these circumstances, external compulsion (such as balance of power dynamics) plays little role in constraining an actor's behavior; this constraint has to come from its self-restraint. Given this perspective, a country's domestic policies present a useful basis for foreigners to discern its character (Kydd 1997). If a government treats its own citizens, such as political dissidents and racial minorities, shabbily, foreigners will probably not be accorded better treatment. In this context, domestic variables showing disparities in the legal treatment and life opportunities of citizens of different ethnicity or political persuasion would be illuminating (e.g., differences in their rate of incarceration, life expectancy, and household income).

Still other situations can disclose a state's character. How has it conducted itself in circumstances that can be reasonably expected to shroud this conduct in secrecy? That is, how has it behaved when it does not expect this behavior to be exposed? Does it eavesdrop on leaders of friendly countries, undertake covert activities to overthrow democratically elected governments, or abuse enemy combatants held in captivity? Recent revelations on such conduct have hurt US reputation, showing inconsistencies in its words and deeds. Democratic institutions and processes make such revelations possible and even likely. Democratic transparency therefore has a double-edged quality. This transparency can more readily expose those occasions when democracies are insincere. But precisely because of this heightened danger of being exposed as a result of democracies' domestic politics, foreign governments should have a higher level of *ex ante* confidence in the sincerity or trustworthiness of democratic leaders. Their domestic media and political opposition can be expected to be in a more independent and influential position to hold them accountable in comparison to the typical situation facing authoritarian leaders.

These remarks should have clear implications for China. Because it has an authoritarian system, Beijing faces a greater challenge in reassuring other countries about its peaceful intentions. It will have to work harder to establish its credibility due to the nature of its political system. As already mentioned, it is relatively easy for most analysts to conclude that China's growth trajectory will put it in an even stronger position relative to its neighbors in the coming years. It is, however, much harder to discern and agree on how it will intend to use its increased power. Does Beijing's current willingness to play nice and to delay a resolution of its various maritime disputes simply reflect a strategy to be patient until it has gained enough strength to impose a unilateral settlement? In other words, can Beijing be trusted when it becomes much more powerful than now?

One can look for clues even though there is little prospect of finding a crystal ball. For instance, has China's foreign policy trended in a more moderate direction as it has become more powerful over time? Was its foreign policy more bellicose when it was weaker previously, especially during periods when its government was besieged by domestic political instability, economic setback, and international isolation? How have Beijing's policies toward Tibet and Xinjiang evolved over time? Presumably, how it has dealt with minority rights in these regions can be informative to some extent about its future intentions toward Taiwan in the event of reunification. To introduce another example, if Beijing resorts to force against the Philippines, this action would be more alarming to its neighbors than if it uses violence against Taiwan – because the former case would suggest that China's threshold for accepting armed conflict is lower than might be otherwise expected. This is because Beijing's contest with Manila over the islets in the South China Sea should obviously impinge less on China's core interests than its sovereignty dispute with Taiwan, thereby implying that Beijing should be more reluctant to use violence against Manila. When it behaves contrary to this expectation, its behavior shows that it has a greater disposition to violence.

Similar reasoning would suggest that it was one thing for the US to blockade Cuba and to threaten war when the USSR introduced missiles to that island; it was quite a different matter when it invaded Grenada – a country that cannot be plausibly argued to present a security threat to the US. As already mentioned, when a country is relatively free to act without being constrained externally, it is more likely to show its true character. Naturally, when a country is very strong like the US and China, external constraints become less effective, and self-restraint becomes more important. To the neighbors of these strong countries, trust increasingly means the extent to which they can rely on a hegemon or would-be hegemon's internal impulses (such as its self-professed principles and values, and its domestic alignment of interests and influences) to check its own behavior.

These remarks suggest an additional proposition. When a country is very strong, it can afford to be more generous, even magnanimous, and it should also feel less insecure than others who are much weaker. When this country's actual behavior contradicts this expectation, its conduct reflects poorly on its trustworthiness. Beijing's objective situation was much weaker in the 1950s and 1960s, and it would have been understandably concerned about the threat coming from Taipei espousing an agenda of retaking the mainland, backed by a strong US military presence on the island and a mutual defense treaty with Washington. Since Beijing's relative power has improved significantly and since Washington's support for Taipei has diminished significantly in more recent years, one should expect to see a reduction in this concern. That is to say, with the improvement in China's objective security situation, one should expect to see a change in its policy. Unremitting animosity would imply more of an offensive than defensive motivation in the new circumstances. Similarly, if Beijing were to act assertively in the South China Sea against much weaker opponents, this assertiveness would more likely indicate an offensive rather than defensive agenda.

By the same token, when the US blockaded Cuba and engaged in overt and covert interventions elsewhere in the Western Hemisphere (e.g., Chile, Panama, the Dominican Republic, Haiti, Grenada, Nicaragua, and of course, Cuba in the Bay of Pigs episode) where it had already attained the status of an undisputed hegemon, its motivation and trustworthiness were called into question. Compared to other countries (even major powers like China and Russia), the US faces, objectively speaking, a more benign security environment so far as threats to its homeland are concerned as traditionally defined by realists. When it continues to outspend other countries on its armed forces (specifically, more than the military expenditures of the other top twenty countries *combined*), its behavior again arouses concerns about its intentions.

How often a country wages war and also where are its wars located (on its home territory or along its borders as opposed to distant lands) are also meaningful for inferring whether it has a defensive or offensive motivation. If it is a wealthy, developed country, it should be expected to give proportionately more foreign aid (and domestic aid to its own less fortunate citizens as alluded to earlier) and to act in a less begrudging manner when negotiating trade agreements with others. When it fails to do so, this failure is informative. Finally, for both Beijing and Washington, a reasonable test of their sincerity would be whether they would be willing to submit their own country and their citizens to the same standards of behavior that they expect from others (such as with respect to nuclear armament, internet espionage, prosecution of war criminals, global warming, and the United Nations Convention on the Law of the Sea, which China ratified in 1996, albeit opting out of Article 298's provision for dispute arbitration, and which the US Senate has repeatedly rejected, most recently in 2012).

People infer intentions and attribute motivations to others by judging the consistency of their behavior with their pronouncements across time and cases. That is, people often generalize from precedents involving themselves or others when they search for possibly relevant information to evaluate a current issue or situation. Naturally, consistency tends to bolster believability or credibility. Washington's support for Taipei on the grounds that it is a democracy is likely to encounter a skeptical reception in Beijing because the US supported Taipei even more strongly when it was an authoritarian state (even after the KMT regime's brutal suppression of the local population in the infamous February 28 incident). Nor is Washington's past record of acquiescing to, condoning, and even actively supporting the overthrow of democratically elected governments in Tehran, Islamabad, Santiago, and Cairo likely to gain Chinese converts to its publicized rationale for supporting Taipei now that it is a democracy. Finally, a country's publicized rationale may rightly or wrongly arouse doubts about its sincerity, such as in invading Iraq over "weapons of mass destruction," intervening in Libya for humanitarian reasons rather than "regime change," and bombing the Chinese embassy in Belgrade due to a bureaucratic snafu. The credibility of these rationales can be tested by thinking counterfactually; would one accept similar explanations if the shoe were on the other foot?

With respect to deterrence credibility, past behavior as indicated by China's intervention in the Korean War, is likely to have contributed to Washington taking Beijing's threat to enter the Vietnam War more seriously. (Here is an example where the non-occurrence of an event, overt massive Chinese intervention as in Korea, is significant.) At the same time and as another example of where non-occurrence can matter, according to at least one account (Sartori 2005), Beijing's failure to invade Taiwan (in 1950–51) diminished the credibility of its subsequent threat to intervene in the Korean conflict in Washington's eyes. Proponents of US support for Taiwan often argue that this support is important as a generic indication of the reliability of US commitments to its allies. This rationale, however, is belied by the precedent provided by South Vietnam (but note also the caveat introduced below about whether a state's reputation is specific to a dyad or is generalizable across all counterparts). Moreover, the disastrous consequences that were predicted to follow in the wake of US withdrawal from the Indochina wars were also contradicted by history. The abandonment of US allies in Laos, Cambodia, and South Vietnam did not produce the predicted spread of communism beyond these countries.

Finally, that a similar reasoning about the desirability and even necessity of upholding a country's general reputation for its alliance commitments is rarely applied to the Soviet withdrawal from Afghanistan or, even more consequentially, Mikhail Gorbachev's refusal to use the Red Army to support fellow communist regimes in the late 1980s points to the natural tendency for people to have selective recall. Parenthetically, the idea of abandoning an ally also does not usually occur to Americans when they urge Beijing to pressure Pyongyang. One would presume that if

Americans worry about the repercussion that their reputation could suffer as a result of abandoning Taiwan, the Chinese may have similar concerns about deserting North Korea – especially considering North Korea is right next to China whereas Taiwan is thousands of miles away from the US.

As already touched upon in Chapter 1, states' reputation has been a subject of prior studies (e.g., Mercer 1996; Sartori 2005), and there is a debate about whether a reputation for honesty and firmness is generalizable from one episode to another (i.e., whether this reputation spills over from one situation to another so that a state can acquire a general reputation that affects how others relate to it). The prevailing view is that those that have been steadfast in the past – or at least those that have bluffed successfully in the past (i.e., those that have gotten away with their bluffs) – will likely be taken more seriously than others that have been less steadfast or that have been previously exposed as bluffers (i.e., those whose bluffs have been called). But again and as just mentioned, the relevant effect may be specific to each dyad. X is likely to respond to how Y has acted toward it previously rather than reacting to Y on the basis of how Y has also acted toward A, B, and C. According to Paul Huth (1988a: 81), "The potential attacker did not seem to draw conclusions about the future behavior of the defender based on the defender's behavior in disputes with other states. Rather, the past behavior of the defender was taken as an indicator of behavior in the current conflict only when the potential attacker has been directly involved in past confrontations with the defender." If true, this proposition means that Vietnam and the Philippines cannot necessarily infer China's intentions in their respective maritime disputes from what Beijing did or failed to do in its contention with Japan over the Senkaku/Diaoyu Islands or in its past confrontations with the US across the Taiwan Strait.

One may even question whether reputations have any effect at all on potential adversaries' conduct, to the extent that their effects tend to be self-correcting in the sense described previously in Chapter 1. Reputation, after all, refers to information that is publicly available and commonly shared. Thus, if I know that you know, and you know that I know you know, and I know that you know I know, and so on, this information would have been fully incorporated in both parties' decisions. The party with a stronger reputation for resolve may be expected to bluff more often, and its counterpart is aware of this tendency and is therefore more motivated to call the perceived bluff, a prospect that is in turn anticipated by the first party, and so on and so forth.

Significantly, other states are likely to interpret a failure to uphold a country's commitments as a result of its circumstances rather than its disposition (i.e., they are likely to decide that this failure is not indicative of this country's basic motivation or its inherent character but is primarily the product of its challenging, even dire circumstances; Mercer 2007). An example of this interpretation may be that the US withdrawal from the Vietnam War had less to do with US leaders' genuine wishes or instincts (Gerald Ford had wanted to continue the war but was overruled by Congress), and more to do with their circumstances (e.g., adverse public opinion, the Watergate scandal). These propositions warrant further investigation to determine the extent to which they receive empirical support.

In addition to reputation which relates to how states have acted on comparable prior occasions, an inclination to trust others and, conversely, to be trusted by others appears to be related to relative power and relative stake. The latter variables speak to the structural conditions (or circumstances) that states find themselves currently in (in contrast to those reputation effects that are due to their prior behavior). When states have stronger capabilities, they have less need to trust others – simply because instead of relying on others' words, they are in a better position to take matters into their own hands. Thus, strong states are less disposed to trust others (Kydd 2005). Conversely and as realists would argue, strong states tend to arouse others' security concerns simply by virtue of their strength. Some have even argued that "It is possible that, when states are approaching capabilities of hegemonic proportions, those resources alone are so threatening that they 'drown out' distance, offense-defense, and intentions as potential negative threat modifiers" (Elman 2003: 16).

As for relative stakes, a state whose core interests are obviously engaged in a situation will not need to bluff, because others are inclined to believe its seriousness in the first place. Conversely, those with only a small stake are disinclined to bluff, because others are likely to question their true commitment (i.e., to call their bluff). States with an intermediate amount of stake are most likely to bluff, because their statements of concern will make more of a difference in others' perceptions than when they have objectively a very high or very low stake (Sartori 2002). Moreover, when states are more equally matched in their capabilities, their show of determination (whether sincere or insincere) will make more of a difference in tipping a situation in their favor. As mentioned earlier, a much weaker contestant in a dyad runs the severe risk of being punished if it tries to bluff and if its bluff is called. Conversely, a much stronger contestant can more afford to bluff because the negative consequences of being caught in bluffing are less serious for it. Moreover and more pertinent to the current context, this country stands a better chance of getting away with bluffing simply because others that are much weaker are more reluctant to call its bluff (due to the heavier penalty they will have to pay if their decision turns out to be mistaken) – which means that these counterparts won't be able to find out whether it was or was not actually bluffing.

These remarks produce straightforward hypotheses. When a much weaker side in a confrontation takes a stand, its credibility is higher than when a much stronger side does the same. As well, contests of will – and mutual bluffing and misjudgments of each other's resolve – are more likely when the contesting sides' capabilities are more equally matched than when they are lopsided. Applied to China, these propositions argue that when Beijing threatened to intervene in the Korean War at a time when it was much weaker than the US, it was not likely bluffing (as we now know in hindsight). As well, now that the Sino-American balance of power has become less asymmetric, the tendency by both sides to bluff has increased.

For democracies, the extent to which domestic groups align themselves with an incumbent government's announced policy provides clues about the credibility of this announced policy (Schultz 2001). This alignment by groups that typically have a vested interest in criticizing or opposing incumbent officials demonstrates a unity of national purpose and implies that the administration in charge is serious about its announced policy – and enjoys domestic support for this policy. The reactions of domestic opposition groups therefore provide a sort of "truth serum" for gauging an administration's policy credibility. Thus, when a foreign policy or international agreement enjoys widespread bipartisan support, an administration is more likely to be sincere and can be relied on to carry it out. (The political opposition now has a stake in this policy or treaty's implementation, and will therefore "enforce" the incumbent officials' "compliance" with their announced intentions.) This interpretation is quite separate from the idea, to be discussed in Chapter 5, that foreign deals require domestic ratification.

Recent research suggests that when an authoritarian regime mobilizes public opinion and escalates media attention to an ongoing controversy, such behavior also lends credibility to its announced policy (Weiss 2012, 2014). As I will expand further in later discussion, such behavior indicates this regime's deliberate investment in its reputation. To the extent that other states and officials believe that reputation is important (but see the preceding discussion), such efforts are in themselves informative. This view suggests that officials can try to contrive or manufacture reputation in order to bolster their credibility. In the next chapter, I will discuss the idea of "tying hands," whereby officials can deliberately commit their reputation to an announced course of action in order to enhance this policy's credibility in foreigners' eyes.

Finally, financial markets both at home and abroad will also attend to officials' words and deeds, thereby providing an independent source for assessing the credibility of their verbal and nonverbal behavior. These markets try to anticipate or at least adjust quickly to those developments that affect corporate profits, interest rates, and currency values. Not surprisingly, in the days immediately before and after World War I broke out, the price of gold, wheat, and Swiss franc rose whereas the value of the belligerent states' currencies fell. More recently when Greece and other southern European states were beset by economic distress in 2012–13, the value of the euro fell as investors sold this currency in an expression of no confidence in the respective European governments' credibility in managing their financial problems. These financial actors did not evidently trust, at that time, that the pertinent governments would carry out their announced plans, nor did they apparently believe in the efficacy of these plans to resolve the ongoing economic challenges.

The market gyrations in 1914 also reflected the investing public's judgments about the sincerity of the belligerent states' announced resolve to go to war and to prosecute a prolonged struggle. I mention the financial markets' reactions because, as will be taken up in greater detail later, they capture the unbiased judgments of self-interested parties. Officials often have an incentive to misrepresent their positions to their audiences (such as when they exchange threats and counter-threats in a confrontation, or when they publicize the prospective benefits of a pending economic accord), but those who buy and sell financial instruments (stocks, currencies, loans, real estate) do not have an incentive to lie to themselves when deciding these transactions. They have the opposite motivation of trying to be as unbiased as possible in making these financial decisions in order to maximize returns and avoid losses. Thus, the reactions of financial markets offer another independent and impartial source of information for judging officials' sincerity and reliability. If, for example, the pertinent officials are seriously threatening war across the Taiwan Strait, the share prices in Hong Kong, Taiwan, and China's stock markets, real estate values in these places, and global interest rates and currency exchange rates (including the value of the US dollar) should reflect the gravity of this situation. If, alternatively, the financial markets fail to react sharply to the pertinent officials' words or deeds, this phenomenon is also meaningful. The investing community is in that event dismissing their pronouncements as "hot air" and their actions as "empty gesture."

Cross-Strait commerce as credible commitment

How does the discussion so far pertain to relations across the Taiwan Strait and to China's relations with the other contestants in the East and

South China Seas? To a greater or lesser extent, Beijing's counterparts in these disputes face a trade-off between promoting thriving economic relations with China and contesting vigorously its sovereignty claims. Arguably, this tension is more acute for Taiwan than for the others. When the issue is framed in this way, the pertinent leaders have to sub-optimize between the economic and political dimensions. In Taiwan's case, its officials can pursue the political goal of independence at the expense of destabilizing the island's economic relations with the main-land. Alternatively, they can expand and deepen cross-Strait economic relations at the cost of their aspirations for political independence. Naturally, the choices implied by this conundrum are not necessarily dichotomous in nature. Rather, they obviously involve a matter of relative emphasis and even deliberate and creative ambiguity to advance the two seemingly incompatible objectives simultaneously.

Nevertheless, the basic tension posed by the competing political and economic desiderata should be clear. Voters expect incumbent officials to deliver on both objectives, that is, they want to achieve good economic performance and defend national honor and sovereignty at the same time. However, given China's increasing centrality in the other involved coun-tries' external commercial profiles, its counterparts' economic perfor-mance (especially for Taiwan, which has become heavily dependent on the mainland market) requires them to mute political contention with Beijing. Political tension can roil financial markets, undermining business confidence and hurting foreign trade and investment. Put starkly, politi-cians are pressured to choose – even though for obvious reasons they want to avoid being trapped by their choices and to also appear as a virtuoso capable of balancing two seemingly conflicting pursuits. However, at the end of the day they will still have to set priorities. Are they the "economics first" type or the "politics first" type (Benson and Niou 2007)?

What has just been said about China's commercial and financial part-ners is also applicable to China itself. It can dial down its maritime disputes in order to foster a stable external environment so that it can focus on its various domestic challenges. Or it can give priority to these disputes and as a consequence, cause changes in both the regional and domestic contexts to the detriment of its agenda of economic develop-ment. My discussion in the subsequent chapters will argue that Beijing has pursued a policy of "reactive assertiveness." It has shown a general inclination to postpone confrontation unless it perceives the other party in a dispute to have taken unilateral actions to breach or threaten the status quo. In that event, it will push back forcefully in order to oppose the other side's perceived encroachments and to deter such conduct again in the future. This behavioral pattern does not conform, or at least has thus far not conformed, to offensive realism's expectation that as a country gains more power, it will become more aggressive and expansionist. By assuming a deterrence posture, Beijing has appeared to be playing more of a defensive game, such as to stop what it perceives to be salami tactics undertaken especially by Chen Shui-bian, actions that sought to move Taiwan gradually toward *de jure* independence. The description just given does not deny that Beijing has sometimes taken offensive actions and unilateral initiatives that alter "facts on the ground." China attacked South Vietnamese forces on the Crescent group of islands in the Paracels in 1974 when the US was unlikely to intervene. This episode contradicts the characterization of reactive assertiveness, and also undermined Beijing's trustworthiness in the eyes of other countries.

How can Chinese officials tell whether Taipei's leaders are truly committed to pursuing the island's independence or conversely, whether they are more interested in seeking détente with Beijing, raising the prospect that economic integration and political accommodation will in the long run lead to reunification? How can China's leaders distinguish statements made by Taiwan's politicians intended for consumption by their domestic constituents, especially in the heat of electoral contests or while trying to gain media publicity in partisan posturing, from communications that should be taken more seriously? How can Taiwan's leaders demonstrate their resolve to pursue political independence or alternatively, to show the sincerity of their desire not to rock the political boat – notwithstanding what they may say publicly? These questions relate to the challenges of judging others' trustworthiness and also communicating one's own trustworthiness (or credible commitment to a policy course, whether announced or unannounced).

Relating back to the discussion in the last section, the more acute a policy dilemma faced by a politician, the more this situation resembles a "stress test." This individual is compelled to choose between two competing desires, such as between economic intercourse with China and political independence from it. Also in line with the logic presented earlier, the choice made by this politician is more informative when it contradicts this person's known political disposition. Therefore, it is much more significant that Taiwan's trade with and investment in China took off during the administrations of Lee Teng-hui and Chen Shui-bian than had they done so under the current government led by Ma Ying-jeou. When a person acts contrary to his/her natural political inclination or preference (or fails to act according to this inclination or preference), this action is more credible and meaningful than otherwise.

As an example from US politics, when Democratic politicians support limiting imports of cheap Chinese manufactures, their action can be construed as disguised protectionism intended to benefit blue-collar workers in the pertinent industries, workers who are their natural constituency. Their behavior can therefore be interpreted to have a hidden domestic agenda rather than being designed necessarily or even primarily as a signal of serious displeasure with Beijing. Conversely, when a Republican administration orders export bans – such as the sale of grain and pipeline equipment to the USSR when Ronald Reagan was the president – these gestures can be taken as an indication of its genuine displeasure rather than partisan posturing or domestic rent-seeking. This is so because these embargoes contradict the economic philosophy and political interests that have been traditionally associated with Republicans and their supporters.

As also mentioned earlier, when people's choices are relatively unconstrained, such as when Taiwan's businesses could have traded with and invested in Southeast Asia, Latin America, North America, and Western Europe but have instead decided to march *en masse* to China, their choice is revealing. Why would they want to do this when they should have known that their commercial deals could be held up as an economic hostage for political ransom by Beijing? Moreover, uncertainties about the legal enforcement of contracts, protection of property rights, and pervasive corruption should have discouraged and even deterred these businesspeople from going to China. This awareness would make their decision to enter into large commercial deals (which sometimes require huge sunk investments and entail many years of operation before any profit may be realized) with their mainland counterparts more puzzling. Finally, that Taiwan's businesspeople had to actually overcome the political barriers and to bypass the legal obstacles imposed by their own government intended to impede cross-Strait commerce in the earlier years is even more remarkable. According to the logic of inference presented earlier, these businesspeople (and many of their political representatives) must have been very optimistic about being able not only to make large profits in China but also to preserve their capital there. Their behavior is also tantamount to a strong vote of confidence in the future stability of cross-Strait relations. Why else would they want to (knowingly) jeopardize their capital (for the politicians this capital would be mainly political rather than financial)?

As suggested by the reasoning of strategic anticipation, Taiwan's businesspeople would not have entered into those relationships that in their view would be unrewarding. Thus, by their actions they are predicting stable cross-Strait relations or, in other words, voting with their money that there will not be a political rupture between the two sides (they would be grievously hurt in such an event). Moreover, given the high costs of misjudgment, their actions must mean a rather strong conviction in and even commitment to being the "economics first" rather than the "politics first" type. Finally, the actions of Taiwan's businesspeople represent a form of credible commitment not to destabilize cross-Strait relations. The more costs their financial or commercial undertakings will entail in the event of a political breakdown, the more credible these actors' commitment not to destabilize or reverse cross-Strait relations (those who are insincere or unreliable would not have taken on such prospectively heavy costs in the first place). Because Taiwan's businesspeople have now acquired a large stake in the stability of these relations, they can be expected to self-mobilize to ensure this stability. In other words, their actions contribute to creating and sustaining a new and more stable situation.

That Taiwan's officials did not effectively stop their firms' initial commercial forays to the mainland and subsequently approved and even supported the further expansion and consolidation of cross-Strait economic integration is also highly significant. These officials' behavior indicates that they too are the "economics first" type and not the "politics first" type (contrast their behavior with that of the North Koreans, the Iranians, and the Cubans until President Barack Obama's announcement in December 2014 of the easing of the travel and financial bans imposed on the latter). When faced with a tough decision between choosing economic performance and political independence, they have chosen the former by their action or inaction (Chan 2006, 2009a). Without their implicit or explicit concurrence, cross-Strait economic integration would not have reached the current stage. From Beijing's perspective, it is only natural to ask the following question. If Taiwan's leaders, especially Lee Teng-huai and Chen Shui-bian with their strong pro-independence sympathies, were either unwilling or unable to stop or limit cross-Strait commerce at a time when the political and economic costs of doing so would have been comparatively lower, what are the prospects for their future successors to undertake actions that would be inimical to the island's economy when the pertinent costs will have become much greater?

Taiwan has in some recent years sent over 40% of its exports to China plus Hong Kong, and it has also directed over 70% of its outbound investment to the mainland. It offers an exceptional case of heavy and asymmetric economic dependency. The other countries involved in sovereignty disputes with China show less pronounced profiles in these respects. The US Central Intelligence Agency's World Factbook (https://www.cia.gov/library/publications/the-world-factbook/) reports that in 2012, Japan sent about 23% of its exports to China plus Hong Kong and received about the same proportion of its imports in return.

Vietnam was more dependent on China plus Hong Kong for its imports than for its exports (about 32% and 13% respectively), whereas the situation was reversed for the Philippines (about 11% and 21% respectively). Taiwan's situation has been more similar to that of the Philippines in that it has depended much more on China plus Hong Kong as a market for its exports (over 40% as mentioned already) than as a source of its imports (about 16%). It has enjoyed a chronic trade surplus with China in addition to having been accorded favorable investment treatments on the mainland.

Taiwan's economic dependency on China is large and asymmetric. It is much more dependent on the mainland market than vice versa. Realists have repeatedly warned against trading with potential adversaries because this trade has a "security externality," by which they mean that it can benefit this counterpart and provide it with economic returns to be used to strengthen its military (for some pertinent discussions, see Morrow 1997, 2003; Kastner 2006, 2007; Liberman 1996; Papayoanou and Kastner 1999). Furthermore, dependency scholars have decried that an economic reliance on foreign capital and markets can result in excessive external influence in a country's domestic politics, even to the point that foreigners can co-opt this country's ruling elite.

Taiwan's officials are not unaware of these security and political consequences. One may perhaps argue that these consequences are less dire or obvious for the Philippines and Vietnam (two countries that have contested China's sovereignty in the South China Sea), or for Japan, which is a large and developed economy. Unlike Taiwan, these countries do not face an existential threat from China. Beijing has not challenged their legal status as an internationally recognized political entity. Taiwan is the only one facing this threat, and Beijing has not disguised its intentions – that is, one cannot accuse Beijing of trying to "set up" Taiwan surreptitiously for a hidden political agenda (as the Nazis had done in their trade policies toward the Balkan countries before World War II). Beijing's agenda has been transparent. So what can explain Taiwan's decision, by both its businesspeople and its politicians, to enter into a highly dependent and very significant economic relationship with China?

One plausible interpretation, one already suggested above, is that this economic dependency is a form of credible commitment. It is a tacit commitment, albeit one that is sometimes contradicted by some politicians' avowed dedication to the cause of Taiwan independence. This relationship would appear to outside observers, including those in Beijing, to be tantamount to an act of "hostage giving" by Taipei and "hostage taking" by Beijing. The basic logic of this exchange is not difficult to grasp. A parallel is offered by the agreement reached by

Moscow and Washington in the Anti-Ballistic Missile Treaty, whereby they pledged to leave all but one of their urban centers undefended against a possible nuclear strike from the other side. The unprotected status of their cities offered a credible commitment not to start a first strike against the other side (if either party should start a nuclear war, its unprotected cities would be destroyed by the other side's retaliation). This example describes an outdated situation: since withdrawing from the Anti-Ballistic Missile Treaty, the US has launched missile defense systems which are perceived by both Moscow and Beijing to be aimed at them rather than at Washington's professed targets (Iran and North Korea). In Taiwan's case, its trade with and investment in the mainland promise implicitly not to declare independence – a development that will surely devastate its economy. Incidentally, this line of reasoning suggests that economic coercion or trade embargo is a far more likely contingency than an outright military invasion in the unlikely event that cross-Strait relations were to deteriorate seriously.

Fixed assets that require a significant amount of time before realizing profits naturally signal that the firms involved (and presumably their home governments) have sufficient confidence in the stability of long-term relations. Moreover, distribution networks and production equipment that are dedicated to serve particular foreign markets (such as in order to meet their specific safety and health standards, labor conditions, or local tastes and content requirements) often represent non-salvageable investments. As such, they again indicate a credible commitment to long-term cooperation. The parties involved will jeopardize, even forfeit, their large investments if this cooperation is stalled. Business joint ventures and participation in cross-border production chains provide other examples whereby the partners commit themselves to cooperate. The larger the amount of their collateral that can be lost should there be a setback or even a rupture in their relationship, the greater their expression of commitment and also of their confidence in the durability of their partnership. Their behavior is similar to depositing money in an escrow account such that one will lose this fund should one renege on a deal. It is also similar to diplomacy of a bygone era when rulers literally took and gave hostages (usually close family members) as a sign of their goodwill and peaceful intentions. Arranged marriages between royalties followed the same idea.

Intra-Asian trade has taken off sharply in recent years. This phenomenon suggests that Taiwan's bilateral relations with China also affect its economic competitiveness relative to its other neighbors. Taiwan's businesses would have been placed at a severe disadvantage relative to their East Asian competitors had Taipei not signed the Economic Cooperation Framework Agreement (ECFA) with Beijing, an accord that has helped to offset the effects of similar trade liberalization agreements that Beijing has entered into with the ASEAN countries, Japan and South Korea. Because other countries are reluctant to enter into trade agreements with Taiwan over China's objection, Taiwan's access to regional free trade arrangements has to be gained by first negotiating and implementing the ECFA with Beijing. Put differently, in the absence of such an accord with China, Taiwan is likely to be locked out of East Asia's rising economic integration. The pertinent economic consequences (both benefits and costs) extend beyond just bilateral trade across the Taiwan Strait. In this light, how Taiwan's Legislative Yuan would proceed with an accord to open up cross-Strait trade in the service sector will be highly informative. This accord was negotiated by Ma Ying-jeou's government before the 2014 landslide victory in local elections scored by the Democratic Progressive Party, and its ratification has been stalled due to a student-led protest (the so-called Sunflower Movement). This legislation's fate would provide another indication of the evolving balance of forces on the island, between those favoring "politics first" and others preferring "economics first."

Taiwan's trade with China provides an exceptional case but other countries, such as Japan, Vietnam, and the Philippines, have also increased their commercial ties with China in recent decades. When countries engage in intense trade, they in effect create a larger economic zone. They produce more of certain goods than their domestic economy can consume, and their surplus production capacity is intended for exports. Their firms become more specialized in order to maximize comparative advantage to serve a larger market that includes foreign clients. This effort to capture economies of scale by selling to a larger (international) market implies a basic reorientation of the domestic economy, which in turn becomes more vulnerable to the perils of foreign market closures, supply disruptions, and idle production capacity should overseas demand decline or be shut off.

Both businesspeople and government officials are surely aware that this internationalist transformation may subject them to opportunistic behavior by their counterparts. As I have argued elsewhere, the pertinent risks are not limited to just the most overt or blatant forms of political coercion such as outright nationalization, expropriation of foreigners' investments, or embargo against their products. The pertinent risks also involve subtler means intended to hamper or harass foreign businesses, such as limiting their profit repatriation, requiring minimum domestic content, imposing ostensible safety and pollution standards, alleging dumping violations, instituting countervailing duties, or initiating tax auditing or corruption investigation. Although couched in these other terms, these actions may be politically motivated. Whether this political motivation is actually involved or not, for the smaller economies that trade with a larger one like China (again Taiwan comes to mind) they are drawn into the latter's economic orbit and as a result, their economic fate becomes tied to that of their larger partner (just as in the cases of Canada and Mexico in their relations with the US). Being aware of these possible consequences, when those countries involved in contested sovereignty enter into intense commercial relations with China, their behavior is significant as a form of credible commitment to not let their disputes get out of hand.

Whether voters and their representatives are the "economics first" or "politics first" type should be gauged by their actions rather than their statements. Surely both the politicians and businesspeople in Taiwan should know that as they become more economically dependent on China, they also are more vulnerable to being held up politically by Beijing – that is, they run a greater risk of having their economic dependency exploited by Beijing as a bargaining chip for political concessions. The longer this dependency lasts and the deeper it becomes, the greater the economic and political costs of extrication and resistance. If ardent pro-independence politicians such as Lee Teng-hui and Chen Shui-bian were unable or unwilling to put a decisive stop to cross-Strait commerce when it was still relatively small in scale, then it would be even less likely for someone who is less committed to this cause to reverse ongoing economic integration now that the stakes are higher and the stakeholders in this integration are stronger.

Put differently, if Taiwan's officials were unwilling to pay the economic price for pursuing their goal of political independence when this price was still relatively low, others (especially those from the KMT camp) are even less likely to pay this price when it is higher. The higher economic price that can ensue from a political rupture stems from the fact that much of Taiwan's investments on the Chinese mainland are immobile (i.e., they cannot be easily retrieved) and that their operations have become integrated into the marketing and production networks there. This investment again implies a strong and credible commitment to not destabilize cross-Strait relations. Surely, a politician or businessperson fully committed to the cause of Taiwan's political independence would not have acted in the manner in which recent cross-Strait relations have evolved. This person would have favored stopping the commercial relationship before the costs of doing so became politically and economically difficult to bear. Extensive economic ties tend to undermine a state's deterrence threat against another state which has become an important commercial partner (Papayoanou 1999). Its deterrence threat becomes less credible because there is now a stronger disincentive to incur the large opportunity costs stemming from rupturing these ties (i.e., the large amount of economic benefits that would be lost should there be a rupture) and because officials issuing this deterrence threat will now face greater difficulties in mobilizing domestic support and forging national consensus to oppose the perceived foreign threat.

The very enormity of Taiwan's business stake in the Chinese market is a form of reassurance to Beijing. This phenomenon is contrary to many politicians' partisan rhetoric directed at the domestic audience, suggesting their support for the independence cause. Deeds speak louder than words. Moreover, the greater the self-imposed costs that a person or state is willing to accept, the greater is its credibility (because those who are insincere or untrustworthy are not likely to accept these costs and run the risk, for example, of forfeiting their large sunk investment). Returning to the question motivating this chapter, a person or state's sincerity and trustworthiness are shown by the size of penalty that this actor knowingly submits itself to should it turn out to be insincere or untrustworthy. Thus, the larger the amount of "earnest money" that a buyer is willing to commit as a down-payment for a purchase, the more serious is this person's likely intention to conclude the deal in question.

This presentation suggests that economic exchanges are "endogenous" to stable political relations. That is, these exchanges are not just determined by the state of political relations but also are in themselves an indication of the state of these relations. Because firms and states select themselves into those relationships that they expect to be rewarding rather than harmful, the level of current economic exchanges also predicts the future stability of political relations. In the case of Taiwan especially and to a lesser extent also for China's other commercial partners that are involved in sovereignty disputes with Beijing, intense economic interdependence portends less danger of future political upheavals. To repeat the point about strategic anticipation, ongoing economic exchanges not only reflect the current state of political relations but are also harbingers of future political relations. They provide one means of discerning intentions by separating the more serious and believable signals from the noises created by political rhetoric and posturing. Because commerce can have security externalities, countries and businesspeople who expect an armed conflict with their counterparts are unlikely to get themselves involved in intense commercial relations in the first place. This observation does not deny that wars have happened between close economic partners (such as the major belligerents in World War I). At the same time, quantitative research has consistently shown a strong cross-national pattern: countries that trade heavily with each other are more likely to keep peace between them than those that do not.

Those who disagree with my interpretation may invoke different reasons to explain the increasing economic integration across the Taiwan Strait. They may point to the great disparity in power between the two sides, their geographic proximity, their cultural similarity, and/or their economic compatibility to explain this development. However, these alternative explanations run into problems if we consider changes over time and the experiences of other contentious dyads. After all, some of the factors just mentioned also existed when trade and travel were banned between the two sides of the Taiwan Strait during the 1950s and 1960s. Economic and cultural conditions have not changed fundamentally since those earlier years but political conditions have. Furthermore, cross-Strait economic integration between these two historical adversaries occurred even though this development did not happen for other pairs of such countries characterized by similar factors – such as between the US and Cuba (at least until Washington's policy change announced in December 2014), South and North Korea, Israel and Egypt, Greece and Turkey, and Pakistan and India. In these latter cases, politics has thus far trumped economics. This digression therefore argues again that it is useful to introduce both a historical and a comparative perspective instead of analyzing a situation or country in isolation.

Other examples of reassurance signals

There are other instances where intense economic relations point to security reassurance. Again, as suggested earlier, when a person or state appears to act "out of character" or contrary to seeming circumstantial dictates, this behavior is noteworthy. Political adversaries and especially states that pose a potential threat to each other are not expected to enter into significant economic exchanges. This is so because foreign trade and investment can have security externalities as mentioned earlier. The economic returns from these exchanges can be used by one's opponent to develop its military and therefore to present a greater security challenge to one's interests in the future. Hence, allies are much more likely to enter into deep and broad economic relations than adversaries (Gowa 1994). For the same reason, adversaries are likely to limit and boycott economic exchanges, such as when the US imposed economic embargoes against the USSR and China during the Cold War (Mastanduno 1992). Certainly, one should expect political adversaries and security competitors to be wary of getting themselves into a relationship that would increase their vulnerability and contribute to their counterpart's relative gain (Grieco 1988).

When states act contrary to these realist expectations, their behavior is meaningful. The huge amount of US debt owned by China is a case in point. Why would China want to hold this vulnerable asset which could potentially be subject to US default or other kinds of defection (such as currency depreciation, debt repayment moratorium, and even outright repudiation of loans)? Why would Beijing want to subsidize US expenditures that could be used to improve Washington's military capabilities in a potential showdown with it? Why would it want to finance the US budget deficit so that the Pentagon could follow through its announced "pivot to Asia," which is widely seen as an effort to contain China? Why would it want to keep interest rates low in the US, thereby helping this country's economic recovery? Liberals could conceivably argue that a healthier US economy would increase demand for Chinese products but this is not a reason that realists would be inclined to offer. Realists, at least most traditional realists, would argue that security should always trump economics (Brooks 1997). From the US perspective, why would Washington want to borrow from Beijing (which is now the largest foreign source of financing US public debt), thereby becoming dependent on this foreign creditor and risking the hazard of a possible future Chinese boycott of US debt instruments and even a dumping of existing Chinese holdings – which could cause havoc to financial markets not only in the US but worldwide (Drezner 2009)? Some have argued that such a scenario is highly unlikely because Beijing's interests would also be hurt enormously in the process. This is of course true but, as has been remarked previously, states have been known to fight wars when the costs (and not just financial costs) can be expected to be enormous.

I have argued elsewhere that the behavior of China and the US in this example can be interpreted as strong reassurance signals, intended to convey a credible commitment not to destabilize their relationship (Chan 2012d). As suggested earlier, the costlier that this destabilization could be, the more persuasive is this gesture – because those who are insincere will be deterred by the prospect that they will have to suffer these costs when they undertake destabilizing actions in the future. The large stake involved in the creditor–debtor relationship between China and the US is a product of these countries' own actions and provides a form of credible commitment – albeit one that is tacit rather than publicized as such. This heavy financial engagement (in addition to bilateral trade and investment) suggests a binding relationship – Zachary Karabell (2009) describes it as "superfusion" – such that one cannot hurt one's counterpart (or defect) without also grievously harming oneself.

Significantly, the above costs are self-imposed – being initiated voluntarily by the parties themselves rather than being forced upon them by an external authority. In this context, the decisions by Japan and Germany to eschew nuclear weapons and to agree to the stationing of US troops on their soil present another example of reassuring their neighbors. By binding themselves to the US in their respective alliances, these countries in effect indicate by their actions that they renounce the option of "going alone" in security matters. Accordingly, these alliance ties are important not so much for their ostensible purpose of power accretion (since by definition, both two superpowers in the bipolar world of the Cold War were so much stronger than their respective allies that they did not need the latter countries' contributions to maintain their dominant status). These ties are rather more meaningful as credible commitments by Germany and Japan to be "leashed" voluntarily. In various forms and ways, these two countries subordinate their respective military to US control – thus providing reassurance, in this case provided by Washington's influence exercised through its treaty arrangements and command integration, to their respective neighbors. Paul Schroeder (1976) has described this latter purpose of alliances as *pactum de contrahendo* or pact of restraint.

In the case of Germany, its officials' decision to embed their country deeply in the multilateral institutions of the European Union and the North Atlantic Treaty Organization offer additional evidence of self-binding, so that Berlin cannot plausibly take unilateral assertive actions without being stopped by the other member states. Moreover, by recognizing Germany's postwar borders (such as with Poland) and showing contrition for crimes committed during World War II (He 2009), Berlin again signals its peaceful intentions. In the case of Japan, its postwar constitution and self-imposed capping of its military expenditure at about 1% of its gross domestic product also furnish reassurance. To the extent that public opinion in both countries leans heavily against militarist policies (Berger 1998), it further reassures foreign audiences because any reorientation of these countries' foreign and security policies (in a more assertive or belligerent direction) would require overriding strong domestic opposition or at least skepticism. Naturally, this observation cuts both ways – if or when nationalist politicians are able to persuade Germany or Japan's public to accept or support a more independent posture (such as Prime Minister Shinzo Abe's seeming intention to revise Japan's "peace" constitution, which forswears this country's military ambitions), this development will also be highly alarming to their respective neighbors.

Following the logic of reasoning presented earlier, how a country reacts to its counterpart's conduct and circumstances is informative. During the Asian financial flu of the late 1990s, several of the adversely affected countries undertook currency devaluation in order to promote their exports. Beijing refrained from engaging in similar behavior – that is, it eschewed the option of also devaluing its currency and thereby accepted an export disadvantage caused by those countries that did depreciate their currencies. Its self-restraint offered a meaningful indication of its cooperative intention. In contrast, the US demanded that as a condition for IMF (International Monetary Fund) emergency assistance, South Korea must deregulate its market, a move that was widely perceived to advance the interests of US financial firms (Kirshner 2014).

As another example, although China has been accused by some US officials of being a "currency manipulator," the *renminbi* has continued to rise in value, albeit not as fast and as much as market conditions would perhaps have warranted. During the recent past, however, Japan, the US, and the eurozone countries have all undertaken massive monetary expansion, dubbed "quantitative easing" in the US. These policies have the effect of depreciating their respective currencies and in view of the vast amount of US debt held by the Chinese, these loans would as a consequence be repaid in cheaper dollars. Beijing has not joined in competitive devaluation of its currency as evidenced by the behavior of major trading countries during the Great Depression. The latter countries undertook beggar-my-neighbor protectionist measures (shown especially by the Smoot-Hawley legislation enacted by the US) and engaged in competitive currency devaluation, such that their collective conduct exacerbated this global economic downturn. As a third example, in recent years NATO expanded its membership eastward to include countries in Russia's near abroad. The Russians perceived this move to represent a violation of the mutual understanding that ended the Cold War. Whether the expansion of NATO membership was in fact an act of reneging on a tacit accord or an informal pledge, it is not difficult to appreciate Moscow's strong misgivings about and even outright opposition to this development (especially given Washington's own insistence on the Monroe Doctrine seeking to keep foreign influences out of the Western Hemisphere). All three examples given in this paragraph refer to an actor's behavior when its counterpart(s) is (are) in distress. In the context of this chapter's discussion on trustworthiness, its behavior in such circumstance can be especially revealing. Does it choose to "pile on," "turn up the heat," or respond to its counterpart's behavior in kind? Having the self-restraint to refrain from taking advantage of a weakened counterpart's difficult, even dire, circumstance is generally indicative of one's trustworthiness.

Reactions of financial markets

One does not have to rely on politicians and officials' self-serving statements commenting on their own or their counterparts' sincerity or reliability. Before the onset of globalization, bringing about the increasing integration of financial markets on a worldwide basis, states had to resort to military displays in order to lend credibility to their pronouncements. They relied on actions such as mobilizing troops, deploying naval ships, and putting their strategic forces on alert in order to back their threatening words with actual deeds. That is, they had to undertake risky military actions in order to convince their counterpart(s) that they were not just engaging in "cheap talk" or bluffing. They continue this practice today. But they now also have another means to communicate their resolve. As several researchers have pointed out (e.g., Gartzke and Li 2003a, 2003b; Gartzke *et al.* 2001), recent developments in globalization have enabled leaders to rely on financial markets to convey their intentions. The level of economic interdependence among countries and the interconnections among global financial markets are such nowadays that leaders can deliberately engage in market-destabilizing behavior in order to call attention to the seriousness of a situation. The more their statements and actions cause havoc to the financial markets and shake business confidence with heavy costs to their own investors and constituents, the more credible is their announced agenda.

Government leaders operating in a world of mobile capital, flexible production, and hypersensitive and highly informed currency, bond, stock, and commodity traders cannot effectively communicate with their counterpart leaders without at the same time also disclosing their professed intentions to financial markets. They cannot very well threaten to go to war against another country while trying to keep this threat a secret from the financial markets – because such concealment will necessarily mean that their threat is not very credible. Thus, leaders cannot easily misrepresent themselves by pretending to be the "politics first" type without having to pay a price in hurting their own businesspeople and investors. This observation in turn presents another implication. It follows that when leaders want to demonstrate that they are resolved to have their way in a crisis, they can now resort to deliberately causing market turmoil as a means of telling their adversary to pay serious attention. The more market panic they cause and the more self-inflicted costs they suffer as a result of this panic, the more credible are their announced intentions. Thus, for example, the more Washington is willing to accept a spike in interest rates that could derail the fragile US economic recovery in a hypothetical confrontation with Beijing, the more credible is its professed resolve.

International tension will make investors and businesspeople in general nervous and insecure. Thus, when leaders declare that they are determined to carry on a political and even military struggle, their actions can roil the financial markets – causing capital to flee, currency value and stock prices to plummet, and commodity prices and interest rates to jump. When Taipei talks to Beijing, businesspeople in Taiwan and abroad are also listening. A demonstration of political resolve to declare Taiwan's independence cannot but have the effect of unsettling the markets and alienating investors. This interconnection between the world of foreign relations and the world of financial markets is important because in the era of globalization, leaders have to be cognizant that their words and deeds in one arena will have repercussions in another. As already noted, they cannot escalate foreign tension without paying an economic price. Potential market reactions help to discipline leaders and discourage them from bluffing by introducing an added cost to this behavior. Leaders can expect markets to react adversely to their escalatory actions, and this anticipation of adverse market reaction should in turn introduce a disincentive for leaders to misrepresent their intentions. The more severe the prospective adverse market reaction, the greater is this disincentive to misrepresent. (Imagine the effects that suspicions of a forthcoming declaration of Taiwan's independence would have on its stock and real estate markets, or that rumors of a Chinese boycott of the US debt market would have on the exchange rate for the *renminbi* and the value of those US bonds already owned by China.)

One can tell the same story from a different perspective. If a leader should really want to communicate the gravity of a situation – getting a counterpart's attention and making this person take his/her communication seriously – this individual now has an alternative to resorting to military displays. He/she can now deliberately roil the financial markets to achieve the same purpose of demonstrating that he/she is not just blowing "hot air." The logic explained in this chapter suggests that the more this leader knowingly causes severe market turmoil, the more credible are his/her declared intentions. Naturally, one cannot cause such market havoc if there are no ongoing financial relations or only very limited economic exchanges – an observation which in turn explains why foreign countries have so little effect on Pyongyang when they threaten the latter with sanctions. The credibility of market signals stems from the fact that one has a large stake in an ongoing economic relationship (described sometimes as "having skin in the game") and when one deliberately imposes heavy costs on oneself by threatening to destabilize the financial markets. To reiterate an important point made earlier, the higher the self-imposed costs, the greater are this actor's sincerity and credibility. These remarks in turn suggest that when leaders are reluctant to unsettle financial markets and alienate potential investors, their behavior suggests that they are likely to be subordinating their political objectives to economic priorities. A "politics first" leader would have behaved in the opposite way, demonstrating his/her political commitment by deliberately shaking financial markets in order to show that he/she is willing to sacrifice economic performance for political or security goals.

This line of reasoning thus contends that whether leaders are willing to resort to actions that upset financial markets or refrain from such actions can disclose their true valuation of political or security objectives relative to economic objectives. Foreign observers can try to infer the pertinent leaders' sincerity by discerning whether they just talk the political talk, or whether they also walk the economic walk. When they knowingly engage in and repeat behavior that has negative market consequences, these market consequences reveal their resolve and motivation. When some pro-independence politicians in Taiwan avoid taking actions that would frighten businesspeople involved in cross-Strait commerce, their inaction speaks volumes. Those politicians behaving in this manner are probably the "economics first" type disguising themselves as the "politics first" type.

This discussion suggests another proposition. One can use the financial markets' reactions to gauge the current and likely future relations between two states. Market actors have an incentive to adjust quickly to and even to anticipate political changes that will influence their economic returns. If so, US interest rates should rise quickly if these actors expect the Sino-American relationship to deteriorate seriously. Likewise, stock and housing prices should fall precipitously and, conversely, shipping insurance rates and freight charges should rise sharply if traders expect cross-Strait relations to deteriorate seriously. The value of gold and commodities should rise. The obverse should also apply. When financial markets fail to react to political events, this information is highly informative. It means that these events or the pertinent politicians' pronouncements are not being taken seriously by the investment or business community.

Thus, interestingly, during the period when Taiwan's Chen Shui-bian was preparing to introduce a popular referendum to coincide with the 2004 presidential election, its financial markets (including the stock prices of those companies that had large business transactions with the mainland) did not respond with a sharp negative correction (Chan 2009a). This referendum consisted of two questions asking for the voters' opinion on the management of cross-Strait relations but was originally supposed to raise the much more controversial issue of whether Taipei should apply for United Nations membership using the name Taiwan rather than the Republic of China (this development would have been interpreted by Beijing as a clear sign that Taipei had declared *de jure* independence). The absence of adverse market reactions in this case was informative because this non-occurrence implied that investors did not expect this referendum to cause serious repercussions for the profitability of cross-Strait economic exchanges. The market's non-reaction indicated that this referendum was being interpreted as political posturing intended to reap domestic partisan gains and that investors were expecting it to fail to receive the required popular support for passage, and it was thus being dismissed by them as an empty gesture.

Financial markets provided similarly reassuring signals in 2012 when a large number of Chinese protestors demonstrated against Japan over these countries' dispute over the Senkaku/Diaoyu Islands. Japanese companies with a large exposure to the Chinese market are obviously vulnerable to a consumer boycott there. One indirect source of information pertaining to the escalatory potential of bilateral tension would be the equity value of major Japanese automobile companies such as Honda and Toyota. Did the share prices of these and other companies with a large exposure to the Chinese market fall precipitously? That these share prices were able to maintain their equilibrium indicated that investors were relatively sanguine about a stable Sino-Japanese relationship. If they had expected this relationship to deteriorate seriously, one would have seen a sharp correction in the stock prices of such companies. In this example and the one presented in the last paragraph, reassurance was provided by the financial markets. As already mentioned previously, unlike politicians and officials, those engaged in financial transactions do not have an incentive to misrepresent. They rather have an interest in "getting the price right" for their own sake. Although participants in the financial markets are obviously not omnipotent, their reactions to politicians and officials' words and deeds are telling. If their initial judgments turn out to be wrong (when security prices are set either too high or too low), these biases should be corrected quickly as these opportunities will be seized swiftly by others who seek to profit from them. As the saying goes, the market is efficient in correcting these misjudgments. The efficient-market hypothesis contends that the current prices of financial instruments have already incorporated all the available information pertaining to existing and anticipated conditions affecting business profit.

As a final illustration drawing on recent events, student protestors stormed and occupied Taiwan's Legislative Yuan in March 2014 to oppose the ratification of an accord that would open up cross-Strait commerce in the service sector. This opposition and the prospect of possibly reversing recent progress in advancing free trade alarmed the business sector. Reflecting this unease, the island's stock index fell by 1.8% in the week ending March 21, or a loss of 154 points that translated to 533.7 billion new Taiwan dollars or US$17.46 billion (http://focustaiwan.tw/news/aall/201403230033.aspx). A drop of this magnitude suggests that the financial market took the student protest seriously and that it had real concerns about Ma Ying-jeou's ability to gain this treaty's ratification (hence, the idea of involuntary defection as mentioned earlier).

The matter of payoff divisibility

Some objects of dispute can be more easily divided among the contestants than others. Money and territory are tangible and quantifiable, and they should at least in principle lend themselves more easily to settlement than values that cannot be easily divided. Naturally, even quantifiable objects can be endowed with important symbolic value, thus making them in practice difficult to partition because they have become emotionally charged. Sacred places, such as Jerusalem, or places with unique historical significance, such as Kosovo for Serbs, are examples. Moreover, territorial contests can be entangled with competition for regime legitimacy, thus making these contests more difficult to resolve. Disputes across the Taiwan Strait, on the Korean Peninsula, and formerly between the two halves of Germany come to mind. Finally, territorial disputes can be compounded by ethnic tension, religious animosity, and historical legacies. When these additional factors are involved, such as in those disputes over Kashmir, Cyprus, and the Senkaku/Diaoyu Islands, they become more intractable. In short, when the issues being disputed involve multiple and highly charged and indivisible matters, they are more difficult to settle.

Still, clever arrangements can be imagined to finesse difficult disputes. For instance, joint custody and "time sharing" for divorced parents with children provide one such arrangement (as a child obviously cannot be divided physically). A compromise was proposed (but failed) prior to the Falklands/Malvinas War; it involved recognizing Argentina's sovereignty claim but retaining Britain's administrative control by leasing these islands back from Buenos Aires. The Svalbard settlement, also mentioned earlier, involved Norway's guarantee to demilitarize the area and to accord to the other signatories unimpeded access to the archipelago's surrounding resources. Power-sharing arrangements were tried (though subsequently failed) between the Greek and Turkish Cypriots with

Britain in the role of an external guarantor to this agreement. Finally, an impartial external mediator provided a face-saving way for Argentina to settle its Beagle Channel dispute with Chile. The Vatican's role in this episode made compromise easier from the perspective of Argentina's domestic politics (it would be easier for any regime to bow to the judgment of an impartial international mediator than to appear to have succumbed to its competitor's pressure). Finally, resource-sharing arrangements can be devised as they are common between multinational corporations and their host governments involved in mineral extraction. As well, federalism as a form of government provides a means to accommodate some level of autonomy for the constituent entities belonging to the same state. In one way or another, all these examples would still require credible commitment to abide by a settlement. Naturally, concerns about the future unenforceability of a deal may hinder the settlement from being reached in the first place.

The above examples suggest that credible commitment is a more important factor in holding up settlements than whether the values being contested are inherently divisible or not. Cases of contested sovereignty become intractable because they impinge on a regime's legitimacy in important ways and because they become entangled in domestic partisan competition to exploit nationalist sentiments. Concerns about credible commitment are especially palpable in attempts to end civil wars (e.g., Cunningham 2011; Fortna 2004; Walter 2002; Werner and Yuen 2005). At the end of these conflicts, the combatants have to be disarmed and a new national army will have to be created. This process naturally creates concerns that one's counterpart may be opportunistic and revert to armed coercion after it has gained control of the military forces and security apparatus. The allocation of commanding officers in an integrated national army to each of the erstwhile combatants in a civil war is therefore an especially contentious issue, one that can obviously impede an agreement to stop the fighting. Significantly, the higher the irreversibility of potential losses, the greater will be the parties' insistence on compelling evidence that their counterpart(s) will eschew opportunistic behavior in the future. It may be possible for a firm to write off its financial losses and bounce back from this setback in the event of confiscation by a foreign government, or for rebel groups to pick up arms again after a failed truce. It is, however, more difficult to recover from a legal concession – such as for Taipei to acknowledge that its relations with Beijing are a matter of China's internal affairs.

This point explains why the 1992 "one-China consensus" has been so controversial in Taiwan's partisan politics. This idea has provided the foundation for cross-Strait talks, and it basically commits both sides to agree that they belong to one China while allowing them to disagree about who represents this China and even what this China stands for (does it stand for the Chinese nation, the constitution of the Republic of China or that of the People's Republic of China, or the government in power on each side of the Strait?). The Democratic Progressive Party has thus far rejected even the existence of this agreement, not to mention support for it. Its inability to reach an intra-party agreement about how to proceed in the future with respect to this matter (which is the one principle that Beijing has insisted on in entering into negotiations with Taipei) has left it in a weakened position in its competition for votes with the Kuomintang, as this impasse has left it without a policy on how to manage relations with Beijing should it come to power in the next presidential election. The DPP's official position on this issue (which is to reject the existence of a 1992 agreement) has proved to be a non-starter with Taiwan's voters, and the option of declaring Taiwan's independence has also been vigorously opposed by both China and the US (as well as a large portion of Taiwan's electorate). This option appears to have been at least temporarily dropped from the public agendas of those DPP leaders who are contenders to represent this party in the next presidential election, as shown by recent events such as the DPP's Huanshan conference in July 2013.

Concerns about the "one-China consensus" articulated by those DPP members committed strongly to the cause of Taiwan independence are understandable. Once the DPP acknowledges this principle as the KMT has, it has implicitly agreed that cross-Strait relations are within China's domestic jurisdiction – no matter how the term "China" is defined. From these individuals' perspective, Taiwan would thus have given up its claim to be recognized as a *de jure* state (unless, of course, it should secede from the one China that it has already acknowledged belonging to). Once Taipei agrees that cross-Strait relations are within the domain of "one China" it is on a slippery slope, as an overwhelming majority of the international community recognizes Beijing as the sole legal representative of China. Taipei can of course contest this view by arguing, for example, that "China" should mean the "Republic of China." But the latter's constitution was initially adopted by the KMT when it was the ruling government on the mainland, and this document encompasses that territory and Taiwan. This document is repugnant to many advocates of Taiwan independence, and has also been used to legitimize the KMT's authoritarian rule for many years since it retreated to the island. Moreover and returning to a point introduced earlier, once Taipei accepts the position that it is a part of China, it becomes difficult to reverse this position by reasserting its sovereignty claim because international perception would have been shifted even more in the direction of treating the cross-Strait dispute as a matter of China's internal affairs as opposed to its being a matter of interstate relations. Should Taipei decide to pursue independence subsequently, it would be seen even more as a breakaway entity, trying to secede from China – a development that would basically validate Beijing's current presentation. Notwithstanding recent interventions by Western countries in Libya and Syria's civil wars and the breakup of the former Yugoslavia, the international community has historically been more inclined to support the incumbent government and reluctant to back separatist movements (as shown most recently in Western countries' reactions to Crimea's attempt to secede from Ukraine).

Finally, the sovereignty issue is important for Taiwan, whether those in the KMT or DPP ranks, because it relates to its exit option. States that enjoy separate sovereignty can consent to join a federal union, a confederacy, a commonwealth, or some other political format such as the European Union, but they presumably also retain in that event the option of subsequently leaving this arrangement. The southern states in the American Civil War contended that they had reserved this right to secede from the Union, a contention rejected by the latter. Therefore, although the assertion that Taiwan is a sovereign actor does not necessarily preclude it from joining a larger Chinese political entity in the future (e.g., Bush 2005, 2013), this claim is not irrelevant to its possible future departure from this entity. From Beijing's perspective, if Taiwan is recognized as a sovereign actor, it would retain the ultimate authority to decide whether or not to be a part of China. This concession by Beijing would in turn be tantamount to recognizing Taipei's right to secede from China whatever its definition or configuration.

There is another reason for Beijing to be adamant on the sovereignty issue. The Republic of China has been Taiwan's formal title, one that it inherited from the KMT government when it ruled the mainland (the DPP charter has called for the establishment of a Republic of Taiwan). Taipei has demanded that Beijing recognize the sovereignty of the Republic of China, and Beijing's refusal has been a stumbling block to reaching a political accommodation across the Taiwan Strait (Bush 2005, 2013). Taipei's demand is equivalent to asking Beijing to acknowledge that Taiwan is an independent and separate political entity, which would entitle it to international recognition. In that event, there is nothing to prevent the US or any other country from extending diplomatic recognition to Taiwan, thereby creating the reality of Taiwan's *de jure* independence that Beijing has so vehemently opposed. Of course, once Beijing recognizes the sovereignty of a political unit called the Republic of China, it cannot easily withdraw this recognition. This consideration of irreversibility in turn heightens concerns about credible commitment. There is therefore good reason why this knotty issue of Taiwan's sovereignty has caused a political impasse. Beijing opposes concession on this sovereignty issue for reasons similar to those given by staunch supporters of Taiwan independence for objecting to the "one-China consensus" as the basis for negotiating cross-Strait relations.

Just as it would be difficult for Taipei to reclaim its sovereign status once it agrees to the "one-China consensus," Beijing faces a predicament when trying to address Taipei's demand to be given more international space. Taipei wants to have greater involvement in various international organizations such as the World Health Organization and the International Civil Aviation Organization. Beijing has dialed back its traditional opposition to Taiwan's participation in such organizations, and it has even counseled some countries that currently recognize Taipei (rumored to be Nicaragua and Paraguay) *not* to switch their diplomatic ties to Beijing. Therefore, it has relaxed to some extent its efforts to isolate Taipei diplomatically. Yet, it would be rightly concerned about whether a future DPP administration might not try to exploit the opening thus far created to push for further diplomatic representation abroad. That is, once granted, it is difficult to retract some concessions, and these concessions may just be the "camel's nose." Credible commitment refers to not just concerns about the extent to which one's current counterpart can be trusted to deliver on its promises but also whether its future successors can be expected to honor an agreement.

As mentioned already, the more closely territorial disputes are tied to domestic politics and embedded in traumatic memories, the more difficult they are to resolve. Moreover, whether these disputes involve just physical space, as opposed to land associated with highly charged emotions and large numbers of people living on it, matters. China's disputes in the South China Sea appear to be more amenable to resolution because they are not saddled with such difficulties. Various formulae are readily available in principle to delineate maritime boundaries and share the ocean's resources (e.g., Tonnesson 2013; Valencia and Nong 2013). The relatively recent nature of these disputes also means that there are fewer domestic vested interests seeking to block settlements and less historical baggage impeding them. Beijing has in fact previously entered into agreements with Manila and Hanoi to participate in joint geological surveys of the disputed areas. Similarly, in the late 1970s and early 1980s, it proposed and entered into talks with Tokyo to undertake joint development in those areas under dispute in the East China Sea (Lo 1989: 162–183). It is possible that the various states involved in the South China Sea disputes, including China (for Beijing's legal arguments, see deLisle 2012), are deliberately padding their negotiation positions by exaggerating their opening bids (i.e., their initial claims). Silence or acquiescence would, legally speaking, be tantamount to forfeiting one's standing. Therefore, all interested parties have a reason to protest loudly and contest visibly in order to maintain their claim, while knowing that the danger of military escalation is relatively low. These remarks suggest that we are likely to witness frequent incidents but at low levels of intensity. Clashing resource claims in the surrounding seas are divisible, and the absence of inhabitants on the contested islets removes one often insurmountable obstacle to an agreement to settle a dispute (how should those displaced by such a deal be compensated and relocated?). Paradoxically, these attributes of the South China Sea disputes also suggest that the relevant leaders lack an urgency to settle, a motivation that would be more strongly felt by all the involved parties if the current situation were perceived to be fraught with an unacceptable risk of uncontrollable escalation. Therefore, protracted stalemate interrupted periodically by low-intensity clashes appears to be a likely outcome for the foreseeable future.

The Senkaku/Diaoyu dispute is much more complicated, even though it is, strictly speaking, a bilateral contest in comparison to the South China Sea disputes that involve several claimants and even though the islets in question are also uninhabited as in the former disputes. For geographic reason alone, this contest also impinges on Taiwan's interests and given the US–Japan alliance, Washington is also an important indirect party, especially in view of its military presence on Okinawa. The latter defense tie is important because it provides Tokyo a lever with which to affect US policy, raising the prospect of getting Washington involved in an unwanted confrontation with Beijing. Taipei's position is interesting in that it has recently adopted a position that is more closely aligned with Beijing's. It has communicated some subtle and intriguing signals through a vehicle that has caused recurrent and predicable uproar in Sino-Japanese and Korean–Japanese relations, namely, the adoption of history texts for students. Taiwan's education authorities have ruled that these texts should use the terminology of "Japanese occupation" rather than "Japanese rule" in referring to the period when the island was a Japanese colony. While the difference between these two phrases may strike outside observers as slight, they carry strong connotations for Chinese nationalists and also for older generations of Taiwanese, some of whom recall Japan's colonial rule favorably. Attempts by Taiwan's education authorities to revise school texts, however, have recently encountered vigorous opposition from pro-independence students who complain that these revisions are too "China-centric."

The contested Senkaku/Diaoyu Islands have been used by both Tokyo and Beijing to push each other's hot button and as a means to display their displeasure with each other publicly. Unlike the South China Sea disputes, the citizens of both countries are more involved in this dispute. This involvement lends itself to competing elite factions attempting to manipulate nationalism and historical animosity for domestic reasons, and it also points to the potential danger that, thus aroused, public sentiments may make attempts to compromise and settle much more difficult. This dispute, compared to those in the South China Sea, is also more likely to be used by each side's military as an excuse to drive up its budget.

This being so, there could be a perverse interest on the part of hardliners on both sides in keeping this dispute alive rather than having it settled. This interpretation points to the nature of two-level games rather than the inherent divisibility of the payoff or even each side's credible commitment to keeping promises as the driver behind this simmering dispute. Were the dispute to involve only the exploitation of the ocean's minerals and fisheries, it could be rather easily resolved by instituting joint ventures and profit-sharing arrangements. The current deadlock implies that politicians on both sides see more liability in settling this dispute than letting it drag on (but not boil over). Importantly, strong trade and investment ties (not as asymmetric as in the case of cross-Strait economic relations but stronger than those between China and the other South China Sea contestants) tend to contain truly dangerous escalation (e.g., Koo 2009).

As already mentioned, there are ways to work around even the issue of sovereignty, which is supposed to be indivisible. A federal system of government with substantial local autonomy, but one that leaves foreign and military responsibilities to the central government, could be one format. The precedent accorded to the USSR whereby Ukraine and Belarus were each represented in the UN General Assembly could also be applied to Taiwan. Beijing has offered to leave undisturbed this island's political and legal system as well as to permit it to retain its own currency and armed forces. China's bottom line is reasonably clear; it would not tolerate any effort by Taipei to break away formally by declaring *de jure* independence. Absent this move, it is willing to allow ongoing processes to take their natural course – obviously in the belief that closer interactions between the two sides will eventually incline Taiwan's leaders and people to accept reunification.

As will be discussed in Chapter 5, Beijing has engaged in "second face" policies (Lobell 2007) designed to influence important political and economic groups in Taiwan with the aim that they would in turn influence their government to adopt more accommodative policies toward China. These efforts seek to change the domestic distribution of power inside a target country and the perceptions of self-interest by its politically important groups. In contrast, "first face" policies try to affect the target country's government directly. Realists often advocate "first face" policies, such as ramping up one's armament and forming countervailing alliances, in order to contain or balance against a target country's government. As such, these policies typically have the effect of bolstering the influence of inward-oriented nationalists, such as those who advocate import substitution and a hard-line foreign policy, in both one's own country and the target country. Conversely, "second face" policies often engage in selective or "smart" appeasement, focusing on those outward-oriented groups with an internationalist outlook in the target country. By enhancing these groups' domestic standing and promoting their interests, these policies aim to alter the target country's domestic politics, policy institutions, and even eventually their people's identity. Britain in the 1930s pursued such policies toward Germany and Japan, seeking to convert, co-opt, or empower important segments of these countries' societies and economies likely to be sympathetic to London's views of a congenial international order. Proponents of US policies of engaging China have voiced a similar motivation to transform the balance of influences, interests, and even identities in China's society and economy in a direction more aligned with the US conception of a good international order. It is too early to tell whether Beijing's pursuit of similar policies toward Taiwan will eventually succeed in getting its people and government to accept reunification.

Beijing's policies have thus far created important stakeholders in Taiwan in favor of stabilizing cross-Strait relations, and they appear to have arrested the momentum for Taiwan's politicians to promote this island's *de jure* independence and to have steered its businesses in the direction of further economic integration with the mainland. With respect to the topics of this chapter, they have evidently been designed to enhance trust, albeit not in the usual manner in which confidence-building measures (such as to exchange military information or engage in diplomatic dialogues) are discussed. Moreover, instead of dwelling on the division of contested payoff, these policies have focused on pooling and expanding the perceived rewards of cooperation by enhancing a counterpart's linkages to a larger external economic area. Returning to the points introduced at the beginning of this chapter, Beijing's policies have sought to transform what most analysts in the West have considered a zero-sum game across the Taiwan Strait into a positive-sum one. Moreover, although contested identity and disputed sovereignty surely remain highly salient issues, cross-Strait relations have become more nuanced with the introduction of an economic dimension that involves more tangible and quantifiable benefits and costs. This economic dimension helps to redefine this relationship in a positive-sum direction.

Concluding reflections

Trust is a product of a long-standing relationship. It cannot be built in a single interaction or even over a few encounters. Credible commitment requires deliberately bearing costs and running risks that those who do not intend to keep their promises would not be willing to accept. The greater these costs and risks, the more one is able to communicate one's sincerity. When people have, as they say, little or no "skin in the game," they can reverse their course of action without suffering severe repercussions. Conversely, when they have invested heavily in their announced policy, in terms of both the tangible costs of preparation and the intangible engagement of their reputation, they have in effect purposefully imposed on themselves a large penalty that they will have to incur if they do not follow through their words with deeds. When people or states are unwilling to make a costly or risky commitment, this behavior conveys their indecisiveness (which may very well be an honest reflection of their state of mind). Naturally, the obverse can also be true: having said publicly and repeatedly that Vietnam was a test case of US resolve, the protection of this reputation was used to justify expending ever-increasing amounts of US blood, sweat, and dollars on prosecuting this conflict.

One can imagine various formal accords that could provide at least an interim agreement to stabilize a contentious relationship. For instance, Phillip Saunders and Scott Kastner (2009) have sketched a possible peace agreement across the Taiwan Strait, with Beijing pledging not to use violence in return for Taipei promising not to declare independence. The terms of such an exchange, however, could entail considerable ambiguity, as Richard Bush (2013: 106) points out. Instead of issuing a formal declaration of independence, Taipei may revise or abandon its constitution as the Republic of China or apply for membership in international organizations in the name of Taiwan. Beijing may likewise undertake economic boycott or conduct military exercises, actions that fall short of a direct attack on the island. Thus, determining possible violations of such an agreement is not an easy or cut-and-dried matter. More importantly and pertinently, however, who will enforce this accord and administer penalties if it is violated? Only rarely do states submit themselves to the judgments of third parties such as an international organization or a powerful neutral state. A significant feature of those reassurance gestures discussed earlier – such as Taiwan's heavy economic dependency on China – is that they do not require outsiders to enforce an agreement (implicit or explicit). The pertinent arrangements are self-enforcing in the sense that the forfeiture of those benefits from future interactions is the penalty to be paid by the parties should there be a rupture in their relationship (Yarbrough and Yarbrough 1986).

Still another complicating factor pertaining to cross-Strait relations comes to mind. A bilateral agreement between Beijing and Taipei sends signals to other parties. From Beijing's perspective, a renunciation of force in its dealings with what it regards as a subordinate entity communicates a lack of resolve. Barbara Walter (2003, 2006) introduces reputation concerns as the key variable in influencing whether states resist secessionists' demands. Her research argues that when a state is likely to face such demands from multiple quarters, it is less inclined to accommodate rebels seeking self-determination or autonomy. Such a state's hard-line policy is attributed to its investment in its reputation for resolve and firmness in order to discourage other potential independence movements in the future (for China, Tibet and Xinjiang come to mind). The larger the number of such potential movements, the more reluctant a state is to accommodate the current group's demands. Walter's analysis agrees with the proposition that conflicts are interdependent (a view that is subscribed to by most analysts of deterrence theory to be discussed in Chapter 4) but applies it to civil wars rather than interstate clashes.

Territories are divisible. Therefore, territorial disputes do not have to be "winner-takes-all" contests. The problem with indivisible payoffs impeding settlements stems from the fact that territorial disputes are often entangled with more intangible values or issues such as national identity and regime legitimacy. In post-material societies, people become less attached to land and nationalism (Inglehart 1977, 1990, 1997). In terms of their people's income levels and consumption patterns, many East Asian economies have already become comparable to their European counterparts. Moreover, East Asian ruling regimes have increasingly turned to economic performance rather than security rivalry as their chief credential for governing (Solingen 2007). Economic performance has hinged on an internationalist outlook that promotes economic openness and stable external relations, conditions that have buttressed the rapid growth of East Asian economies in recent decades (including China's). The turn to emphasize economic performance based on international interdependence by most East Asian countries has in turn affected the domestic distribution of influences and interests in the relevant countries, and even evolving identities in the case of Taiwan. These changes have generally enhanced the power of the more internationalist groups in domestic ruling coalitions, and diminished that of the nationalist ones that are more attached to policies favoring economic autarchy and territorial sovereignty. These reciprocal influences between external and internal developments tend to generally augur well for dampening China's maritime disputes, keeping them from escalation. The broad, long-term trends also favor the peaceful resolution of these disputes – although in the intermediate term when

countries navigate through the process of democratization or the phenomenon of rising populist pressure, it is quite possible for them to find
themselves caught in political and even military confrontations.

Of China's various maritime disputes, the one involving Taiwan has the
most potential to escalate and also to involve the US. Former US
Ambassador to China Stapleton Roy has stated flatly that it is inconceiva-
ble that the US could become militarily involved in a Sino-Japanese confrontation over the uninhabited rocks in the East China Sea (http://www
.youtube.com/watch?v=kibpu7qHVLY), although more recently US
President Barack Obama has said publicly that the US defense treaty
with Japan will cover contingencies involving this dispute. Beijing has
been careful to avoid direct military confrontation in the South China
Sea disputes, but has undertaken a series of land reclamation projects in
order to expand the surface areas of some islands under its control and to
build infrastructures on them. Importantly, that the Taiwan issue may be
more combustible is not likely to be due to the usual reason presented,
namely, that Taipei may precipitate a crisis by declaring independence.
That this act would cross Beijing's red line is well understood by all sides,
and Taiwan's voters (as will be discussed in more detail in Chapter 5) are
not pushing their leaders in that direction. The most likely time for such a
move was during Chen Shui-bian's administration, and its prospects
appear to have diminished distinctly since that time. Moreover, Taiwan's
economy is becoming more integrated with China's with the passage of
time. Rather, and ironically, the danger of escalation across the Taiwan
Strait is more likely to have its source in China – and not because of this
country's rising military capabilities as typically suggested. Instead, this
escalatory potential is likely to stem from the democratization process as
reflected by the increasing role played by public opinion and elite competition in Chinese politics (e.g., Christensen 2011; Goldstein 2013). The
Taiwan issue is the most potent issue for Chinese nationalists, and is a
natural choice for them to mobilize popular support in domestic partisan
maneuvers. Sagging regime legitimacy, mass discontent, and intense fac-
tionalism within the ruling elite may create a dangerous brew for the
diversionary incentive – to exploit or manufacture a foreign crisis for
domestic partisan gain. Conversely and ironically (from the perspective
of those who see a democratic China to be also a more peaceful China), a
more secure, united communist government is a more self-confident one,
one that is in a stronger political position to resist public opinion and to
make concessions to foreign counterparts in order to reach settlements on
disputed territories or contested sovereignty. This proposition applies as
much to China's relations with Taiwan as to its relations with the other
countries contesting China's maritime claims.

4 Deterrence theories
Bringing in the US

In this chapter, I take up the role of the US, specifically in the context of empirical research on extended deterrence and pivotal deterrence. Washington is generally perceived to be the most important indirect party to China's maritime disputes. It has professed a strong interest in preventing armed hostilities involving China and US allies (even if the protégé state does not have a formal defense treaty with Washington as in the case of Taipei). It also has the undisputed wherewithal to intervene militarily on behalf of its allies if China resorts to force. US policies in these situations are accordingly often seen as deterrence efforts to prevent an outbreak of war.

There is a large literature on deterrence, some of which relies on comparative case studies while others undertake statistical analysis based on a relatively large number of historical episodes (e.g., George and Smoke 1974; Jervis *et al.* 1985; Huth 1988; Huth and Russett 1984, 1988, 1990, 1993; Lebow 1981; Lebow and Stein 1989, 1990). Although some of this literature stresses the cognitive and affective errors in past failures of deterrence attempts, there is also a substantial body of studies that reflects the rationalist or rational choice approach to understanding this phenomenon (e.g., Achen and Snidal 1989; Downs 1989; Fearon 1994a, 1994b; Morrow 1989; Natebuff 1989; Wu 1990). The discussion below reflects the latter approach with the view that states are strategic actors which choose to get into, or not, situations of deterrence episodes on the basis of their anticipation of how others are likely to respond to their behavior. They adjust their behavior on the basis of this anticipation. Naturally, their anticipatory judgment is not infallible, thus accounting for the fact that wars and confrontations happen even though deterrence efforts try to avoid them. By identifying and establishing common baseline expectations, the rationalist (or rational choice) approach helps us to see how states typically conduct themselves and when and where their behavior deviates from the norm. Both the general patterns of behavior and the departures from them provide useful insights about the deterrence phenomenon. I will focus in this chapter especially on US deterrence policy as it applies to the Taiwan Strait, as Washington's military intervention in this case is more likely and it also carries with it more ominous consequences compared to China's other maritime disputes.

The problems with standard deterrence accounts

It is typically argued that a defender of the status quo must communicate persuasively that it has both the capabilities and the will to punish a prospective offender should the latter undertake the undesirable behavior that is the object of deterrence. Richard Ned Lebow (1981: 84–85) spells out especially clearly the necessary conditions for successful deterrence according to this prevailing understanding on the subject: "Nations must (1) define their commitment clearly, (2) communicate its existence to possible adversaries, (3) develop the means to defend it, or to punish adversaries who challenge it, and (4) demonstrate their resolve to carry out the actions this entails." These injunctions are not wrong but they tend to overlook some of the pertinent practical difficulties, countervailing considerations, and hidden premises.

The basic idea of the above-mentioned conception of deterrence is to warn a prospective offender that it would suffer more severe costs than it can expect to gain by undertaking the objectionable behavior. Several problems follow from this perspective. First, the offending behavior is not always easily subject to clear stipulation. To cite an obvious example, the development of nuclear weapons is not a dichotomous matter of "yes" or "no," but is rather a scalar question of "closer to" or "farther away from" crossing several thresholds for achieving an operational and deliverable warhead. To stake out a clear marker against an offending behavior can produce the perverse effect of encouraging the target state to inch as close to the red line as possible without actually crossing it. Conversely, deliberate ambiguity to obfuscate this red line in the hope of preserving the defender's policy flexibility invites doubts in the mind of the target state (i. e., the potential challenger), which is left with uncertainty about what exactly constitutes the offending behavior. Indeed, when put in such circumstances, it would not be unreasonable for the prospective challenger to question whether it is being put on a treadmill whereby the goal posts are subject to being moved constantly. Ambiguity therefore arouses concerns about the sincerity of the country issuing the deterrence threat, and invites probes to test the limits of this country's tolerance – with the attendant danger of miscalculation leading to crisis escalation (e.g., Goldstein 2013). Washington's objection to any "non-peaceful" means to change the status quo across the Taiwan Strait leaves enough ambiguity to give itself substantial policy space to maneuver if it decides not to intervene in a future crisis. Beijing can try to exploit this ambiguity. For instance, instead of launching a large-scale military invasion against Taiwan, it could initiate an economic embargo (something that was anticipated by the Taiwan Relations Act) or even a silent (i.e., unannounced) trade boycott. Washington would face greater difficulties in mobilizing domestic and international support to intervene in such a situation.

The parties to a dispute can always engage in actions that leave some room for different interpretations as to what is the status quo and who is trying to alter it. Each side may take actions that in its view are intended to defend the status quo but are seen by its counterpart in the opposite light (Goldstein 2013). Issues such as US arms sales to Taiwan and the deployment of Chinese missiles across the Taiwan Strait illustrate such divergent interpretations. Moreover, the parties can make subtle gestures that are tantamount to "salami tactics" – actions that are not sufficiently provocative to elicit a strong response in isolation but can cumulatively alter "facts on the ground" over time. For instance, Taipei can make changes to the map (such as showing the island of Taiwan rather than the territorial expanse claimed by the Kuomintang government when it ruled China before 1949) and title (such as putting the word "Taiwan" beneath "Republic of China") featured on its passport cover without formally declaring independence. It can remove portraits of Sun Yat-sen, the founding father of the Republic of China, from official functions and public places to suggest political separation both from China and from its own past practices (these portraits were ubiquitous in Taiwan under the rule of Chiang Kai-shek and Chiang Ching-kuo).

The definition of the status quo and the identification of its defender are often a matter of contesting interpretation and indeed, competing construction (on the question of whether China is a status-quo or revisionist state, see Chan 2004; Johnston 2003; Kastner and Saunders 2012). Was China acting as a defender of the status quo when it intervened against US forces which had crossed the 38th parallel on the Korean Peninsula? Was the US the protector of the status quo when it intervened against North Korean troops crossing this same line of demarcation, but the challenger when it sought to reunify Korea under a pro-US government? It would appear that the Korean War features multiple deterrence episodes with the pertinent parties taking on different roles. Some deterrence episodes are more likely to be overlooked than others, and some cases of compellence (acts intended to *reverse* another country's acts that have *already* been undertaken) may be mistaken for cases of deterrence (which are policies intended to discourage another country's *potential* acts), as Richard Ned Lebow and Janice Stein (1990) have noted. Thus, for instance, was the US-supported invasion of Cuba at the Bay of Pigs a failure of Soviet extended deterrence, and should the subsequent US blockade of the island to force the withdrawal of Soviet missiles (installed there to deter a possible repeat of US invasion) be interpreted as an act of compellence? Sometimes, the distinction between deterrence and compellence is hardly clear as a binary matter, such as with respect to Chinese, American, and Kuomintang efforts to foil Chen Shui-bian's referendum initiative on cross-Strait relations.

That deterrence success depends on demonstrating to the prospective offender that the punishment for its infraction will outweigh whatever benefits it can expect to gain by this infraction is true, but this is an incomplete picture. From the target state's perspective, it is not just about the probable punitive penalty that it could suffer. Rather, this country is also concerned about whether it will endure even greater costs if it fails to act. Thus, from Tokyo's perspective, inaction (i.e., being deterred by a US threat to fight if Japan were to invade the European colonies in Southeast Asia to make up for the shortfall of strategic resources being caused by Washington's trade embargo directed against it) would be even more unacceptable than mounting a risky attack against Pearl Harbor (as inaction would have meant certain economic strangulation without having put up a fight). The problem faced by the target of a deterrence attempt is often not so much whether the punishment for undertaking the offending behavior will be costly (it can be totally convinced about this action's heavy costs). Sometimes, the target state's decision pertains to a comparison of the expected disutilities of its various feasible options. This point about disutilities is important because rather than the typical emphasis placed by rational deterrence theory on potential challengers' pursuit of possible gains, historically such countries have often been motivated to take risks out of concerns for their existing vulnerabilities or impending losses (Lebow and Stein 1990: 210).

Leaders care about many goals, including their country's national security, political autonomy, territorial integrity, and their regime's or their own personal political survival. Fighting the US in Korea shortly after the establishment of the People's Republic was not something that Beijing welcomed, but putting up with a pro-American government right on China's border was even more distasteful. As other examples, Saddam Hussein and Slobodan Milosevic would surely have preferred to avoid rather than accept a fight with the US. But if they were convinced that Washington could not be appeased or that the price for conceding would be their personal or their regime's demise, their behavior does not appear to be so odd. Thus, returning to relations across the Taiwan Strait, whether the US has the necessary capabilities or will to intervene on Taiwan's behalf is only part of the analytic picture. Both Japan in 1941 and China in 1950 did not doubt that the US commanded superior capabilities and would fight back if attacked. As Robert Jervis (1989: 190–191) has remarked, there is nothing irrational about a state – even a weak one – choosing war if it expects its future position to deteriorate. Most existing discussions on deterrence policy fail to acknowledge that a target state may not have a good reason to expect that the future will be a continuation of the status quo if it does not act. (The prospect of Japan being strangled economically by the US strategic embargo comes to mind; Barnhart 1987; Russett 1969.) Similarly, serious domestic political fallout would surely represent a significant factor in Chinese leaders' calculations if they should fail to act against Taiwan's *de jure* independence.

This discussion holds some clear and important policy implications. If a target state is motivated by fear rather than greed, then threats are likely to further exacerbate its insecurity and contribute to the escalation of tension and even invite its attack. For such a state, a policy of reassurance would be more appropriate. Conversely, if the target state is motivated by a greed for aggrandizement, a policy of deterrence based on threats of denial and punishment would be more appropriate. It is therefore important to distinguish the nature of the target, separating the greedy from the fearful type (Davis 2000). This question addresses the fundamental issue of whether a counterpart's actions are motivated by defensive or offensive reasons. For instance, what was the motivation behind China's intervention in the Korean War and, should a future confrontation occur over the Taiwan Strait, what would be the most likely cause for each side's bellicosity?

Another implication follows from the above discussion. Prospect theory contends that states in the domain of loss are more inclined to take risks (Kahneman and Tversky 1979, 2000; Kahneman *et al.* 1982). This argument in turn leads to the proposition that attempts to deter a state that is trying to avoid a loss (e.g., North Korea) will require more resources and effort than those aimed at a target hoping to make a gain (Davis 2000). Ironically, this reasoning also implies that Beijing is more likely to put off forcing a definitive resolution of the impasse in its maritime disputes when it is becoming stronger – because it feels time is working in its favor. Conversely, this reasoning suggests that it will become more impatient and bellicose when it senses its position is weakening and its growth is tapering off. Similarly, Beijing is more likely to undertake military escalation if it perceives itself to be in the domain of impending loss, whether this loss pertains to domestic political setback (e.g., challenges from opposing elite segments, popular backlash) or foreign policy defeat (e.g., decisive electoral victory by pro-independence forces on Taiwan, the island's formal declaration of independence).

Discussions on deterrence typically assume that there is an interdependency connecting events and actors. That is, they assume that a failure to resist a challenge on one occasion will embolden the same challenger in the future (thus the imperative not to engage in appeasement policy) or that this failure will encourage copycats to repeat similar behavior (and hence, worries about falling dominoes). The prevailing tendency is to emphasize the reputation of the country issuing the deterrence threat – suggesting that this country has to stand firm and if necessary, to fight in order to protect its general reputation. In this formulation, a country's commitment to an ally becomes a national interest in and of itself – rather than the reverse of this proposition, which asks whether a country's national interest should justify making a particular foreign commitment in the first place (Kaufman 1956). These remarks about a country's reputation for keeping its commitments are pertinent to recent debates about US support to defend Taiwan and the broader regional security implications should Washington abandon this long-time ally (e.g., Gilley 2010; Glaser 2011; Rigger 2011; Tucker and Glaser 2011).

I will return later to this topic but would for now note that this consideration for reputation should apply to the target state as much as to the state undertaking the deterrence effort. Having backed down previously in the face of a defender's threat, a target state may harbor increasing resentment and grievance and it may be more resolved not to suffer similar embarrassments in the future. For example, having yielded previously to Germany's pressure, Russian leaders were determined not to be humiliated again in the July 1914 crisis. Thus, that a defender has prevailed militarily or diplomatically in prior deterrence encounters does not necessarily mean that it will be able to repeat this success in the future (Huth and Russett 1988). Its reputation for firmness is built on its counterpart's weakness and setback in prior confrontations, a record that should incline this counterpart to care even more about its (deteriorating) reputation.

Those cases mentioned earlier, as well as others such as the Vietnam War, also suggest that a military imbalance in favor of the country making the deterrence threat is not the crux of the key analytic problem in studying deterrence successes or failures. Existing discourse on the Taiwan Strait and the East and South China Sea disputes tends to focus much attention on the contestants' relative military balance, especially the capabilities of US armed forces. The Japanese in World War II, and the Chinese and Vietnamese Communists in the Korean and Vietnam Wars, could have hardly doubted their severe military disadvantage relative to the Americans. This fact constitutes mundane information and public knowledge available to even non-officials like journalists, scholars, and other common folks. As such it should not in itself be the decisive factor in explaining why deterrence threats by the strong often fail to have the desired effect on the weak – since this factor would certainly have been considered and discounted by the weaker side when it decided to take on its stronger opponent. The weaker belligerent does not necessarily have to believe that it can prevail militarily over the strong. It just has to perform better on the battlefield than expected by its adversary (as most dramatically shown in Somalia in the episode popularly remembered as "Black Hawk down"). In deciding to fight, the private information available to it – such as its beliefs about its own leadership quality, troop morale, geographic advantage, strategic ingenuity, popular support for its cause, and its greater national resolve – must have convinced it that it can gain more favorable settlement terms than its stronger opponent is willing to concede to it without a fight. Fighting then becomes a form of bargaining intended to influence the terms of an eventual settlement.

Although Washington clearly enjoys an asymmetry in military capabilities in its favor, it suffers from a disadvantage in asymmetric stake with respect to the Taiwan Strait. Whatever it says or does, it will have a hard time convincing Beijing – and Taipei – that it cares more about Taiwan than Beijing. It is not unreasonable for both Beijing and Taipei to believe that Taiwan is important to Washington more for its derivative than its intrinsic value. That is, Washington may care about Taiwan because Beijing cares about Taiwan and Washington cares about what Beijing cares about. Even proponents of US support for Taiwan often formulate their arguments in terms of the negative ramifications that abandoning Taiwan could have for Washington's regional security arrangements (or the damage that this abandonment could do to Washington's other important objectives such as discouraging nuclear proliferation). This is another way of acknowledging implicitly that Taiwan's importance to Washington tends to be secondary to its higher priorities. Moreover, the policy context is such that the US always has the option of "going home" but Taiwan and China will continue to be "stuck" with each other as close neighbors. This asymmetry in intrinsic stake and thus inherent credibility describes the fundamental structure of the situation facing the three parties.

Outside analysts obviously cannot be certain about the felt stake and private resolve of the parties involved in a deterrence relationship. Indeed, even the parties themselves have great difficulties in making these determinations (or else they would not be subject to miscalculation). Physical distance, however, provides a possible basis for inferring the relative stake a defender has in deterring an attack against its protégé, and hence its willingness to fight on the latter's behalf (Danilovic 2001b). The closer this protégé is located to the defender, the greater is this defender's willingness. Conversely, the closer this protégé is located to the challenger, the greater is the challenger's stake. This inferred stake, in turn, provides a strong hint about the respective parties' resolve to have their way. Leopoldo Galtieri, the head of the Argentine junta, reportedly remarked, "Why should a country [Britain] situated in the heart of Europe care so much for some islands [the Falklands/Malvinas] located far away in the Atlantic Ocean; in addition, islands which do not serve any national interest? It seems senseless to me." (quoted in Lebow 1985: 118). Although Galtieri was incorrect in this case, it is not unreasonable to expect as a matter of general proposition that physical distance indexes the relative importance of felt stake by the contestants.

In general, in asymmetric contests where one side enjoys a large advantage over the other, the weaker side's perceived resolve can be a decisive factor; "the driving force behind the outcome [of a conflict] is the contest of will rather than of brute numerical strength" (Slantchev 2010: 379). Indeed, in contests involving asymmetric capabilities, the weaker side can only prevail by demonstrating that it is more resolved – being willing to fight harder and make more sacrifices for its cause than its opposite number or, in Thomas Schelling's (1966) well-known formulation, being willing to take more competitive risk. As scholars such as Avery Goldstein (2013) and Thomas Christensen (2001) have argued, China can challenge the US even when it suffers from a severe disadvantage in relative capability.

This hypothesis suggests that *ceteris paribus*, extended deterrence should encounter increasing resistance as a defender seeks to protect allies that are farther away from its home turf, and this policy's rate of success should decline as this distance increases. For example, in the Cuban Missile Crisis, the US evidently had a stronger stake and greater resolve than the USSR – not to mention that it also enjoyed a large advantage in both conventional and strategic forces. Parenthetically, physical distance as a proxy for a country's stake or resolve in a dispute is also reflected in situations of direct deterrence between two great powers; these countries are more likely to escalate a conflict which is located close to their homeland – either in the role of a defender or that of a challenger (Huth et al. 1992).

These general remarks about the influence of geography buttress Thomas Schelling's important insight (1966: 33): there is a fundamental difference between a state's deterrence threat to fight back if its homeland is attacked on the one hand, and its threat to defend an ally on the other hand. The former threat is inherently believable, whereas the latter threat has to be made believable to others by credible action. When threatening to defend its homeland, a country is engaging in direct deterrence, whereas when declaring its intention to intervene on behalf of an ally, it is undertaking indirect or extended deterrence (Morgan 1977). This distinction is crucially important when discussing US protection of Taiwan. Washington has to make credible that which is inherently not believable, persuasive, or rational (Danilovic 2001b) – that is, to fight for an ally seemingly in disproportion to its intrinsic stake in a dispute and against another large and nuclear-armed country – and indeed for a protégé about whose status it has chosen not to contest Beijing's claims in various formal communiqués with China. In contrast to homeland defense, a reputation for resolve and firmness has to be invented in attempting extended deterrence.

To a much lesser extent, the general points made above about the "tyranny of distance" and "intrinsic stake" also pertain to the US role in China's other maritime disputes in the East and South China Seas. China currently faces a situation whereby the US is a formal or informal ally of various countries involved in disputes with it, countries that are located next to China or that are relatively close to it (such as Vietnam, Japan, and the Philippines). The Pentagon's declared intention to "pivot to Asia" has been widely understood as a redeployment of US military assets to contain China. However, this new containment policy is different from the one previously implemented against the USSR in one key respect.

During the Cold War, Washington basically conceded Eastern Europe as a Soviet sphere of influence. As Evan Resnick (2013) observes, the US containment policy against the USSR succeeded in large part because it sought to deter Moscow from attacking those countries (the Western European members of the North Atlantic Treaty Organization) that Moscow was only weakly motivated to attack (it was far more interested in maintaining its dominance in the USSR's near abroad in Eastern Europe) and that Washington was strongly motivated to defend. The current situation in East Asia departs from and, in some cases, even reverses this description – such that Beijing is strongly motivated with respect to Taiwan and in its East and South China Sea disputes to assert its interests whereas Washington's resolve, as already noted, is more questionable (many Asians still remember what happened to South Vietnam). Moreover, whereas the US implicitly recognized a Soviet sphere of influence in Eastern Europe during the Cold War, this accommodative stance seems to be missing in East Asia today (even in the case of China's lone formal ally and next-door neighbor, North Korea). This asymmetry in stake and motivation as reflected by geography has heretofore been offset by a large asymmetry in national capabilities as suggested by the huge US military advantage. This advantage, however, is being decreased by ongoing power shifts between China and the US and, as already mentioned, a defender's military superiority is not necessarily the most important factor in determining the success of its extended deterrence.

My earlier remarks suggesting that a weaker challenger may be undeterred by the threat from a stronger defender are often related to the former's disposition to wage a war of attrition to wear down its stronger opponent. In making this calculation, the challenger's perception of its opponent's time horizon and its own time horizon are obviously critical factors (e.g., Kirshner 2000). The greater the defender's tendency to discount the future relative to the present, the more likely this strategy of undertaking a protracted struggle is to prevail. Moreover, this defender's overall military advantage matters less in determining its deterrence success than the resources that it can summon to bear on the immediate vicinity of a conflict. The pertinent literature shows that the balance of aggregate and potential military capabilities between a challenger and a defender (i.e., capabilities that can be mobilized in the long term by each country's economic, industrial, and demographic assets) is less important for the latter country's success in attempting deterrence than the military assets that it has available locally to use immediately in a fight (e.g., Huth 1988b; Huth and Russett 1984, 1988). That London and Paris did not have troops deployed to stop a Nazi invasion of Poland made their deterrence threats appear as "empty talk" to Adolf Hitler. Had they undertaken this deployment (as a form of "sunk investment" to be discussed later), their deterrence threats would have been more credible.

The logic of selection to be discussed further below also argues that when a defender has sufficient local assets to prevent a quick, decisive victory by a potential challenger, it is less likely to be challenged in the first place (i.e., extended deterrence is more likely to succeed in the first place). Understandably, a potential challenger is also more likely to be deterred if the defender and its protégé are joined by a formal alliance and, as already mentioned, if the two countries are located within close physical proximity to each other (e.g., Danilovic 2001a; Huth 1988b; Huth and Russett 1988). These conditions are weak or absent when considering extended deterrence by the US with respect to the Taiwan Strait.

The credibility of US commitment

As already mentioned, in a situation of direct deterrence, a defender declares its serious intention to fight back if its homeland is attacked. In contrast, in a situation of extended deterrence, it announces publicly its intention to intervene militarily on behalf of a protégé if the latter is attacked by a third country (the challenger). The relationship between the defender and the protégé can vary in strength, and the distinction between what is "homeland" and what is "abroad" is also not always clear. The Falklands/Malvinas are tied to Britain by historical, cultural, and ethnic ties, but they are separated by a large physical distance. Portugal can claim Goa to be part of its legal jurisdiction, but the emotional and physical distance separating them makes Lisbon's announced intention to resist Indian annexation of this territory unpersuasive. As a third example, the US threat in 1940 to fight Japan if the latter were to invade the European colonies in Southeast Asia indicates that the strength of ties between the defender and the protégé(s) can be even more indirect (as this deterrence effort was aimed not at the homelands of the European countries but rather at their overseas territories).

The general implication following from the point about the strength of ties binding a defender and its protégé should, however, be relatively clear. The more distant or attenuated are these ties, the greater the need for the defender to make credible its commitment to come to the protégé's aid. As already noted, this credibility involves demonstrating that it has both the capability to thwart a challenge mounted by a third party and the will to use this capability in a military showdown. As conventionally understood, these two items – capability and will – are individually necessary and jointly sufficient in order for extended deterrence to succeed. These items are conceptually distinct even though in practice they are intertwined. For example, prior to Argentina's invasion of the Falklands/Malvinas, Britain decided to recall its one remaining naval vessel stationed in the South Atlantic, the icebreaker *Endurance*. When actually carried out, this decision would have further diminished Britain's military capability to resist an Argentine assault (this assault occurred before *Endurance* was scheduled to be withdrawn). But the news of this decision was in itself important because it signaled a weak will to defend the islands. Similarly and as already mentioned, Adolf Hitler dismissed London and Paris's declaration that they would come to Poland's aid if it should come under attack. Because neither Britain nor France had troops in a position to actually block a German advance, their deterrence threats appeared hollow.

Bargaining theory addresses how states try to communicate to each other their capabilities and intentions (or resolve or will). Because states have been known to bluff or deliberately misrepresent their capabilities and intentions, they have to demonstrate to their counterparts that they are sincere and should be taken seriously. Of course, the insincere states will try to disguise themselves as sincere. Their actions will accordingly try to mimic those of the sincere ones. James Fearon (1995) shows the consequent need for states to demonstrate their sincerity (or truthfulness or reliability), so that their declarations will not be dismissed as "hot air." In order to distinguish (or "separate") itself, the sincere type will have to take on costly actions and run policy risks that the insincere type would be unwilling to accept (Kydd 2005). *Ceteris paribus*, the heavier the costs and the greater the risks entailed by a state's behavior, the more credible are its declared intentions. As the saying goes, this country not only talks the talk, but also walks the walk – or puts its money and troops where its mouth is.

When is bluffing (pretending that one will fight when one really does not intend to do so) more likely? The really weak states are generally not disposed to do so when confronting others that are much stronger – for the simple reason that their bluff is likely to be called and when it is they can expect to pay a heavy price for this misrepresentation. Presumably, the really strong states can better afford to bluff because they understand that the other (weaker) states are reluctant to challenge them – and hence, they can more reasonably expect to get away with their bluff. The weaker states' reluctance stems from their awareness that they will have to pay a heavy price if they should make a wrong judgment, mistaking their counterpart's serious threat as a bluff (such as if Saddam Hussein had thought Washington was bluffing). Knowing this tendency, strong states are more tempted to bluff – and their bluffs are less likely to be exposed. One would also surmise that even if occasionally exposed as a bluffer, a really strong state is in a better position to withstand the consequent damage to its general reputation by this dishonesty. Given its overwhelming power, it will still have to be reckoned with by others.

The tendency to bluff should also be related to the stakes involved in a contested issue. Because China has a greater stake in the resolution of its dispute with Taiwan, one would expect that its leaders' reputation – whether in domestic politics or foreign relations – is more engaged in this situation than the US leaders'. When little is at stake, the incentive to bluff is weak. When very high stakes are involved, there should also be little need to pretend. In the latter situation, a state's interest – such as in defending its homeland – should be evident to all concerned, and bluffing is unnecessary. The probability for a state to bluff should be the highest for those issues involving an intermediate level of stakes (Sartori 2002). Such issues are most likely to present the more ambiguous situations where greater efforts are required to communicate one's resolve and credibility – and where such efforts are more likely to actually make a difference to the outcomes of contests. For the US, the situation involving Taiwan's status belongs to this middle range of stakes. The power balance between the US and China has also become less asymmetric than before. As a consequence, this discussion on signaling also gains greater relevance and importance for this other reason.

How can officials make their deterrence threats credible? That is, how do they persuade their counterparts that they are not bluffing? Fearon (1997) presents two general approaches: tying hands and sinking costs. Officials tie their hands by deliberately committing their personal and their government's reputation to an announced policy. In democratic countries, public and repeated assurances conveyed to domestic and foreign audiences that a government will follow a particular course of action (such as to support an ally in distress) gain credibility for this announced policy to the extent that the officials and politicians in charge would suffer serious political repercussions if they were to renege on these promises. For example, they can be criticized by the media and challenged by their political opponents if they fail to honor their pledges (Schultz 2001). By deliberately exposing themselves to the risk of being censured by their domestic constituents and political opponents if they fail to follow through their announced policy, these democratic leaders make their policy more credible to foreigners.

As a corollary to this proposition, when the political opposition in a democracy does *not* criticize the incumbent government's announced policy or when it offers vocal support for this policy, its behavior presents a strong indication that the country is united and resolved – and that the policy in question is not a bluff (Schultz 2001). From this perspective, a democratic government's domestic critics are perhaps the ones most informed about and most strongly motivated to expose its possible insincerity and in doing so, to make partisan gains. Foreign observers can accordingly learn much by listening to a democracy's political discourse. The transparency of a democracy's political processes provides a better opportunity for such observation compared to its authoritarian counterparts whose decision processes are shrouded in secrecy.

One may be able to make some further inferences from this discussion. Knowing that a national policy debate can be used to demonstrate its country's unity and resolve – an inherent advantage enjoyed by the nature of its political system – a democratic government's reluctance to invite such a debate can also be informative. Foreign observers may infer that this reluctance is due to the incumbent officials' awareness that the policy in question could be controversial, and that they are consequently hesitant about publicizing political divisions and disclosing them to pertinent foreign audiences. A similar interpretation can be applied when democratic leaders choose to be deliberately silent or ambiguous – that is, when they knowingly forfeit what amounts to a powerful advantage in being able to demonstrate their credibility by publicly, clearly, and consistently linking their own and their administration's reputation to an announced policy, thereby exposing themselves to political damages should they renege on their pledges. These remarks suggest that a democracy's political transparency and its leaders' ability to resort to "tying hands" as a means of credible commitment can present a double-edged sword. This double-edged quality also pertains to another aspect of interstate bargaining. A democracy's transparency makes it more difficult for it conceal its intention for the sake of fostering a sense of false optimism on the part of its counterpart – that is, to abet the latter's complacency and overconfidence and therefore to set it up for a strategic surprise in a forthcoming showdown (Slantchev 2010).

The extent to which democratic leaders have deliberately promoted audience costs to enhance foreign perceptions of their resolve has been questioned by Snyder and Borghard (2011) and Trachtenberg (2012). Moreover, although domestic audience costs have typically been associated with political processes in democracies, recent research shows that authoritarian leaders can also be subject to these costs, such as when they are challenged by their domestic rivals and constrained by their country's political institutions (e.g., Weeks 2008, 2012). By deliberately arousing public attention and encouraging mass participation such as through popular protests, authoritarian leaders can communicate their firm commitment to a particular policy position (Weiss 2012, 2014). Such actions intentionally expose the authoritarian leaders in question to the danger of a popular backlash (which can result if they are seen to have compromised national honor or interest), thereby providing a means for them to convey their resolve to their foreign counterparts. Authoritarian leaders have been known to lose the confidence and support of their powerful colleagues, or face an even worse political fate in the wake of their foreign policy setbacks (e.g., Nikita Khrushchev, Slobodan Milosevic). Naturally, to the extent that there are costs for failing to deliver on one's public pledges, their effects need not be limited to the domestic arena. States that acquire a reputation for having been dishonest or unreliable in the past may have to pay a price in international audience costs as well – other states may become more skeptical about their policy pronouncements in the future. In short, by their public rhetoric and engagement of important audiences, both democratic and authoritarian leaders can make their deterrence commitments more credible. They can do so by making a policy reversal or retraction more politically costly to themselves, although recent research indicates that democratic leaders have not resorted to this method very often in the past.

When leaders tie their own hands, they pay a price in their reputation or political standing only if they fail to honor their announced commitment. These are *ex post* costs that occur only when leaders are exposed as insincere or unreliable (i.e., only when their bluffs are called). Alternatively, leaders can try to enhance the credibility of their deterrence commitments by taking on *ex ante* costs (i.e., before a target of deterrence actually mounts a challenge). They can "sink costs" by investing in preparations that a less committed defender would be reluctant to take on. These costs include tangible ones such as stationing troops and establishing forward bases on a protégé's soil, and also more intangible ones such as creating joint command structures that would entail not insignificant costs in decision autonomy and freedom of action. Weapons transfers and other forms of military assistance provide another example. The ratification of a mutual defense treaty lends further credibility to a defender's commitment to its protégé, and this example illustrates elements of both sinking costs and tying hands (as a legal instrument, such a treaty formally commits a country's current and future administrations and reduces their discretion if an ally should come under attack). From Beijing's perspective, it is only natural to ask about the extent of US commitment or resolve, as indicated by the presence of US troops and bases in and defense treaties with Japan and South Korea, but their absence in US – Taiwan relations.

There is relatively little doubt that US armed forces have a commanding military advantage over China, even though Beijing has managed to develop some important capabilities recently that will enable it to complicate the unimpeded freedom of movement that the US has enjoyed heretofore almost right up to China's coastline. In contrast to the relative strength of its military capabilities, the credibility of Washington's commitment poses a more challenging analytic and policy question when discussing extended deterrence by the US in China's sovereignty contests. With respect to China's disputes in the East and South China Seas, the US has formal security treaties with some of the other parties involved, such as Japan and the Philippines. Even with respect to the latter two countries, public US statements on whether it will involve itself in a military confrontation with China over these maritime disputes have been equivocating on some past occasions (e.g., Green 2001: 90–92; de Castro 2013: 170; Samaniego 2012). More recently, however, senior US officials, including the president and secretary of state, have publicly declared that the US – Japan defense treaty will apply to any Sino-Japanese conflict over the Senkaku/Diaoyu Islands. US commitment to the defense of Taiwan has been more ambiguous. Both in its public statements (such as in its joint communiqués with Beijing, which in effect acknowledge Taiwan to be part of China) and in its actions (especially its unilateral abrogation of its defense treaty with Taiwan), Washington has sent mixed signals.

The presence of formal alliance ties presents one clue to the seriousness of a defender's commitment to its protégé. Bruce Bueno de Mesquita (1981a) reports that during 1816–1965, 76% of allied states had received outside support after they were attacked, compared to only 17% of the non-allied states receiving such support in similar situations. According to Paul Huth and Bruce Russett (1988), the probability that a defender will come to a protégé's military aid increases by 40% when they are allies. Other studies based on different data report that alliance ties either contribute to the success of extended deterrence or they at least do not diminish this prospect (e.g., Huth and Russett 1984; Levy 1981; Siverson and Tennefoss 1984; Smith 1998; Tillema and Van Wingen 1982). Although much recent literature has mentioned the Taiwan Relations Act enacted by the US Congress as evidence of Washington's support for this island, the replacement of a formal defense treaty by this unilateral legislation cannot be interpreted to indicate a strengthening of Washington's commitment to Taiwan's defense. In view of those studies just cited, this change can only be seen as a weakening of its commitment.

Quantitative research has investigated other factors that have influenced the outcomes of deterrence efforts. Much of this evidence speaks to those "sunk costs" that can make a deterrence threat more credible. Huth and Russett (1984) find that arms sales by a defender to its protégé and the size of their bilateral trade tend to improve the odds of success in attempting extended deterrence. But Huth (1988a: 93) reports subsequently that arms sales to a protégé have not had this positive effect. At the same time, one would expect that a heavy volume of trade between a protégé and a challenger (as in the case of Taiwan and China, whose bilateral trade has exceeded that between Taiwan and the US) has the effect of undermining the defender's deterrence threat. As mentioned earlier, geographic location seems to matter a great deal (although this factor obviously cannot be considered a "sunk cost"). The probability of deterrence success decreases if a challenger (i.e., the prospective attacker) is located near the protégé, whereas the defender is farther away.

Finally, whether the defender has deployed sufficient military forces in the immediate vicinity of a possible military assault by the challenger makes a difference (e.g., Huth and Russett 1988). The local and short-term balance of military forces affects the defender's ability to thwart a quick, decisive victory by the challenger and to render immediate assistance to the protégé. Deterrence failures often happen when the defender is not in a position to act quickly. Conversely, when the defender and protégé command a local military advantage, deterrence efforts have succeeded in 88% of the sampled cases (Huth 1988a: 75–76). These tendencies are understandable since a challenger is likely to judge a defender's resolve by studying its allocation of the necessary resources ("sinking costs") to assist a protégé in an emergency, such as the (misleading) clue conveyed to Buenos Aires by London's decision to withdraw *Endurance* from the South Atlantic (as well as other signals indicating to the Argentines that London's commitment to defend the Falklands/ Malvinas was sagging; e.g., Kinney 1989: 60; Lebow 1985). The marginal effect of changing the immediate balance of military forces (i.e., in the immediate area of a challenge), however, appears to be relatively low. When this balance changes from a 1:4 disadvantage for the defender's side to a situation of parity, the probability of deterrence success only increases 16%. It goes up by 27% when this balance changes to a 3:1 advantage for the defender's side. This relatively small effect, albeit in the expected direction, is likely due to a selection effect.

As I will discuss in more detail below, a prospective challenger like China must have already been fully aware of the various factors mentioned in the preceding two paragraphs. The geographic location of the parties, the amount of their respective trade and arms transactions, the presence or absence of formal alliance ties, and the relative balance of military forces are public and indeed common knowledge. As such, this information must have already been taken into account by the challenger in its process of deciding whether to initiate a confrontation. Having already considered them, the influence of these variables on the challenger's subsequent behavior should be greatly attenuated (Fearon 1994a, 1994b; Lemke and Reed 2001). Indeed, Huth (1988a: 82–83) shows that alliance ties have only a weak impact on the outcomes of immediate extended deterrence, and foreign trade and arms transfer do not influence these outcomes significantly. These outcomes should only be affected by information that becomes available subsequent to a challenger's initiation of a confrontation (such as information conveyed by additional diplomatic communications after the onset of this confrontation, as argued by Sartori 2005). The information that was known before the challenger's decision to initiate a confrontation (and that which has already been factored into this decision) should not affect these outcomes. This discussion calls attention to the important distinction between factors that motivate decisions on whether to initiate a confrontation and factors that affect decisions to further escalate a confrontation after it has already started.

Parenthetically, just like the other variables, the nature of a country's political system is well known to all concerned parties. Leaders in

Beijing, Taipei, and Washington are surely aware whether their counterparts have a democracy or authoritarian regime (even academic researchers know *this*!). If so, they must have already taken this knowledge into account when they decide whether to select themselves into a deterrence encounter. That is, they must have already considered this fact in deciding about the *onset* of militarized disputes. The democratic peace theory concerns whether a state's political system is systematically related to this decision (i.e., whether democracies are less likely to *start* a conflict, or whether they are more likely to pursue negotiations to settle their differences). The logic described in the preceding paragraph would argue, however, that once they are *already* in a conflict, the nature of political systems should not make a difference to subsequent decisions to escalate militarily. That is to say that democracies and non-democracies may differ in their disposition to initiate militarized interstate disputes, but it is quite a separate matter whether they will respond differently once they find themselves already in these conflicts. One would not expect them to react differently in the latter situation. A democracy is no more likely than an autocracy to refrain from fighting back after it has come under attack or to back down when challenged or provoked militarily. Democratic leaders are generally no less likely to escalate in such a situation than their authoritarian counterparts (Huth and Allee 2002: 241, 285).

In his classic study on alliance politics, Glenn Snyder (1997) points out that alliances serve various purposes other than the obvious one of aggregating the capabilities of their members to confront a common enemy. In addition to the purpose of power accretion, alliances serve to restrain one's partners and to deny potential partners to one's adversaries. Given the obvious lopsided nature of US alliances with its partners in Asia, especially at the time when these treaties were initially formed, these are clearly not reciprocal arrangements (whereas the US is expected to protect its allies, the latter are not expected to return the favor). Compared to Europe, the role played by these alliances (even including the one with Japan) in providing power accretion appears less important than their role in restraining these allies (such as "leashing" Chiang Kai-shek and Syngman Rhee so that they would not ensnare the US in a war to retake territories controlled by their respective communist nemesis). These considerations explain in part why there is not a multilateral defense organization like NATO in Asia, where the US has forged an alliance system following a hub-and-spokes pattern. In this system, US allies (e.g., Japan, South Korea, South Vietnam, the Philippines, and Taiwan) do not have bilateral treaties, but are instead each linked to Washington separately (Cha 1999).

There are several plausible reasons for this phenomenon. One of them is that Washington does not have to face collusion among its weaker allies in a multilateral setting. Another possibility is that it makes Washington's attempts to manage each of its allies easier, thereby reducing the danger, from Washington's perspective, of becoming trapped in an unwanted conflict instigated by one of its junior partners. More recently, this concern has been reciprocated by these partners, so that Tokyo and Seoul have increasingly engaged in creative ambiguity in their statements about whether US military bases located on their soil can be used in a Sino-American confrontation over the Taiwan Strait and in Japan's case, in military contingencies on the Korean Peninsula (Chan 2012a). These remarks therefore argue that alliances may have been intended to serve purposes other than or at least in addition to their publicized purpose of deterrence.

This discussion also suggests that formal alliances do not remove all uncertainties about US intentions should any of China's maritime disputes come to blows. Washington's ambivalence is most noticeable in the case of Taiwan. After abolishing its defense treaty with this island, Washington undertook the unilateral step of adopting the Taiwan Relations Act, which is a domestic law. This Act expresses a concern for the wellbeing of the inhabitants *on* Taiwan (as opposed to the people *of* Taiwan) and objects to any non-peaceful way to resolve the current political impasse between the two sides of the Taiwan Strait (Chan 2010). The enactment of this public law occurred in the context of the US breaking its diplomatic ties with Taiwan (thereby enabling Washington to switch its diplomatic recognition to Beijing) and of its withdrawing armed personnel and military installations from the island. These moves were not consistent with efforts intended to "tie hands" or "sink costs" in order to increase the credibility of one's deterrence commitment.

This said, Beijing cannot necessarily conclude that the US will henceforth disengage itself from the Taiwan Strait. Events since 1979 have indicated otherwise, such as when US President Bill Clinton ordered two carrier battle groups to the Taiwan Strait in March 1996 in the midst of heightened tension caused by Beijing's missile tests aimed at affecting the outcome of Taiwan's presidential election. Presumably, Korea and Vietnam also rank quite high in their importance to China's border security in the minds of Chinese officials. These officials are therefore most likely to recall US involvements with these two immediate neighbors of China. In July 1950, the US intervened in the Korean War – even though US Secretary of State Dean Acheson had stated as late as January of that year that Korea was outside the US defense perimeter. Immediately after the outbreak of this conflict, US President Harry Truman ordered the Seventh Fleet to intervene in the Taiwan Strait – with the practical effect of preventing the Communists from invading this last refuge of their civil war adversary. This intervention again occurred after much public indication that the US had decided to abstain from further intervention in the Chinese Civil War after the Kuomintang, whom it had supported, had been decisively defeated on the mainland. In Vietnam's case, the US eventually decided to withdraw from that conflict after having committed its reputation and enormous resources to support its ally in Saigon. These salient episodes happened in recent years and to China and its immediate neighbors. They cannot but remind Beijing that it is difficult to be definitive about Washington's intentions.

This conclusion, in turn, relates back to Thomas Schelling's (1966: 92–105) well-known remark describing deterrence attempts as competitive risk-taking. According to him, it pays sometimes to deliberately leave something to chance and not to appear entirely rational or consistent. The current US policy of strategic ambiguity regarding Taiwan's defense seems only to make sense in this light. It is purposefully vague and evasive, as Washington declines to be pinned down *a priori* about its future intentions in a possible contingency involving Taiwan. This posture is somewhat similar to statements made by Japanese officials about contingencies under which their country would support US military actions in "areas surrounding Japan" (Green 2001; Heginbotham and Samuels 1999), and others made by unnamed US sources about whether the Philippines can count on its defense treaty with the US in its confrontation with China in the South China Sea (Samaniego 2012). A strategy of deliberate ambiguity naturally goes against the grain of "tying hands" or "sinking costs" with the intent of enhancing and demonstrating the credibility of one's deterrence threat. Whereas these two approaches try to communicate an impression of "we will fight you if you cross the red line," an ambiguous posture conveys the message of "we may fight you if we think you have crossed the red line." By providing loopholes for itself, a policy of strategic ambiguity reduces the credibility of a defender's commitment to its protégé. This is the necessary price to be paid for not locking itself into a predetermined decision to defend an ally and in so doing, motivates a prospective challenger to probe and test its resolve (e.g., as Beijing appeared to act in the 1954–55 offshore confrontation with the US, Wang 2002; Zhang 1998: 210–224). At the same time, this policy preserves the defender's discretion, reserving for it the right to decide at a later time how to respond to a situation. A policy of strategic ambiguity lowers the danger of entrapment for the defender whereby its protégé might otherwise exploit its commitment in order to deliberately embroil it in a conflict against its wishes or interests.

The idea of pivotal (or dual) deterrence

On its face, the current US policy pursues pivotal deterrence (Crawford 2003). Sometimes also described as dual deterrence, this policy involves a situation whereby a third party intervenes to maintain peace and stability between two direct disputants. It tries to take on the role on an impartial intermediary even though its intervention is intended to protect and advance its own interests. This approach has been used by the US in disputes between its allies, such as Greece and Turkey over Cyprus and Ecuador and Peru over their contested sovereignty in the Cenepa Valley. When used to characterize the situation across the Taiwan Strait, this US policy is supposed to discourage both Beijing and Taipei from undertaking unilateral actions that disturb the status quo. It warns Beijing against the use of force, and Taipei against declaring de jure independence. This posture of dual deterrence assigns to the US the pivotal role of a third party, which will act against the side that has in its view destabilized the current situation.

As Timothy Crawford (2003) points out, however, it is rarely possible in international relations to determine "who started it." There are bound to be situational ambiguities and competing interpretations that make this judgment more difficult and controversial in comparison to refereeing a sports match. This inherent uncertainty, in turn, provides the US with leeway to decide – when it comes time to make a decision. Moreover, one or the other party (sometimes both) involved in a dispute often has serious doubts about Washington's impartiality in trying to mediate a dispute or prevent a war. The Argentines were bitterly resentful of both covert and overt US support for Britain (including sharing intelligence information with London) while US Secretary of State Alexander Haig was engaged in shuttle diplomacy between Buenos Aires and London, with an exasperated Leopoldo Galtieri finally professing that "Argentina has lost faith in the United States" (quoted in Freedman and Gamba-Stonehouse 1991: 291). Finally, the US executive branch has been known to bypass or finesse legal mandates such as those banning funds assisting the Nicaragua contras or those armed forces (such as Egypt's) that have overthrown their elected government. Therefore, the interpretation and implementation of US laws are not as straightforward as is sometimes implied in the current discourse on the Taiwan Relations Act.

Drawing on lessons from Argentina's experience (a country that was after all a US ally and a US surrogate in supporting the contras in

Nicaragua) as described by Freedman and Gamba-Stonehouse (1991), Beijing would be understandably guarded in its judgment of Washington's impartiality in dealing with cross-Strait relations. The US policy of strategic ambiguity is also burdened with considerable tension and contradictions (Chan 2008). Why should Taipei believe that its intrinsic importance to Washington would be any less due to an act of declaring its *de jure* independence? Why, in other words, would the US want to change its view about Taiwan's value as an ally today when it enjoys *de facto* independence, compared to tomorrow if it were to announce *de jure* independence? Why would a change in just its name entail a complete reversal in Washington's attitudes toward Taipei? From Beijing's perspective, why should it agree to renounce the use of force in return for Washington's help to dissuade Taipei from declaring *de jure* independence if this arrangement means that it will have to accept the latter's *de facto* independence indefinitely, even perhaps in perpetuity? By agreeing, even if tacitly and implicitly, not to use force, won't Beijing give up the most effective means to deter Taipei's *de jure* independence? After all, public opinion polls in Taiwan have rather consistently shown that the people there would prefer independence – were it not for their fear of China resorting to military force in that event. In other words, these survey results suggest that China's deterrence policy, based on the threat of military coercion, has actually worked to preserve the status quo.

In various communiqués and presidential statements, the US has repeated its commitment to a policy of "three nos" – that the US would not support two Chinas or one China, one Taiwan; that it would not support Taiwan's independence; and that it would not support Taiwan's membership in those international organizations that require their members to be states. While declaring that it does not support Taiwan's *de jure* independence, Washington's policy (including its arms sales to Taiwan and its dual deterrence policy described above) protects its *de facto* independence by objecting to any attempt by Beijing to resolve the impasse by armed means. Although Washington characterizes its policy as one of dual deterrence, Beijing perceives the US as the main reason for Taiwan's resistance to China's pressures and overtures, the chief obstacle standing in the way of its reunification agenda. On the one hand, the US states that it is agnostic about the status of Taiwan as a sovereign entity, but on the other hand, it declares that it does not support its (*de jure*) independence but would somehow guarantee Taiwan's safety as a separate political entity (Bush 2005: 302).

Former US National Security Advisor (and subsequently Secretary of State) Henry Kissinger captured the US policy predicament well in a conversation with his assistants. Even if Mao Tse-tung were to guarantee a peaceful solution of the Taiwan issue as part of the deal to establish Sino-American diplomatic ties, "it would be a fraud" (quoted in Tyler 1999: 225). If China were to attack Taiwan, what would the US do? "Go to war?" Kissinger continued, "If Taiwan is recognized by us as part of China, then it may become irresistible for them. Our saying we wanted a peaceful solution has no force. It is Chinese territory. What are we going to do about it? For us to go to war with a recognized country where we have an ambassador over a part of what we would recognize as their country would be preposterous" (quoted in Tyler 1999: 225).

The text of the 1979 Sino-American joint communiqué establishing these countries' diplomatic relations, negotiated subsequent to Kissinger's remarks quoted above, states: "The United States of America recognizes the Government of the People's Republic of China as the sole legal Government of China. Within this context, the people of the United States will maintain cultural, commercial, and other unofficial relations with the people of Taiwan." Moreover, it declares that "The Government of the United States of America acknowledges the Chinese position that there is but one China and Taiwan is part of China" (http://www.taiwandocuments.org/communique02.htm).

Changes are of course occurring in the domestic economies of all three sides (the US, China, and Taiwan), so that with the passage of time their relative bargaining power and their incentive structures will also evolve. An interim deal to freeze the current political situation could buy some time (Lieberthal 2005), letting the maturation of ongoing trends to take their course – most likely to Beijing's benefit. The evolution of domestic politics in China (in the direction of greater pluralism) means that patience and moderation may be in shorter supply in the future. The domestic costs and benefits for Beijing's leaders to make foreign concessions will change with greater elite competition and mass influence (the mass public tends to be more nationalistic than the elite). Because democratization means a larger number of veto groups, Beijing's domestic win set (Putnam 1988; Tsebelis 2002) will shrink. That is, its range of acceptable and feasible negotiation outcomes will become more restricted, making an agreement with Taiwan more difficult to reach. Moreover, incumbent officials are less likely to offer concessions and seek accommodation when they believe nationalism will pay political dividends or when they fear conciliatory policies will expose them to assaults from their domestic opponents (Huth 1996). A deterrence strategy relying on ambiguity works as long as it is not challenged. Several scholars have therefore called for a timely reexamination of the US policy toward Taiwan to avoid the danger of miscalculation implied by the current policy, and their call for change has, in turn, invited responses in favor of maintaining US support for Taiwan (e.g., Betts 2012; Gilley 2010; Glaser 2011; Rigger 2011; Tucker and Glaser 2011).

What about strategic ambiguity?

A policy of strategic ambiguity buys time. But as noted above, time may soon run out. We already know that territorial disputes are the most likely source for producing militarized interstate disputes. What specific characteristics of these disputes are especially likely to cause escalation? Historical evidence from quantitative research points to those territorial disputes that involve ethnic irredentism and national unification, especially when the disputed territory also impinges on the contesting parties' geostrategic interests (Huth 1996: 108). Moreover, and understandably, a challenger is more likely to escalate when its military position has improved. A past history of militarized disputes also predicts the increased probability of subsequent confrontations (Huth 1996: 114, 132–133), thus endowing an adversarial relationship with a serial quality (such that each clash increases the odds of another one). In addition, a challenger is less likely to compromise if national unification is intertwined with the issue of disputed territory, and when its incumbent officials' domestic legitimacy and political support are shaky (Huth 1996: 149, 192). Finally, there appears to be a general cross-national tendency whereby challengers are more willing to compromise when they are involved in multiple disputes concurrently. One would infer conversely that they are less willing to compromise when their counterparts are parties to other conflicts (Huth 1996: 178, 184).

As remarked earlier, important qualifications are necessary, especially with respect to the distinction between the original initiation of a conflict and its subsequent escalation. In conflicts involving just the great powers, those contestants already involved in another militarized dispute are more inclined to escalate the current one. Being already entangled in a militarized dispute should lower the probability that a great power will be disposed to *initiate* another one. However, its involvement in a prior dispute implies that it must be highly resolved if it decides to enter into another one, and this resolve is reflected by its greater disposition to *escalate* this current dispute (Huth *et al.* 1992). These remarks on general tendencies offer some baseline expectations about China's intentions as it has recently become involved in several maritime disputes concurrently, even though most of the other disputants involved are minor powers. Of course, the US is also currently involved in several conflicts, such as with Iran and Russia, in addition to military engagements in Afghanistan, Iraq, and Syria.

Significantly, a policy of strategic ambiguity pertains to several empirical patterns reported by past research. Lebow (1981: 97) concludes from his study of past deterrence episodes that whether a defender is in fact firmly committed or not, a challenger's perception of this commitment's vulnerability motivates its decision to engage in brinksmanship. Strategic ambiguity would contribute to this perception, if the challenger's wishful thinking was frequently the primary cause for deterrence failure, as Lebow argues. Almost every challenger in his sample of cases misjudged the defender's willingness to accept war for the sake of honoring its commitment (Lebow 1981: 271). Paul Huth and Todd Allee (2002: 275–276) report that when democratic leaders demonstrate their resolve early in the history of these contentious relations, their deterrence efforts are more likely to succeed. In light of this statistical evidence, a democratic defender's failure to act in the expected manner is also significant. This defender's policy of strategic ambiguity thus contradicts the implied suggestion for effective policy that one would have drawn from this evidence. The implicit recommendation from this evidence is that a democracy should publicize its deterrence commitment early and often in order to maintain its credibility.

A policy of strategic ambiguity works if the challenger refrains from probing. But when and if faced with a probe, the defender has a choice of standing firm or backing down. Standing firm means to engage its reputation and to clarify its intention in a way that a policy of deliberate ambiguity has heretofore sought to avoid. This choice also runs the risk of further escalation if the challenger persists in pushing. The question then becomes whether a fight is "worth it" – a debate that deliberate ambiguity has tried to postpone. Backing down avoids a confrontation but also exposes the defender's policy of deliberate ambiguity to have really been a bluff. Whether such a called bluff is costly to Washington's general reputation in conducting its foreign relations and whether Taiwan is in and of itself worthy of US support (even at the risk of fighting China) are questions that have been asked by different analysts in one way or another. Current US policy puts off this debate until a crisis happens – "just when either action or restraint would be most urgent and most fraught" (Betts 2012: 286).

Reputation should matter most when the two sides of a relationship are closely matched in their capabilities. When their relative power is more symmetric, a reputation for being "hard to be pushed around" becomes more relevant and important. That is, establishing sincerity and resolve looms as a larger concern among states that see themselves as peers – or when their capabilities are actually becoming more equal. Conversely, a hegemon – a country that is by definition peerless – has less need to invest in its reputation, because its overwhelming capabilities are obvious for all to see. This relationship between capability balance and concern for reputation bears directly on how ongoing Sino-American power shifts are likely to affect Washington's attempts to signal its resolve to defend Taiwan. Both sides are aware of the general tendencies just described: China knows them, the US knows China knows them, China knows the US knows it knows them, and so on and so forth.

Regarding the question of general reputation, Anne Sartori's (2005) recent research contends that states recognized by others as having been generally honest in their diplomacy are less likely to be challenged by others in militarized interstate disputes. This reputation for honesty includes those instances when a state acquiesces when it does not really intend to fight, and of course also instances when it actually fights when it says it will. This reputation is also maintained when its bluffs are not called. Sartori's theory and quantitative analysis suggest that when a defender does not actually intend to fight, its timely concessions actually enhance its general reputation and endow its diplomacy with greater credibility, thus making this diplomacy generally more effective in the future. The thrust of Sartori's argument of course contradicts those who tend to see concessions as appeasement and who claim that accommodation will necessarily undermine future credibility in other diplomatic or military settings. Her conclusion questions the wisdom of states trying to invest in their reputation for firmness for the sake of deterring future challenges (such as the tendency observed by Barbara Walter's studies referred to earlier and again below).

Taking a social psychological perspective, Jonathan Mercer (1996) also contends that concerns for states' reputations are overstated and, therefore, efforts to invest in their reputation for firmness and reliability are unnecessary (see also the exchanges among Copeland 2007; Huth 2007; Mercer 2007). He argues that when a state does something desirable from another state's perspective, this action tends to be explained away according to its circumstance. Thus, when a country comes to its ally's defense, this ally will be inclined to make a situational attribution (i.e., the defender's action is likely to be seen as stemming from its circumstance rather than its disposition). From the perspective of an adversary, the failure of a defender to support its ally would be a desirable development and as such, the defender's inaction will also likely incline this adversary to adopt a situational interpretation. Accordingly, providing help to an ally will not enhance the defender's reputation for reliability in this ally's eyes, nor will a failure to do so hurt its reputation for resolve in a challenger's perception. The interpretive logic being applied here is that if the defender's action is due to situational factors, its response may be different next time when circumstance changes.

The above social psychological formulation would imply that an ally is prone to explain a defender's failure to support it according to this defender's disposition, and an adversary is likely to apply a similar dispositional explanation to the defender's support for its ally. Mercer (2007: 108), however, argues that such dispositional attributions are not the same as acquiring a reputation. They are necessary but not sufficient for establishing a reputation. For a reputation to form, an ally or adversary must also use this dispositional interpretation for a current case to predict the defender's future behavior.

In contrast to Mercer, Barbara Walter (2003, 2006) argues that a concern for its reputation often plays an important role in an incumbent government's resistance to demands for secession or political autonomy. The focus of her studies is on civil wars stemming from demands for self-determination. She finds that when a government faces the prospect of many other minority groups with similar interests, it is less likely to accommodate demands from the current rebel group. She explains this phenomenon by arguing that this government rigidity reflects a desire to establish a reputation for firmness in order to discourage other secessionist challenges in the future. This logic also led Walter to expect that states with many neighbors would be more likely to be concerned about their reputation for firmness, and that "neighboring states are more apt to go to war to settle their territorial disputes because these are the cases in which reputation-building is most important" (Walter 2003: 150).

In his study of China's management of its territorial disputes, Taylor Fravel concludes that Beijing has not been hesitant to compromise with a given counterpart out of an apparent fear that its concessions will be perceived by other countries as a sign of weakness. In his words (Fravel 2008: 310), China "repeatedly pursued compromise without any apparent concern for the effect that its concessions would have on its reputation or for appearing weak to other states. This suggests that, under some conditions, states may seek to create reputations for cooperation instead of toughness." Beijing has of course resorted to force in several border disputes, and this practice could have conceivably contributed to its reputation for taking military action even when facing a strong adversary or one that is seen to challenge the status quo. Fravel's analysis, however, also points to the importance of fostering a reputation for conciliating, such as a willingness to settle border disputes on terms generally more favorable to China's counterparts and to eschew opportunistic behavior when these counterparts are vulnerable to exploitation. This observation is pertinent because states' reputation is usually discussed in terms of how others perceive their resolve – and only rarely in terms of how others perceive their honesty and disposition to conciliate. Moreover and as already mentioned, a country's reputation for resolve and firmness is often built on the basis of its counterpart having backed down in a previous confrontation, that is, on the basis of the latter's lack of resolve – a development that would presumably make this counterpart more concerned about its reputation for resolve and contribute to its determination to stand firm in a subsequent confrontation.

It is pertinent to ask whether a US commitment to defend Taiwan will have ramifications for other states' perceptions of Washington's commitments to them. Would a decision to abandon Taiwan destabilize the other security arrangements that the US has fostered in the region? In other words, is a country's behavior in an individual episode or relationship likely to affect its reputation in general? On this question, there is room for debate. Other researchers have introduced evidence seemingly in contradiction to that presented by Sartori (2005). Paul Huth's (1988a: 81) research indicates that a defender's prior behavior toward other challengers offers a poor basis for inferring how the specific challenger in the *current* episode will react to it. In other words, the current challenger does not seem to use the defender's previous behavior toward other states – as opposed to itself – as a guide in formulating its policy. If true, this tendency would suggest that a country's reputation is not necessarily generalizable to parties involved in other disputes although it can affect future interactions within a specific dyad. Huth's work also speaks to the oft-heard advice for officials to stand firm in the face of foreign challenges. Intransigence on the part of a defender and its protégé in prior episodes appears to have the opposite of the intended effect: a rigid, uncompromising posture tends to encourage the challenger not to back down again and be humiliated in a subsequent encounter (Huth 1988a: 218).

This observation, in turn, raises another question: what would motivate a disputant to start or accept yet another confrontation after its setback in a previous one? Huth's (1988a: 182) quantitative research of past episodes of extended deterrence suggests that "if the potential attacker was forced to accept a diplomatic setback in a previous confrontation with the defender then the probability of deterrence success would decrease because the attacker would be determined to avoid another blow to its bargaining reputation." This topic will be taken up in the next section.

Whether explicitly or implicitly, much of the US discourse has focused on Taiwan's derivative rather than its intrinsic importance to the US – whether in terms of serving as a geostrategic asset (an "unsinkable aircraft carrier") to contain China, as a showcase to demonstrate US general resolve to resist aggression, as a point of bargaining leverage to gain

Chinese cooperation or concessions elsewhere (e.g., Iran, North Korea), or simply as a continuing source of irritation to Beijing (a "thorn in its side") and a key to denying or frustrating its core national agenda. There are, of course, also arguments made in favor of Taiwan's intrinsic values such as its democratic politics and the right of its people to self-determination. These are important and laudable values worthy of US support, even though they may not be consistently applied across cases (for instance, should the people of Crimea be also entitled to self-determination by way of a referendum to secede from Ukraine?).

From Beijing's perspective, however, these latter arguments are not likely to be taken seriously because US support for Taiwan predates the latter's democratization (if anything, this US support was stronger when Taiwan had an authoritarian government and it has waned since then even while Taiwan has become more democratic). When Washington supports or acquiesces to the overthrow of democratically elected leaders (e.g., Iran's Mohammad Mosaddegh, Chile's Salvador Allende, and Egypt's Mohamed Morsi), and when it intervenes militarily in various small states in the Western Hemisphere (e.g., Grenada, Nicaragua, Panama, Cuba, Haiti, the Dominican Republic) that cannot be easily construed to pose a tangible threat to US national security, its past conduct undermines the sincerity of its publicized rationale for supporting Taiwan, and also the credibility of its declared intention.

Moreover, the right to self-determination has evidently been applied only selectively; it has not been accorded a priority in US policies toward those living in Crimea, Palestine, and Kashmir, for example. Of course, when Washington practices dual deterrence that has as one of its announced objectives the prevention of Taiwan's *de jure* independence, its policy directly opposes the expressed preference of a majority of Taiwan's people and subordinates their self-determination to some other higher goal. Beijing obviously also opposes Taiwan's independence but its argument, based on the claim that there is a single political entity called China and that Taiwan is a part of it, treats Taiwan as a province that tries to secede from China (analogous to the Confederate States' attempt to withdraw from the Union). It argues that as such, the people on the mainland should also have a say. (Washington has used a similar argument in its opposition to Crimea's attempt to break away from Ukraine, suggesting that this attempt violates Ukraine's constitution and denies *all* its citizens a voice in deciding Crimea's status.)

It is not clear from much of the current US discourse why Taipei should be any more reassured by Washington's unilateral abrogation of their mutual defense treaty and its replacement by a much weaker document, the Taiwan Relations Act. If Washington truly cared about protecting

Taiwan as its top priority, it would not have canceled this defense treaty or derecognized Taipei in favor of Beijing. Thus, obviously, there are other more important goals than its commitment to a long-time ally. For those who stress the importance of US credibility, it is hard to argue that the aforementioned acts would have enhanced Taipei's or other US allies' confidence in US reliability. Much of the reputation costs to US reliability would have already happened at that previous time, and Kissinger's reflections quoted earlier anticipated the subsequent turn of events. The repercussions suffered by Washington's reputation as a result of its exit from the Vietnam War were largely self-inflicted; Vietnam was important because Washington had said publicly and repeatedly that it was important and that this war was a test of US will. Some critics of the current US policy on Taiwan have wondered, to quote Macbeth, "If it were done when 'tis done, then 'twere well it were done quickly."

Finally, one should recall that US credibility pertains to multiple parties. Its reputation is also at stake since it has publicly and repeatedly committed to Beijing its policy of "three nos" and its pledge to reduce arms sales to Taiwan over time. From Beijing's perspective, whether Washington has met its expectations in past bilateral deals is naturally also consequential. Thus, what has been argued to bolster one's credibility relative to one party (e.g., Taiwan) can be detrimental to another (e.g., China). In the 1972 Shanghai communiqué, "The US side declared: The United States acknowledges that all Chinese on either side of the Taiwan Strait maintain there is but one China and that Taiwan is a part of China. The United States Government does not challenge that position. It reaffirms its interest in a peaceful settlement of the Taiwan question by the Chinese themselves" (http://history.state .gov/historicaldocuments/frus1969-76v17/d203).

Discerning China's resolve

It is useful to remember an important conclusion from a careful study of past episodes of international crises and deterrence encounters. "In the United States we probably devote too much attention, in theory and practice, to the credibility of our commitments and not nearly enough to trying to understand what might actually prompt an adversary to challenge these commitments" (Lebow 1981: 279). The empirical pattern emerging from these past episodes suggests that an adversary's objective weakness does not prevent it from challenging the country issuing the deterrence threat, nor is this defender's professed resolve to carry out its threat necessarily the primary determinant of the challenger's decision. The challenging state is often motivated less by its perception of a strategic opportunity to undertake its objectionable behavior, and more by its sense of a compelling need to do so (Lebow 1981: 276). This felt need often stems from domestic pressures and vulnerabilities. Both Argentina and Britain would have preferred to avoid fighting over the Falklands/Malvinas. But these countries nevertheless ended up in an unwanted war because their leaders were convinced that they would not survive politically had they decided otherwise.

These remarks echo Thomas Schelling's important insight. He points out that in addition to considering its own credibility, it is "[e]qually important [for the defender] ... to help to decouple an adversary's prestige and reputation from a dispute; if we cannot afford to back down we must hope that he can, and if necessary, help him [to do so]" (Schelling 1966: 125). In other words, if it is costly for one to make concessions, it can also be for one's counterpart to do so. Making concessions easier and more palatable for the other side (e.g., not to make it lose face or suffer a loss in reputation) is germane. As the metaphor of two-level games reminds one, the pertinent costs also include severe domestic repercussions for appearing weak in dealing with a foreign adversary. Conversation between the Kennedy brothers at the height of the Cuban Missile Crisis indicated their belief that the president would be impeached if he were to fail to act resolutely (www.gwu.edu/~nsarchiv/nsa/cuba_mis_cri/audio.htm). Similarly, the Argentine junta and foreign minister reportedly feared a "lynching" by their citizens if they were to succumb to a humiliating settlement over the Falklands/Malvinas (Gamba 1987: 155). Serious domestic backlash was also feared on the other side of the Atlantic, with one British cabinet member confiding to a reporter that, "To be frank, I don't see how she [Margaret Thatcher] can survive [politically] if she shrinks from a military showdown" (quoted in Lebow 1985: 117).

It takes a politically secure and confident leader to make concessions in order to reach a foreign deal. This leader is more risk acceptant in this particular sense because he/she has less fear of a rebuke from his/her domestic opponents (Huth and Allee 2002). Because a deal requires at least two sides, the domestic situations for both parties have to align so that mutual accommodation can occur. Domestic political security means a strong incumbent with a high level of support from different elite segments and the public, and a weak and disorganized opposition. This political security is higher when leaders do not need to submit themselves (at least not in the near future) to a referendum (e.g., an election, a parliamentary vote of no confidence, an occasion for leadership succession). Leaders who are politically secure are more likely to be in a position to offer concessions and to also gain domestic ratification of those deals that they have negotiated with their foreign counterpart. This being the case, each side has a vested interest in its counterpart's popularity.

An unorthodox implication follows from this observation. Authoritarian leaders like Mao Tse-tung are in a better position to strike and deliver deals than less authoritarian ones. Democratization by definition introduces institutional constraints that limit leaders' discretionary power and hold them accountable to various veto groups and constituents (including the mass public or the electorate). Contrary to the view that democracy can provide a definitive solution to resolve interstate disputes (and especially to dampen Sino-American tension as some contend; e.g., Friedberg 2011), democratic leaders "can be quite aggressive when they anticipate that confrontational policies will generate political support at home" (Huth and Allee 2002: 153). When applied to China, this observation would imply that Beijing's leaders will not necessarily be more inclined to compromise and less motivated to escalate a confrontation when the Chinese political system evolves in a more democratic direction. On the contrary, a process of democratization tends to have the effect of engaging Chinese leaders' domestic reputation more publicly and subjecting their nationalist credentials more to the scrutiny of their political competitors and the mass public (e.g., Christensen 2011; Goldstein 2013). As highlighted by Lebow and Schelling's remarks introducing this section, such developments are likely to restrict the domestic win set for China's international negotiation space and also to increase the political vulnerability faced by its negotiators for making real or perceived concessions.

I have mentioned earlier the idea of selection, that is, the general proposition that people and states alike make choices about which encounters (or relationships) to enter into, and which ones to refrain from joining. They choose to become involved in those episodes that they expect to turn out profitably for them or at least not to become detrimental to them, and this choice is based on their anticipation of how others are likely to react to their conduct. History reflects such selection in that it only records those occasions when people and states decide to initiate an encounter (if they decide not to become involved, these decisions are not recorded by history because the episodes in question are non-occurrences).

One implication of this observation is that history is biased, for example, in over-reporting the success of insurgent or secessionist movements. Why? Only those rebels with the highest expectations of success or the greatest commitment to their cause would have chosen to confront an incumbent government. Others with weaker capabilities, less resolve, and thus lower expectations of prevailing in their contest would have been self-deterred from starting this challenge. That only those who believed that they had a strong prospect of succeeding would have made this move is analytically consequential. Because of this self-selection, the *a priori* odds of succeeding should be in favor of those rebel challenges that did take place. When most of these attempts fail, their observed frequency should therefore indicate that secessionist or insurgent movements face even poorer prospects than is indicated by their historical failure rate.

As a result of the selection process, analysts can expect certain events to occur more frequently under some conditions than others. Thus, for example, friendly countries should be more willing to quarrel when they expect their more stable and robust relationships to reduce the danger of escalation. Conversely, when states worry about the danger of a conflict spiraling out of control, they should be more reluctant to initiate a dispute in the first place. Reflecting this selection dynamic, we know as an empirical fact that most wars of aggression tend to be bilateral affairs – a tendency that reflects the aggressors' anticipatory calculation that their victims will not receive help from other countries (Gartner and Siverson 1996). This calculation is obviously not infallible (i.e., the aggressors' prognosis can turn out to be wrong) but it exemplifies the selection logic. This logic suggests that aggressors tend to pick vulnerable targets – those unlikely to receive international support – as their victims. These aggressors also avoid potential targets that are likely to receive this support.

What does the selection logic have to do with Beijing's resolve and by implication the odds that another Chinese challenge pertaining to Taiwan will likely turn out to be more successful from its perspective? We know that the Taiwan Strait has experienced several prior crises initiated by China in 1954–55, 1958, and 1995–96. Each of these military confrontations concluded after Beijing decided to deescalate. In other words, these previous episodes ended with China terminating its challenge without achieving its declared objective of nudging Taiwan closer to national reunification. In terms of Thomas Schelling's (1966) frame of competitive risk-taking, Beijing decided on each occasion that it was not willing to accept the increasing risk of war that would be entailed by taking the next step on the escalation ladder. To use a phrase attributed to US Secretary of State Dean Rusk in the Cuban Missile Crisis, Beijing was the one that "blinked."

In each of the previous crises, Beijing failed to accomplish its announced goal of "liberating Taiwan." These episodes were not without costs to Beijing, costs that included the adverse consequences for its leaders' domestic political standing and international reputation – considerations that according to our earlier discussion should have mattered less when

China was more authoritarian previously than now. In view of these known and possibly cumulative costs, one would naturally want to ask: why would Chinese leaders want to initiate another challenge? Having drawn lessons from their prior experience, one would infer that they should be more cautious and more reluctant to start another confrontation unless they have new information stemming from developments since the last episode, information that has had the effect of boosting their confidence and/or their resolve. The logic of selection would suggest that with each successive failed challenge, a challenger should be more discouraged from initiating another one. However, should it decide to launch another confrontation, it must be subjectively more optimistic – and/or feeling more desperate.

These attributions need not be mutually exclusive. A country's leaders may feel more confident if they believe that the military balance has shifted more in their favor (or less to their disadvantage), but they may also sense greater urgency or political insecurity due to domestic pressure. Leaders' relative optimism or pessimism may also relate to developments abroad, such as their perceptions of their foreign counterparts' growth trajectories, political cohesion or discord in these other countries, and changes in these countries' public mood and mass identity (e.g., the evolving level of Taiwanese identity; Rigger 2006). A sense of desperation, mentioned above, could stem from a feeling that, for example, pro-independence forces are gaining strength in Taiwan and that the prospects of this island's reunification with the mainland are slipping. In this hypothetical context, desperation could point to pessimism and even despair that one's situation is deteriorating with each passing day. In the Pearl Harbor example given earlier, Japan's leaders decided to gamble on a surprise attack not because they were confident of their chances of success but rather because they were trying to escape from an increasingly dire dilemma (posed by the perils of both action and inaction; e.g., Barnhart 1987; Russett 1969).

Having failed before, one would at least expect the leaders of the challenging state to be more determined if they should decide to renew their challenge. The logic of selection implies that *ceteris paribus* the odds for a challenger's success should rise with each successive challenge. This is so because the less determined challengers would be discouraged from repeating their behavior after having suffered prior setbacks. Drawing on this inference from selection logic, James Fearon (1994b) presents an important insight in distinguishing between two different kinds of deterrence situations. A situation of *general* extended deterrence involves the defender declaring its intention to protect its protégé when there is no evidence that the challenger is actually preparing to attack the latter. In contrast, a situation of *immediate* extended deterrence involves the defender declaring the same intention after a challenger has made tangible moves to attack this protégé. Fearon argues that the conditions for successful general extended deterrence should predict failures in immediate extended deterrence. The following evidence and logic are germane to this phenomenon.

According to Huth and Russett (1984), immediate extended deterrence succeeded in only 57% of the sampled cases during 1900–80. This seems to be a rather low figure, considering that it is not too different from the even odds of 50% each for a successful outcome and a failure. The reported evidence shows that the presence of an alliance between the defender and its protégé is related *negatively* to such deterrence success. Moreover, the defender's possession of nuclear weapons, its military advantage over the challenger, and its behavior in prior deterrence episodes (e.g., whether it stood firm or conceded) do not contribute to this success (thus belying the injunction that one should avoid appeasement and weakness because these traits damage one's reputation and ability to resist future challenges). After being challenged (i.e., after general extended deterrence has failed), a defender is more likely to fight on behalf of its protégé if the latter is a large state comparable to itself, and if these two countries are tied by a formal alliance. The extent of trade and arms transfers between the two, however, does not necessarily increase the defender's willingness to fight (Huth and Russett 1984: 520–521). One can discern rather readily the relevance of these empirical tendencies to the specific case of US extended deterrence with respect to Taiwan. But what can explain these tendencies?

The defender's military capabilities (including its possession of nuclear weapons and the number of carrier battle groups in its fleet), its formal alliance obligations (if any) to the protégé, its past behavior in honoring its treaty commitments, and other such factors are public information and well known to a potential challenger. They should have an effect in discouraging this challenger from starting a confrontation. That is, variables such as those just mentioned should contribute to successful *general* extended deterrence, discouraging potential challengers from initiating a deterrence episode in the first place. However, if a challenger nevertheless decides to initiate a confrontation even while being quite aware of the aforementioned factors, it must be highly resolved. Indeed, the greater the defender's military superiority and the stronger its political and economic ties to the protégé, the more highly motivated must be the challenger for it to start a confrontation – that is, to bring about a situation of *immediate* extended deterrence. The challenger's higher motivation or greater dedication to its cause – or some other private information only known to it – must be at work to offset the known facts about the defender's stronger military capability and its steady support for the protégé in past crises. This being the case, variables that contribute to success in *general* extended deterrence should predict failure in *immediate* extended deterrence. Fearon's (1994b) analysis has provided empirical support for this inverse relationship.

Huth and Russett (1993) have found a similar pattern, showing that a protégé's alliance ties are positively related to the success of general extended deterrence but negatively to that of immediate extended deterrence. That is, if and when a challenger actually makes preparations to attack a target with allies, it must be more resolved compared to when its victim is not allied. These authors also report several other intriguing statistical tendencies. States experiencing political instability are not more likely to be targeted by challengers. It appears that this phenomenon stems from the potential challengers' expectation that politically vulnerable leaders in the target states will be more disposed to stand firm and retaliate than to concede. That is, in line with the somewhat counterintuitive hypothesis proposed earlier, *ceteris paribus* politically insecure leaders will be more confrontational, whereas those who are politically secure are in a better position to make concessions. Contradicting this pattern, however, is the finding that leadership discord and elite conflict tend to encourage challenges. Moreover, and as suggested earlier, changes in the direction of more balanced power between a defender and a challenger also tend to have this effect.

Finally, public opinion should have a greater influence in the policy processes of democratic countries even though it is not irrelevant in authoritarian ones. Officials will have an easier time if their policies have the backing of supportive public opinion compared to when their policies have to face popular views that are skeptical or even hostile. According to recent polls conducted by the Chicago Council of Global Affairs (2010: 14,17), the American people strongly prefer more policy emphasis on fixing problems at home (91%) compared to addressing challenges abroad (9%). Moreover, 79% of those surveyed agreed with the view that the US is playing the role of world policeman more than it should. More specifically on the issue of supporting Taiwan, only 20% thought that a cross-Strait confrontation would present a critical threat to the US (Chicago Council of Global Affairs 2010: 42, 51, 65), giving this contingency the least importance among the seventeen foreign policy items surveyed. When asked directly about whether the US should use troops to help Taiwan if China invades it, 71% were opposed compared to 25% in favor (Chicago Council of Global Affairs 2010: 52, 65). These popular views obviously present more severe constraints to the policies of those incumbent leaders who are facing political difficulties (such as when they face a divided government, low popular support, or more intense electoral contests) than others whose political position is strong. This information on the American people's views is available to foreign leaders, including those in Beijing and Taipei, who will naturally take it into account when they formulate their respective policies (even though they are also aware that public opinions can change).

Successes in general extended deterrence are by definition non-events – a prospective challenger chose not to start a confrontation. We can never be absolutely sure whether the supposed challenger actually had the intention to attack a protégé and was only prevented from carrying out this attack by the defender's deterrence threat. Did the USSR ever seriously consider invading Western Europe and was it only stopped by the US deterrence effort? We do not know, and there is always the risk of false attribution (giving credit to deterrence policy when it does not deserve it). This analytic risk is less serious in situations of immediate extended deterrence because the challenger has actually made moves to upset the status quo, as in the case of prior crises involving the Taiwan Strait. Of course, we do not know for certain the extent to which Beijing's behavior in these prior episodes of military confrontation might have also been motivated by a desire to probe US intentions or even by its own efforts to seek immediate deterrence against Taiwan's creeping *de jure* independence in the events leading up to heightened tension during 1995–96.

Whether Beijing will initiate another military episode is difficult to predict. The preceding discussion argues that if it does, it must have some reason to believe that its odds of succeeding have improved since last time – or that its stake has increased even if its odds of succeeding have not. This remark points to a simple but important consideration: a country's behavior is influenced by its expected utility or disutility – which is a joint product of two variables, probability and payoff. The probability of a particular event coming to pass is pertinent to its decision process, but its subjective sense of the size of prospective benefits and costs resulting from this event is also relevant. Traditional deterrence theory has focused on minimizing the probability that a challenge to the status quo will succeed (primarily by focusing on a defender's capabilities and its resolve to thwart a challenge), but it has given less attention to a challenger's assessment of the importance of its interests at stake (whether these interests pertain to its prospective gains or losses). A challenger, such as Japan with respect to its decision to attack Pearl Harbor, may be motivated to act when it believes that its interests at stake are great and the opportunity costs of inaction are also huge – even though the odds that the contemplated action will produce a successful outcome are judged to be low.

A final proposition seems reasonable and important even though it is not usually emphasized enough. With respect to breaking the impasse in cross-Strait relations, military force is a last resort rather than a first choice for Beijing. War will be costly ("inefficient" in the parlance of bargaining theory), and not just in economic terms. If it happens, it must mean that Beijing believes that it has exhausted the other available options to settle its dispute with Taipei. Having already waited for about sixty-five years, a resort to force by Beijing must mean that in its eyes, the costs of continuing the impasse have increased significantly. Moreover, and in line with my earlier remark that the role of a defender can be taken up by more than just one state, a Sino-American confrontation would mean that Beijing has failed to deter Washington from becoming involved in its dispute with Taipei. Contrary to the usual depiction of a latecomer challenging an existing dominant power (as presented by the power-transition theory; e.g., Organski and Kugler 1980), this interpretation suggests that should such a confrontation come about, it would not be because China wanted to fight the US, but rather because it had failed to persuade the US to stay out of a fight. From Beijing's perspective, it would of course greatly prefer to keep its dispute with Taipei as a strictly bilateral affair whereas from Taipei's perspective, internationalization – primarily by engaging the US – would obviously provide the means for it to escape from being pinned to a lopsided, one-on-one bargaining situation with Beijing.

Concluding reflections

The Falklands/Malvinas War happened even though neither Britain nor Argentina had wanted to fight it. London was quite content to have the Kelpers courted by Argentina for some form of eventual integration with the latter country. Buenos Aires was also anxious to gain the islanders' goodwill, relying on economic carrots to entice them to join Argentina. It engaged in negotiations with London over several decades but eventually decided it had been "strung along" like the proverbial donkey (Lebow 1985: 108) – being put to "talking for the sake of talking" (Freedman and Gamba-Stonehouse 1991). Once the issue was defined by London as a matter of self-determination by the Kelpers – who would naturally wish to gain economic benefits from Buenos Aires while continuing to enjoy political protection from London – it was almost certain that there would be a perpetual impasse. The Kelpers would understandably want to have their cake and eat it too, that is, to continue to enjoy the benefits of normal relations with their nearby and more powerful neighbor without, however, accepting its political rule. They would never say "never" to

Argentina's entreaties for political union, and would always profess "maybe later" in order to stabilize their relations and to sustain the flow of economic benefits.

The Falklands/Malvinas are far away from Britain and low on the list of Whitehall's policy priorities. When things were quiet, the resolution of these islands' fate was put on the policy back burner. But when Buenos Aires rattled its saber, British officials would also put off efforts to resolve this dispute, giving as their reason that one should never negotiate under pressure. The result was that there was never a good time to have a thorough and thoughtful debate – neither when the situation was calm (there is no reason to fix something that is not broken) nor when it was tense (one should not compromise under duress). This tendency reinforced the typical impulse to avoid divisive bureaucratic debates and to postpone tough policy choices. As time went on, however, London's capacity to support a large military establishment declined and most of its available resources had to be committed to its NATO obligations – leaving the Falklands/Malvinas an easy prey for Argentina's invasion. It had wanted deterrence on the cheap – but its very reluctance to allocate enough resources to the defense of the islands encouraged Buenos Aires to believe that it would not fight for these islands and that Argentina could have a quick and easy victory. Argentine generals also believed that with Ronald Reagan in the White House, they had a friendly US president who would at least restrain Britain from retaliating and from trying to reverse a *fait accompli*. Their (misplaced) optimism stemmed in part from their (mistaken) belief that their right-wing ideological affinity with official Washington and their acting as a US surrogate in assisting the *contras* in Nicaragua would ingratiate them with the US administration. When Ronald Reagan telephoned Leopoldo Galtieri to stop Argentina's invasion force on its way to seize the islands, he was told that it was too late to stop this military operation.

In retrospect, we can say that the Argentine generals had seriously misunderstood Britain's intentions and incentives (including those pertaining to its domestic politics). Hindsight, however, is always 20/20. Given the information available to them at the time, the Argentines' calculations and interpretations were not unreasonable. The tragedy of the Falklands/Malvinas episode is of course that war happened even though neither side had wanted it and even though a third party, the US, had tried hard to prevent it. Moreover, domestic dynamics provided much of the impetus to escalating armed hostilities. The unpopularity of Argentina's military junta due to both its "dirty war" against leftist citizens and its mismanagement of the economy put in play those incentives highlighted by the diversionary theory of war: incumbent officials sought to restore their sagging political legitimacy by means of confronting a foreign adversary and recovering lost territory. Similarly, partisan posturing in the name of protecting national honor, defending ethnic solidarity, and opposing aggression and appeasement turned out to be popular on the other side of the Atlantic.

William Kaufman (1956: 19–20) remarked some time ago that there must be some objective correspondence between the value of something and the costs that one is willing to pay for securing it. London's predicament, at least as perceived by Buenos Aires, is that such a correspondence was lacking in the Falklands/Malvinas. Having retaken these islands, it is still not clear how in the long run Britain will be able to muster the necessary commitment and command the necessary resources to protect this overseas territory. Given China's rising power and the greater budgetary constraints of the US, these questions will also become more acute for Washington to address with respect to the impasse across the Taiwan Strait.

Henry Kissinger (1994: 168; quoted in Danilovic 2001a: 9) has remarked,

The Nuclear Age turned strategy into deterrence, and deterrence into an esoteric intellectual exercise. Since deterrence can only be tested negatively, by events that do *not* take place, and since it is never possible to demonstrate why something has not occurred, it became especially difficult to assess whether the existing policy was the best possible policy or a just barely effective one. Perhaps deterrence was even unnecessary because it was impossible to prove whether the adversary ever intended to attack in the first place. (emphasis in the original)

The feedback loops connecting putative causes and effects can indeed be complicated and impossible to prove conclusively. For example, it is not obvious that China would foreswear the use of military force against Taiwan if the US were to stop its support for Taiwan, although it is possible that in that event Taipei would be forced to make such concessions to Beijing that its accommodative policy would greatly reduce China's incentive or perceived need to resort to violent means. At the same time, despite the lopsided balance of power that has worked to its disadvantage (such as shown by its diplomatic isolation and its economic dependency on China), Taipei's ability and willingness to hold out in its protracted dispute with Beijing are not unrelated to the support it has received and that it expects to receive from Washington.

One might add that deterrence works – until it fails, when it is too late to make changes to this policy. The time to make a policy adjustment is not when troops are already on the move – in situations likely characterized by high threat, great surprise, and short response time (the standard definition of a crisis situation; Hermann 1969). China's failure to deter the US in the Korean War (when US troops crossed the 38th parallel) and the failure of the US to reassure China in that episode serve as poignant reminders (e.g., Chen 1994; Slantchev 2010; Whiting 1960). That China went to war at that time when it was much weaker than now suggests that relative military capability is not everything, not even the most important thing – as the quantitative research referred to earlier has established. It also bears reflecting that deterrence policy can in itself contribute to tension and distrust, just as a policy of ambiguity, vacillation, and procrastination (as in the case of Britain's policy toward the Falklands/Malvinas) can have this effect.

5   Taiwan's two-level interactions with China

It takes more than two to reach an interstate agreement. The contracting parties' constituents and interest groups will have a voice and to the extent that these actors occupy pivotal positions in their respective domestic political economy, they can block an agreement's ratification (a term that is used here to refer to more than just formal legislative approval, and that is intended to include political support or at least acquiescence by veto groups in authoritarian systems). In this chapter I turn to a discussion of the evolving distribution of interests, views, and influences on the Taiwan side of cross-Strait relations. Several basic ideas animate the following discussion.

Officials need domestic support in order to enter into negotiations with their foreign counterparts and, once an accord is reached, to gain domestic approval for it. Naturally, an *ex ante* awareness of prospective domestic opposition to an accord will influence officials' willingness to enter into a negotiation in the first place. Moreover, if they do decide to negotiate, the terms of a prospective deal that they will accept and the range of concessions that they will countenance will be influenced by their anticipation of possible domestic reaction. The greater the expected domestic constraints, the smaller the officials' bargaining space. In order for an accord to be successfully negotiated, the contracting parties' bargaining spaces must overlap. The greater the area of this overlap, the higher the chances of reaching an accord. Each side's bargaining space is conditional on its negotiator's political standing relative to his/her own domestic constituents and the extent to which this negotiator's preferences are concordant with those of these constituents. A strong and popular leader has more bargaining room and can afford more to make concessions to the other side. This official is able to withstand domestic criticisms better, including charges of appeasing the other side. Conversely, one who has to deal with powerful veto groups with discordant views and interests will be more severely constrained in his/her work. This leader faces a more constricted win set – the range of negotiated outcomes that will receive domestic approval or at least acquiescence by powerful veto groups.

Ceteris paribus, the larger the number of domestic veto players and the greater the differences in their respective preferences, the more difficult it will be for a negotiator to reach an agreement with his/her foreign counterpart and to subsequently gain domestic ratification for it (e.g., Cunningham 2011; Tsebelis 2002). Almost by definition, authoritarian systems have more centralized decision processes and hence fewer points of access by domestic groups wishing to block an unwanted foreign accord. A corollary of this observation is that generally speaking, domestic interest groups in democracies are more susceptible to being mobilized by foreign governmental or non-governmental actors to lobby or otherwise influence their governments' policies.

Because domestic consent is required for both bargaining parties, timing is important. For a deal to be negotiated and ratified, conditions in both countries have to be aligned in such a way that mutual accommodation becomes possible. In closing the last chapter, I mentioned that during periods of calm, London was distracted to attend to other policy matters considered to be more important than the Falklands/Malvinas. But when Buenos Aires turned up the heat, British officials refused to negotiate under pressure. There was therefore never a good time for this dispute to be accorded the amount of sustained top-level attention that was required to overcome a protracted impasse. A similar story can be told in US–Cuba relations (Nincic 2011), at least until a seeming breakthrough in December 2014. Until then, when Havana was more receptive to improving relations, the incumbent administration in Washington happened to be less willing to make conciliatory gestures. When Washington was more disposed to initiate these overtures, the government in Havana felt less interested in engagement.

The matching and mismatching of these moments is therefore consequential. The usual outcome of mismatching is policy drift or stasis. Occasionally, however, a political system becomes disequilibrated; it encounters what Miroslav Nincic (2011) calls a critical juncture, which opens a window for policy innovation and change to occur. During this period, old policy formulae and ideas are more vulnerable to challenge, and the existing ruling coalition is weakened so that its members are more disposed to look for new ways to shore up their power and to advance their interests. They may even be open to redefining their interests and realigning their politics. In the parlance of Most and Starr's (1989) analytic framework, these are occasions when "opportunity" and "willingness" converge. When these factors are aligned for both sides, they are poised to achieve a breakthrough in their relationship.

These remarks naturally question the assumption that states are unitary actors representing homogeneous national interests. They also introduce the issue of principal–agent relationship, pointing to the possibility that incumbent officials may have an agenda that is independent of and sometimes even contrary to the preferences of their constituents. A possible example is suggested by Mao Tse-tung's rejection of Soviet offers of a deal that would have turned over the disputed islands in the Ussuri River to China – offers that were identical to those Beijing eventually accepted decades later – because concluding such an agreement would have meant accommodating Soviet revisionism and compromising his personal stature and political position both domestically and internationally (Chung 2004).

This acknowledgment of possible tension between a principal and its agents immediately calls attention to the domestic redistributive effects of foreign deals. These deals produce relative losers and winners. Rising trade and investment across the Taiwan Strait, for example, increase competitive pressure on the more labor-intensive sectors of the island's economy while strengthening the bargaining power of large financial institutions and multinational conglomerates. Although much of the scholarship on Taiwan's relationship with China has focused on its people's identity and the political division concerning the question of the island's future status (independence versus reunification with China), economic interests are certainly also engaged and they often coincide with the opposing groups' political preferences. Which economic sectors will have to bear the brunt of the burden of adjusting to rising cross-Strait trade and investment, and who will stand to benefit most from this development (Simmons 1994)? From Mancur Olson's (1965, 1982) seminal writings on collective action, it will surprise few to learn that groups representing concentrated interests are better able to mobilize and organize politically in order to protect and advance their agenda than others with more diffuse interests.

Even though it usually tends to be acquiescent and permissive, public opinion does matter in shaping the general parameters of two-level games – not least because it affects the electoral chances and campaign strategies of political candidates. In a two-party system, these candidates gravitate toward the median voter (Downs 1957). It is a political truism that those politicians and officials who go with the grain of popular sentiments will have an easier time accomplishing their objectives than others who choose to go against it. Most would rather have a tailwind at their back than a headwind in their face.

But when politicians and officials knowingly buck the popular view, their behavior is revealing – this person is probably strongly committed to his/her views and believes that the public's views are malleable and can therefore be altered. An interesting example is presented in the wake of the Liberal Democratic Party's July 2013 electoral victory to win control of the House of Councilors, thereby giving Prime Minister Shinzo Abe control of both chambers of the Japanese parliament. Whereas US news reports stressed Abe's campaign promise to continue his economic reforms, Chinese media focused on his declared intention to revise Japan's postwar "peace" constitution. That latter revision would reduce or remove legal constraints on the overseas deployment of its armed forces, and would communicate to other countries a significant reorientation of its foreign relations. It is a change, however, opposed by many if not most Japanese citizens and could have varying effects on foreign audiences depending on whether Abe's words were merely campaign rhetoric or actually reflected his sincere intention. Whether his proposed constitutional revision prevails over a skeptical public or is forestalled by it will disclose meaningful information about the alignment of opposing forces in Japanese politics, and could obviously send sharply different signals to other countries, including China and the US.

Disregarding important nuances and qualifications, a majority of Taiwan's voters prefer the status quo. This preference reflects a compromise between two seemingly conflicting desires: they want to have the benefits of economic integration with China but do not want to pay the costs of political union with the latter. Taiwan's negotiators are accordingly challenged to sub-optimize across these two dimensions. The nature of public opinion just depicted suggests that while popular views obviously constrain the extent to which Taiwan's negotiators can accommodate China's demand for political reunification, this opinion also opens up possibilities for economic integration across the Strait. Similarly, this double-edged public opinion poses concurrent constraints and opportunities from China's perspective. Its negotiation strategy pivots on linkage politics (Rosenau 1969): how can the mainland use economic inducements to eventually alter Taiwan's political economy to such an extent that its people will approve political union?

Of course, cross-Strait economic and political talks are not formally presented as a matter of *quid pro quo*, but the general relationship between them, as just sketched above, is understood perfectly well by the two sides. Harrison Wagner (1988) has asked about the rationale for issue linkage. Why would the two sides take on two issues jointly rather than dealing with them separately? One would surmise that the answer is that both sides must think that connecting the issues – even if tacitly and implicitly – will help them to better reach their respective objectives compared to their having to deal with the pertinent issues independently.

In the latter situation, impasse and negotiation breakdown are very distinct possibilities in negotiating cross-Strait relations. Linkage gives the side that has made a concession in one arena (such as when it accepts terms of an exchange that are inferior to those which it could have been accorded by prevailing market conditions) the basis, or the leverage, to demand reciprocal concession from the other side in another arena.

In domestic legislation, logrolling and omnibus bills serve roughly the same general purpose of exchanging favors. Such exchanges across issue areas were, of course, also the main conclusion of Albert Hirschman's (1945) classic study of Nazi Germany's economic statecraft before World War II. Berlin offered favorable commercial terms to the Balkan countries so that it could gain political influence over these trade partners. The general idea that developed countries are able to acquire unwarranted political clout in the developing countries due to the latter's external economic reliance is also a foundational idea in scholarship of the dependency school. As a negotiation strategy, issue linkage enables negotiators to expand their domestic win set – foreign pressure or concession are used to overcome domestic resistance that would have otherwise prevented a deal (e.g., Schoppa 1993). Robert Putnam (1988) has used "synergistic linkage" to describe such strategy.

China has incurred a chronic deficit in its trade with Taiwan, and it has extended various forms of preferential treatment to Taiwan's firms doing business with or on the mainland. Its agenda is transparent. Chinese officials have not made any effort to hide their ultimate objective of changing Taiwanese public opinion to accept political reunification with the mainland. This goal represents a tall order because it seeks to effect a basic transformation of Taiwanese people's identity and preference and their government's existing source of legitimacy and support. It seeks a "catalytic" conversion (Nincic 2011). Because this desired outcome will necessarily entail a protracted process, the respective officials' time horizon, that is, their relative preference for meeting short-term versus long-term objectives, becomes an important consideration.

For instance, are politicians facing regularly scheduled elections more prone to discounting prospective future returns in favor of current payoff? Does term limitation for office holders impair or enhance their motivation to undertake bold policy initiatives? These questions are obviously germane to the different circumstances facing democratic leaders and their authoritarian counterparts. The former officials' tenure is more uncertain and they face a larger "selectorate" which can reject them at the polls (Bueno de Mesquita et al. 2003). It seems likely that democratic officials would be more inclined to negotiate for specific exchanges in policy changes as opposed to undertaking influence strategies aimed at transforming their counterparts' basic identities or values (even though one often hears public arguments to the contrary, such as when US officials contend that economic and cultural exchanges with China can be used to alter the latter's society in ways that make it more congenial to Western liberal traditions).

Political opening and economic reorientation

The late 1970s and early 1980s were a critical juncture for Taiwan's political economy. The US decision to break off its diplomatic tie and to abrogate its defense treaty with Taiwan was traumatic, even though the general trend culminating in these events had been unfolding ever since Taiwan lost its right to represent China in the United Nations in October 1971 (Taipei, with the support of the US, was able to occupy the China seat until then, and Beijing was kept out of the UN). This event was followed in short order by Richard Nixon's landmark visit to Beijing in February 1972. The breakthrough in Sino-American relations high-lighted Taipei's increasing international isolation, and Taipei's diplomatic predicament was compounded by mounting domestic challenges to the Kuomintang's (KMT) authoritarian rule. The Kaohsiung incident (December 1979) was emblematic of this political opposition and the regime's attempts to suppress domestic dissidents demanding democratic reform and respect for human rights.

Political opposition to the KMT's single-party rule (this opposition movement was called *Tangwai*, which in Chinese means literally "outside the party") gathered momentum and received popular support mostly from native Taiwanese (as distinct from the so-called mainlanders whose families emigrated to Taiwan in the late 1940s when the KMT withdrew to the island after being defeated by the Communists on the mainland). When Chiang Ching-kuo succeeded his father (Chiang Kai-shek) as Taiwan's president in 1978, it was already becoming evident that the mainlanders' practical monopoly of power could not be sustained for much longer as they represented only about 10% of the population. Chiang chose Lee Teng-hui, a native-born Taiwanese, to be his vice president in 1984, and he legalized political opposition (the Democratic Progressive Party or DPP was established in 1986) and lifted martial law (in 1987), thereby initiating the island's democratization process.

During this period of political change and reform, Taiwan's economy was also confronted with an urgent need for adjustment. It had till then performed remarkably well as a model of export-led development, but was beginning to face increasing challenges from latecomers (e.g., the Southeast Asian countries and China after Deng Xiao-ping's economic reforms in 1978–79) which were competing for the lower end of export markets consisting of manufactured products with high labor input but low technology content. Thus, the forces of globalization provided another powerful impetus for change. The conjunction of developments summarized here threatened the existing equilibrium for Taiwan's political economy and its ruling coalition's grip on power. It presented a critical juncture during which political realignment and economic reorientation became possible.

Political opening and electoral contest gave the DPP an advantage as the natural representative of an overwhelming majority of Taiwan's people (Rigger 2001). Political independence for the island was a popular cause for the DPP's political base. The KMT faced an existential crisis after a split between its "main stream" and "anti-main stream" factions (headed respectively by Lee Teng-hui and his premier, Hau Pei-tsun). For a while, members of the latter faction broke off to form their own parties (the New Party and the People First Party) to participate in electoral contests. This phenomenon, however, turned out to be ephemeral, so that in subsequent years a two-party system emerged, with the DPP and the KMT as its chief protagonists. During this period of transition and evolution, the latter party searched for a new identity and mandate to counter the former's popular call for independence. Not surprisingly, the KMT sought a comparative advantage in presenting itself as a bridge to the mainland and as a superior manager of the economy. The critical juncture of Taiwan's recent history thus provided an opportunity for this party to look for and invent a new basis for its identity and legitimacy.

Although somewhat of a simplification, the general contours of partisan alignment and electoral contest have in recent years revolved around the debate about whether voters should favor "economics first" or "politics first" (Benson and Niou 2007), and thus whether they should support the KMT or the DPP. As already implied, a preference for "economics first" means closer economic cooperation with the mainland and subordinating the island's political independence to this economic priority; conversely, "politics first" means to pursue political independence even at the expense of sacrificing economic growth and stability.

This brief narrative argues that Taiwan's democratization process and the legitimacy and electoral challenges presented by the DPP gave the impetus and incentive for the KMT to reinvent itself from its previous incarnation as an authoritarian party state following the model of a garrison state (Lasswell 1941) and premised on the recovery of the mainland as its main *raison d'être*. External political and economic forces further contributed to the ruling coalition's disequilibrium, presenting both an opportunity and a motivation for its various stakeholders to redefine their interests. This account holds two important points. First, these interests are not fixed. Because preferences can change, the domestic win set can also shift. Second, a chief executive's role as a pivotal veto player can also evolve. By refusing to enter into negotiation with a foreign counterpart or by declining to submit a possible deal to domestic ratification, a government leader serves as a gatekeeper who can block any settlement that he/she dislikes. This was the situation for a long time under Taiwan's old regime. Changes since the late 1970s and early 1980s, however, altered this situation.

For reasons including domestic electoral competition, the KMT began to represent itself as the party that could be entrusted to negotiate effectively with the mainland authorities and to manage the island's economy competently. By emphasizing the danger of destabilizing cross-Strait relations and the importance of economic benefits to be gained from cross-Strait intercourse, it sought to undertake what Putnam (1988) describes as "synergistic linkages." These claims are used as a lever to expand the domestic win set (including efforts to gain mass and elite acceptance to open negotiations with Beijing in the first place) and to situate the KMT in a more advantageous position for electoral contest (in order to counter the DPP's popular appeal as an advocate of Taiwan independence). As the metaphor of two-level games is intended to convey, moves on the international board are sometimes made with an eye to advancing an actor's domestic agenda. Critically and understandably, because Beijing's greatest objection is against Taiwan's independence, which is the DPP's professed goal, it has refused to deal with this party. This refusal in turn strengthens the KMT's domestic position, enabling it to argue to Taiwan's electorate that it is the one to turn to if talks with the mainland are to be undertaken.

Two-level games suggest a two-way street whereby the above situation can be reversed such that one's domestic constraints and opportunities are exploited to improve international bargaining. A smaller domestic win set can sometimes be used to extract concessions from a foreign counterpart (in contrast, a negotiator with a large domestic win set can be more easily "pushed" around to accommodate his/her foreign counterpart). Accordingly, a chief executive facing strong domestic opposition may actually be advantaged to the extent that his/her counterpart prefers a settlement to no settlement (which means continuing with the impasse represented by the status quo). Labor union negotiators, for example, often try to extract concessions from the management by arguing that the current offer made by the latter will be rejected in a vote by their rank and file. By this logic, a skeptical public and a vigorous DPP tend to improve the KMT's position when bargaining with Beijing, because any deal they reach will have to satisfy the KMT's domestic critics. This same logic would explain Beijing's strategy of targeting those groups that can be influential in partisan competition in Taiwan and that are an important element of the DPP's political base.

Thus, for example, Beijing has used side-payments in an attempt to "peel off" those who work in Taiwan's tourism, banking, and real estate sectors and also the island's rice and fruit farmers, in order to influence their economic interests and political preferences. It has also contracted with fish farmers in Xuejia, an economically distressed district in southern Taiwan and one that has been strongly disposed to support the DPP, in order to influence local political attitudes (Huang 2012). Significantly, Beijing does not necessarily have to convert these DPP supporters by completely reversing their political sympathies. Its strategy will have worked if it can cause significant affective dissonance, thereby neutralizing these voters' pro-independence sympathies. The above examples suggest that the more critical opponents or at least the more skeptical voices arrayed against a potential foreign deal tend to be singled out for concessions (such concessions are unnecessary for those who are already supporters of this deal). This tendency in turn implies that strategic actors want to position themselves to be the last holdout to sign off on a deal, as this status will confer upon them the greatest advantage to extract concessions from those who are already on board. These hypotheses of course assume that one's foreign counterpart is politically and psychologically invested in (even committed to) reaching a deal (as Jimmy Carter appeared to be in negotiating the Camp David Accords and the Panama Canal Treaty; Pastor 1993; Stein 1993). If this is not the case, this counterpart may walk away from a deal instead of making additional concessions (after all, it also has to face its own domestic dissenters). Yet, as should already be apparent, authoritarian states are in a better position to ignore or suppress domestic dissidence – and as a result, they are less able to use this dissidence as a lever to threaten the other side with a breakdown in negotiation. This observation reinforces again the idea that when a chief negotiator is politically secure and strong in domestic politics, his/her weaker foreign counterpart will have a better chance of gaining concessions from this individual (a politically vulnerable negotiator will be more reluctant to make concessions which could undermine his/her domestic power and popularity).

Naturally, any change in a state's international relations will face opposition from those domestic groups and institutions whose interests and influence are tied to the old policies. The military-industrial complex, conservative party stalwarts, and bureaucrats in charge of large state enterprises are some examples of the old guard who would have to be somehow mollified or eased out of power if a new era of détente and economic openness were to take hold. Therefore, it is never easy to engineer an international settlement that has the intent or effect of undercutting the status of these stakeholders. Arguably, Taiwan has made this transition much more effectively and peacefully than some other cases that come to mind. Both Anwar Sadat and Mikhail Gorbachev basically offered to exchange international conciliation for foreign assistance to resuscitate their dire domestic economies (Snyder 1993; Stein 1993; Wohlforth 2003). Their search for external détente was an indispensable part of their respective agendas for domestic reform. Whether judged by the political or economic results of their reform efforts, their domestic legacies have been much less impressive than Taiwan's record.

Public opinion and popular expectations

The above discussion is not meant to suggest that policy initiatives stem directly from public pressure. This rarely tends to be the case. Public opinion is most often acquiescent and permissive, thus giving officials considerable room to maneuver. Indeed, officials are often in a position to lead and shape public opinion, and can sometimes even override it (such as when the wars in Vietnam and Afghanistan dragged on long after they became unpopular with the American people). The public's views (sometimes latent) can, however, be mobilized and exploited by the political opposition (such as in the US debate about "who lost China") and a dissatisfied electorate (such as over poor economic performance or foreign setback, as shown by Gerald Ford's bout with domestic stagflation or Harry Truman's "mess in Korea") can censure incumbent officials retrospectively by rejecting them or their political successors at the polls. Not surprisingly, wary politicians often try to preempt their domestic political opponents who are likely to take advantage of voter discontent for partisan gains. This observation suggests that officials naturally try to be anticipatory and to adjust their policies in accordance with what they sense to be the general mood and direction of mass attitudes.

The discussion in the preceding section described the KMT's efforts to reposition itself in Taiwan's domestic politics. If the electoral contest is to be defined along a single issue dimension of independence for Taiwan versus its reunification with China, the DPP will have a huge edge. If, however, the KMT is successful in persuading the voters to accept the management of the island's economy as a second issue dimension, it can reframe the political discourse and create an offsetting advantage for itself. This attempt to persuade Taiwan's electorate was bolstered by Beijing's refusal to negotiate with Taiwan's pro-independence politicians.

Thus, Beijing became a tacit supporter of the KMT's political strategy in an implicit partnership which has enabled the KMT to argue that cross-Strait relations would be put in a "deep freeze" if Taiwan's voters should elect a DPP government. To the extent that Taiwan's economic performance has become increasingly intertwined with its dependency on the Chinese market, the KMT has plausibly argued that the island's economic wellbeing will be jeopardized, should relations with Beijing be destabilized. It has tried to enhance its domestic credentials and expand its win set by proclaiming that it is uniquely qualified to manage this important relationship. Interestingly and significantly, the implicit partnership between China and the KMT also shares some parallels with the US role in Taiwan's domestic politics. It has been an open secret that Washington has also favored KMT rule because it has been critical of the destabilizing effects that the DPP's pro-independence agenda can have on cross-Strait relations (as it did during the administration of Chen Shui-bian). This US connection furnishes another example of two-level transnational coalitions.

As political entrepreneurs, officials are interested in more than winning elections. They also want to fulfill their policy agendas. They therefore try to shape and change public opinion, especially when the opportunity to do so is the greatest when this opinion is malleable and in flux, and when it reflects heterogeneous interests, contingent qualifications, and cognitive and affective dissonance. At the same time, if they want to be elected, politicians have to work within the general parameters of public opinion. Survey data show several central tendencies which in turn capture the predicaments faced by Taiwan's politicians and officials.

A large majority of Taiwan's people prefer independence. Although the intensity of this preference (and of the opposite preference of reunification with China) naturally varies for different individuals, there is an approximate ratio of 4 to 1 among Taiwan's survey respondents (in February 2011) in support of independence (or 80.2% in favor versus 19.8% against; Wang 2013). The survey respondents' preferences on the question of independence versus reunification correlate with partisanship so that whereas nearly 93% of the pan-green (predominantly DPP) supporters favor independence, only 70% of the pan-blue (predominantly KMT) supporters have the same preference (the figure for those respondents who consider themselves political independents is 82%). When presented with more than a binary choice between independence and reunification, a majority of Taiwan's people (about 61% in 2011) avoided choosing a long-term outcome (Bush 2013: 26). Those indicating varying degrees of preference for independence (about 21%) or reunification (about 11%) represent minorities. That these two polar preferences receive much less support than the mainstream view of "wait and see" is highly significant. Richard Bush (2013: 207) has remarked: "Increasingly, the Taiwan public has become so sensitized to the dangers of Taiwan independence for cross-Strait cooperation that it is becoming impossible for an advocate of independence to win a presidential election." Thus, according to this view, democratic politics (more specifically, the majority desire to keep the status quo for an indefinite time) tends to restrain any impulse on the part of leading Taiwanese politicians to "rock the boat."

The preferences of Taiwan's people are not fixed and can be quite context dependent (Hsieh and Niou 2005). Not surprisingly, the two most decisive factors influencing their attitudes are the prospects of US support and the danger of China's resort to force if Taiwan declares independence. A person's preference for independence is related to his/her expectation of US intervention on Taiwan's behalf. Among those who support independence unconditionally, 81% believe that the US will defend Taiwan even if it declares independence. This belief is also related to partisanship – with the pan-green supporters expressing a higher degree of confidence in this US support than the pan-blue supporters. Significantly, more than half of Taiwan's public (56%) believes that the US would come to Taiwan's defense even in the event that it declares independence (this figure rises to 86% among the pan-green supporters; Wang 2013: 98–99). These figures stand in sharp contrast to the survey results reported by the Chicago Council of Global Affairs (2010: 52, 65), indicating that Americans are opposed to military intervention in the event of a war across the Taiwan Strait by a margin of almost three to one.

As just noted, a slight majority of Taiwan's electorate is not persuaded by Washington's policy of pivotal deterrence (or dual deterrence), which threatens Taiwan with abandonment if its government changes the island's political status unilaterally. Over four fifths (83%) expect the US to "send troops to help" Taiwan if China attacks in the absence of Taiwan declaring independence. This figure is also intriguing as it suggests that the remaining 17% of Taiwan's public does not trust Washington's implicit pledge of support if China attacks without being provoked. The pertinent survey figures seem to indicate that about two thirds of Taiwan's people have doubts about the credibility of official US policy for one reason or another. As just mentioned, more than half believe that the US is committed to defending Taiwan regardless of what it does (i.e., even if Taipei upsets the status quo by declaring independence). About one fifth does not believe in US military support regardless of what China does (i.e., even if Beijing attacks while Taipei maintains the status quo). These views also appear to be quite unstable.

In 2008, 47% believed that the US would still defend Taiwan if it were to declare independence, compared to 44% who believed that it would not in that event. These figures changed to 57% and 27% respectively in 2011. As suggested by these figures, there is also a substantial "silent minority" of about 10% that has not indicated an opinion.

In addition to whether the US will intervene militarily to help Taiwan, public support for Taiwan's independence is highly conditional on the respondents' opinion on whether China will respond with a military attack in that event. About two thirds (65.7%) of the respondents indicate that they would not support independence if this action would result in a Chinese attack, but the remaining one third would favor independence even if China attacks. The threat of Chinese military attack has had a greater effect on the pan-blue backers than on the pan-green backers. Only 14% of the former group but 65% of the latter group would favor independence even if it means war with China.

In the aggregate (i.e., taking into account the independents), an overwhelming majority of Taiwan's people in 2011 (91%) support maintaining the status quo, whereas only 2% would prefer immediate reunification with China and 5% would favor immediate independence (Wang 2012: 105). This majority preference against making any drastic change points to an important conclusion from Beijing's perspective: if it were not for Beijing's threat to use force, Taiwan's public opinion would have opted decisively for independence. Therefore, China's military deterrence has been effective in thwarting this development. This observation in turn implies that it would be difficult for Taipei or Washington to persuade Beijing to renounce the use of force since it has been the decisive factor in restraining Taiwan's independence according to its people's own admission. The same survey data also point to the importance of the US factor. For the most ardent supporters of Taiwan's independence, their position is buttressed by the belief that the US will defend their country unconditionally. Given this fact, it is also not unnatural for Beijing to conclude that, whether intended or not, Washington plays a critical role that encourages and sustains the Taiwan independence movement.

It was mentioned earlier that attempts to affect Taiwan people's perception of their identities and interests appear an arduous task from Beijing's perspective. There is some tentative evidence suggesting that its strategy has borne some fruit recently. Although its results are necessarily limited and reversible, the survey reported earlier in Chapter 1 (Kuomintang 2013) indicates that over 90% of Taiwan's respondents have identified themselves as having Chinese ethnicity. According to the same poll, over half of the respondents thought that Taiwan should take advantage of China's economic development as an opportunity and about

15% believed that it should actively participate in this development. Less than 20% perceived China's development as a threat. These figures hint at changing public opinion which, if true, invites politicians and political parties to adjust their positions. They also indicate that the public's views and preferences are not necessarily consistent or stable, and that the malleability and evolution of people's attitudes can create opportunities for politicians to reposition themselves in domestic partisan politics.

Generational differences can be one important and inexorable source for evolving mass attitudes. Older people die and younger people with different historical memories and socialization experiences replace their elders as political participants. With respect to Taiwan's electorate, the younger voters' views appear to be more conducive to breaking the cross-Strait impasse than the older generations' views. Shelley Rigger (2006: viii) remarks: "The attitudes that are most destructive to cross-strait ties are held by older Taiwanese, whose political influence will wane in the coming years. Younger Taiwanese tend to be pragmatic and flexible in their views; they lack the passionate emotion that drives many [of their elders]." She concludes that "current trends suggest that Taiwan's public will demand policies that ease relations between the two sides in the future" (Rigger 2006: ix). Thus, there is some basis for Beijing's optimism that the passage of time will favor its relative bargaining power not only because of its improving capabilities but also because of the changing nature of Taiwan's electorate.

Voters elect their political representatives according to their preferences but political candidates also adapt their policy positions to maximize their prospective electoral support, adjusting their political strategies in pursuit of the so-called median voter. One possible example of such adjustment comes from Frank Hsieh's recent visit to China. He was Taiwan's premier when the DPP was the incumbent government. His visit to the mainland caused controversy within the DPP, and again exemplifies two-level games whereby this trip was deployed in intra-DPP maneuvers. Such maneuvers can in turn present clues to outside observers about the relevant politicians' judgments about how they can position themselves most advantageously to exploit shifting public opinion. Incidentally, if Hsieh's behavior portends a more general move by the DPP to reposition itself in Taiwan's political economy and electoral contests as the KMT has done before, my previous discussion offers a further implication.

To the extent that this move augurs a change in the DPP's position so that it becomes closer to the one adopted by the KMT with respect to Taiwan's relationship with China, this development points to an expanded win set for reaching accommodation with Beijing. Such an evolution in turn implies that Beijing will gain enhanced bargaining power because the prospect of DPP opposition to a cross-Strait negotiated deal will have lessened. This prospect has heretofore given credibility to the KMT's demand for concessions in order to satisfy domestic ratification for any deals reached with Beijing. When the DPP and KMT positions on dealing with China become more closely aligned, this phenomenon naturally means that they are competing more intensely for the support of the median voter on that issue and, as we have seen, there is some tentative evidence that this median voter's views are evolving. While this evolution will reflect ongoing secular trends (such as the replacement of older generations by younger voters, the *embourgeoisement* of Taiwan's society), election returns and partisan support can manifest sharp swings such that voters can provide the KMT with a landslide victory in one election only to be followed by a sharp rebuke in the next one.

Vested interests and distributional coalitions

In seeking to advance international agreements and domestic ratification for these agreements, officials recognize that public opinion typically represents those for whom a particular international deal will introduce only diffused costs and benefits. Unless mobilized by the political elite (or counter-elite), the median voter tends to be generally a passive player in this deal's domestic ratification. In contrast, special interests representing groups with concentrated costs and benefits are more likely to organize themselves to either block or promote this proposed deal (Olson 1965, 1982). These latter groups tend to be the more active and consequential participants in the ratification process. They are likely to self-mobilize to protect or advance their more immediate and substantial stake in an international accord. They are also in a better position to form a transnational coalition with counterparts in the other country to promote a common cause. Taiwan's businesspeople with collaborative projects with local interests and authorities on the mainland provide an obvious example.

Democratization of course gives people a voice at the polls. Electoral contest and voting rights enable people to choose their representatives. An unintended consequence of Taiwan's democratization, however, has been the expensive costs of financing political campaigns. These costs in turn give businesspeople more clout, whether through their campaign donations to political candidates or by their efforts to seek political office directly. "Big money" politics tends to make the political parties beholden to business interests, especially those representing large multinational conglomerates (Kastner 2009). These conglomerates are typically internationally oriented. They prefer stable currencies, low tariffs, a small public sector, reduced government regulations, and unimpeded flow of capital, goods, and people across borders. When Taiwan expands its trade and investment with China, it is tantamount to creating a larger economic zone for these companies. This enlargement in turn has the effect of increasing the mobility of production factors. Because this mobility is greater for capital than for labor (people are less likely to emigrate, although there are now an estimated one and half million people from Taiwan residing in China), economic integration between the two sides of the Taiwan Strait has increased the bargaining power of capitalists at the expense of workers. In short, foreign economic intercourse tends to have a domestic redistributive effect, and not just on various groups' income but also on their political influence and social standing (Abdelal and Kirshner 1999–2000; James and Lake 1989; Lobell 2007). Therefore, the more inward- and outward-oriented groups (often generalized as "nationalists" and "internationalists") unsurprisingly favor different government policies on tariffs and taxes, monetary and fiscal expansion, government regulation of the economy and, not least of all, the maintenance of large state enterprises and government bureaucracy, including the national security apparatus.

There is another way of looking at the distribution of costs and benefits stemming from expanding cross-Strait commerce. The well-known Stolper-Samuelson theorem offers a conclusion similar to the one reached in the above paragraph. Owners of a more abundant production factor will be advantaged by free trade, whereas owners of a scarcer production factor will be disadvantaged. Being relatively capital rich, Taiwan can export this production factor by investing in operations in China in order to take advantage of its larger market and lower labor cost. Conversely, Taiwan's labor being scarcer and therefore more expensive compared to China, its workers will face downward wage pressure from the mainland when trade barriers are reduced or removed. In this scenario, the return for capital improves whereas that for labor deteriorates. Taiwan's small and medium-sized family enterprises, especially in the labor-intensive and domestic service sectors, are most likely to be adversely affected. On the other side of the ledger, large financial institutions and industrial corporations tend to be the chief beneficiaries of expanded cross-Strait commerce.

Expanding cross-Strait commercial ties are but symptomatic of the more sweeping processes of globalization. The changes brought about by these processes have increased the importance of capital assets and financial flows compared to merchandise trade (Frieden 1991). Moreover, although the exchange rates for currencies are certainly not unimportant (just witness the ripple effects caused by the declining value of the yen and euro caused by Japan and Europe's recent "easy money" policies), they tend to operate through the interest rates prevailing in different countries, a phenomenon that is in turn indicative of the relevant countries' macroeconomic conditions (such as the malaise that has afflicted the eurozone countries, especially those located in its southern tier).

These remarks call attention to the discrepant interests and incentives on the part of different economic actors. Multinational corporations, large financial institutions, and companies that export tradable goods would prefer to see monetary expansion and a stable (and even depreciating) currency. Conversely, those firms with a domestic orientation and operating in the service sector would advocate fiscal expansion and favor appreciating currency that would benefit importers. These divergences reflect divisions within the business community and also class cleavages between capital and labor. Although obviously imperfect, these differences tend to correspond to the KMT and DPP's respective partisan base. They also tend to overlap with geographical lines of division with the relative winners of economic opening to the mainland concentrated in Taiwan's more urban north and the relative losers located in its more rural south (which is the DPP's political bastion).

The respective political parties' policies when in charge of the government – such as whether they favored monetary or fiscal expansion, whether they supported a stable currency and low interest rate, and especially whether they tried to stop or promote cross-Strait trade and investment – should disclose their agenda. Significantly, commercial ties between Taiwan and China rose sharply during the administrations of Lee Teng-hui and Chen Shui-bian, two politicians with a reputation for favoring Taiwan's independence. This phenomenon in turn presents an enigma: why did they not act more decisively to curtail these ties, especially when their political constituents are likely to bear the brunt of the consequent adjustment costs? As noted in Chapter 3, the rationalist perspective explains their inaction or at least lethargy by pointing to the difference between political rhetoric for domestic consumption and international signaling to reassure one's foreign counterpart.

In their more recent conduct of two-level games, both sides of the Taiwan Strait have tacitly joined in efforts to expand Taiwan's domestic win set. By agreeing to promote tourism, facilitate mainlanders' access to banking and real estate on the island, permit direct flights and shipping between the two sides, and expand popular entertainment (movies, music, television shows) for shared viewers and audiences, they have created vested interests in several service industries whose continued profitability (in some cases, even their commercial viability) has come to depend on maintaining stable cross-Strait relations. These groups will self-mobilize to oppose any backsliding in these relations. Their expected behavior helps to lock in ongoing commercial relations, prevailing over others whose interests are more diffuse. It is one thing for a government to impose an economic embargo against another country when its companies have very little ongoing business stake in the target country (such as when the US and its NATO partners instituted an economic blockade against the USSR and China during the 1950s and 1960s; Mastanduno 1992). It is a different matter, however, for a government to persuade its companies to join a boycott after they have already acquired a large, irretrievable investment in ongoing commercial relations.

Economic engagement creates stakeholders who are motivated to maintain this cooperation and even to further increase it (Long 1996). When states have a strong financial stake in or are economically dependent on others, it is more difficult for them to mobilize domestic support to oppose these same foreign counterparts in security or political confrontations (Papayoanou 1999: 18). One clear implication is that *ceteris paribus*, when one's economic wellbeing becomes intertwined with another's, deterrence threats directed against that other country become less credible. Officials interested in mounting such threats now have to face an uphill fight to convince their own reluctant domestic interest groups. This is one major reason given by realists who call attention to the security externalities of engaging in commerce with one's actual or potential adversaries (Gowa 1994). Economic interdependence makes it difficult to harm one's commercial partners without also hurting oneself.

Significantly, cross-Strait commerce not only affects people's evolving perceptions of their interests but also shifts the relative influence between contesting groups in domestic politics. Globalization, as suggested above, not only promotes the interests of large international corporations but also enhances their bargaining power relative to labor – and relative to the state. Capitalists can now more easily move their operations to offshore sites, thus escaping the political jurisdiction of their home governments. That cross-Strait commerce has thrived attests to the triumph of Taiwan's more liberal groups favoring international opening and a political setback for those conservative and also pro-independence groups who would put the island's security concerns above its economic performance (which is purchased at the cost of becoming more reliant on the mainland, and thus exposing Taiwan to the danger of being subjected to the latter's political pressure). In its struggle to regulate commerce across the Strait, Taiwan's government has been fighting a rearguard battle in its efforts to manage market forces. As Tse-kang Leng (1996: 127) has remarked, "the [Taiwan] state has been 'chasing' the market mechanism instead of 'governing' it. What the state has done is to partially legitimize the existing [commercial] situation rather than to act as a guide to Taiwanese businesspeople."

Back to synergistic linkages

Robert Putnam's (1988) important insight about two-level games emphasizes the importance of synergistic linkages that resonate with the interests and perspectives of significant domestic stakeholders on both sides of a negotiation table, thereby enabling the successful conclusion of an interstate deal that would not have otherwise been possible.

Increased economic interdependence provides the opportunity for more "synergistic linkages" between the negotiating parties to strike a deal. These linkages do not necessarily attempt to change immediately the existing preferences or beliefs of each party's domestic constituents, although such changes are possible over a longer period of time. (That people's perceptions of their identities and interests can evolve as a result of their mutually beneficial exchanges has been a core proposition of the communications and functionalist schools of scholarship, e.g., Deutsch *et al.* 1957; Haas 1958; Mitrany 1966.) Synergistic linkages facilitate such a deal by creating a policy option that was previously beyond the reach of each side's domestic political economy. For instance, when Chinese tourists are allowed to visit Taiwan, this decision has specific effects on a targeted group – Taiwan's tourism industry – and helps to turn this group into a supporter and advocate of continuing and expanding the economic and even political opening across the Taiwan Strait. Another example is provided when China opens its market to Taiwan's fruit farmers on favorable terms. These farmers are located mostly in southern Taiwan. The political significance of this geographic fact is of course that whereas the KMT's political supporters are found mostly in the north, the DPP's political base is located in the south. The example of fruit farmers points to Beijing's attempt to peel off one of the DPP's key constituencies, and such attempts have at least the effect of getting this traditionally pro-independence party to expend scarce resources (including political capital) to fend off possible dissent within its own ranks. US electoral contests provide a comparable example: sometimes a candidate will try to force his/her rival to divert valuable resources, such as funds for media advertisement, to defend certain districts so that this rival will have fewer resources to deploy in mounting a more effective challenge in other districts.

In the examples of Taiwan's tourism industry and fruit and fish farmers given earlier, the key point is to recognize the distinction between homogeneous and heterogeneous national interests (Putnam 1988). Whereas all (or nearly all) of Taiwan's voters can be expected to favor greater political space for their government in participating in international organizations and forums (a homogenous interest), they can differ sharply among themselves about whether to open trade with China, admit Chinese tourists and students, and permit Chinese investment in Taiwan's real estate (heterogeneous interests). An analytic perspective that assumes a unitary actor (or homogeneous interests) overlooks such domestic divisions and the possibility that these divisions can provide for synergistic strategies. Moves made in attempting to reach a foreign deal do not necessarily work better when they involve general concessions to homogeneous interests (such as China's concessions that enable more extensive participation by Taipei in international organizations or its self-restraint from pressuring countries that currently recognize Taiwan to switch their diplomatic ties), but rather can work more effectively when they are focused on specific target groups with heterogeneous interests. The latter attempts are important not so much for their *average* impact on all voters as for their *marginal* effect on specific pivotal groups.

These observations should be familiar to strategists of US presidential campaigns. Democratic candidates do not typically waste their time and effort on deeply red states like Texas where they are unlikely to win no matter how hard they try, or in deeply blue states such as New York and California where they already have a very large lead. Republican candidates behave according to the same logic. In going after the maximum number of electoral votes, they both focus on a dozen or so battleground states such as Pennsylvania, Virginia, and Colorado, spending most of their media resources and organizational efforts on a rather small number of swing voters in these states.

The general point about heterogeneous interests in a foreign counterpart's domestic political economy is also exemplified by several recent episodes pertaining to disputed sovereignty in the South China Sea. In spring 2013, a Philippine marine patrol vessel shot and killed a Taiwanese fisherman. In the ensuing quarrel, Taiwan applied its economic leverage, threatening to deny or delay applications by Philippine citizens who want to work as domestic helpers in Taiwan. The foreign revenues provided by these workers are a considerable source of income for Manila. In another episode in spring 2012 that pitted the Philippines and China in a confrontation over the Scarborough Shoal/Huangyan Island, Beijing advised its citizens to avoid travelling to the Philippines. The suspension of organized tours again threatened a vital source of income for Manila. In both of these examples, economic incentives rather than military forces were deployed to influence soured relations stemming from maritime clashes.

Significantly, synergistic linkages are not just a means that incumbent officials can deploy to expand their domestic win set. Groups within a government as well as outside it can resort to the same strategy. For instance, Taiwan's businesspeople (many of whom reside in China) have lobbied long and hard for direct travel between the two sides (previously, flights and shipping had to be routed through a third party such as Hong Kong). Their efforts have broken down the official stance of Taiwan's government for a long time that it would not negotiate with or approve any direct contact with its mainland adversary. Nowadays, officials on both sides of the Strait are in constant communication with each other, and nearly all barriers to their contact have been removed (Gilley 2010). Moreover, and as alluded to earlier, those who are in favor of further rapprochement and cooperation are by the very nature of their relationship in a position to build a trans-border coalition to promote their common goal. In contrast, those who are opposed to this development cannot obviously enter into an organized coalition, although in their reciprocal hostility they may be able to sustain a rivalry by feeding on each other's distrust and enmity.

Expanded linkages and increasing exchanges can promote mutual benefits but they can also provide the leverage for one side to coerce the other. An obvious concern for Taiwan is whether its economic dependency on China can be used by Beijing to extract political concessions. As mentioned earlier, the success rate of overt economic sanctions has not been high (Hufbauer *et al.* 1990; Pape 1997). For example, Cuba held out throughout decades of economic blockade by the US, as acknowledged by President Barack Obama when he decided to reverse this policy in December 2014. Similarly, Iran (until the recent limited agreement to freeze its nuclear program), Iraq (under Saddam Hussein), and North Korea have shown strong resistance to making political concessions in return for the lifting of sanctions directed against them. The targets of past economic sanctions have typically been authoritarian systems. As a democracy, Taiwan's situation would be different if it were to face an economic blockade by Beijing. We know that one variable that has contributed to past sanction failures has been the role played by a "black knight" or a "sanction buster" (Chan 2009b). When alternative suppliers or markets are available to make up for the resource or financial shortfalls caused by a sanction, this sanction is more likely to fail (such as past Soviet assistance to Cuba and Chinese aid to North Korea). Thus, whether the US and Japan, for example, would be willing to replace

Taiwan's lost trade with China in the event of an economic embargo initiated by Beijing would be a critical factor.

Another relevant factor, mentioned already, pertains to those distributional coalitions which have a vested stake in maintaining economic relations with China. In the event of a political rupture, these groups not only risk losing their existing investments on and trade with the mainland, but also suffer the opportunity costs of forfeiting future business transactions. As argued in the last chapter, the credibility of a deterrence threat depends on a target audience's assessment of the relative deprivation caused by complying with the coercive demand versus that which would ensue from defying this demand. Moreover, the experience of pre-1914 Europe suggests that elite cohesion and national consensus are critical in mounting an effective national defense in the face of a looming foreign threat (Schweller 2006). Some segments of Britain's ruling elite, for instance, judged the challenge coming from its own working class to be even more threatening than the menace posed by imperial Germany. In the absence of a unity of purpose and popular commitment to a political community as an ongoing concern deserving of shared sacrifice, a government's attempt to mobilize the necessary support will be severely hampered.

Concluding reflections

To paraphrase Karl Marx, people make choices but not necessarily under circumstances of their choosing. Structural conditions determine the menu of choice for officials, and set broad limits to the range of feasible strategies and the probabilities that these policies will succeed. The circumstances in which officials find themselves can constrain their policy freedom severely or extend to them considerable discretion. *Ceteris paribus*, policies that face prevailing headwinds are less likely to be adopted and if adopted, they are less likely to succeed. This said, political entrepreneurship also matters and can sometimes overcome structural constraints or take advantage of emergent opportunities.

The general idea of bargaining provides the context for our discussion on how states and their significant domestic groups can try to influence one another (including efforts by domestic actors to form cross-border coalitions to influence their own government) in order to achieve a more satisfactory outcome for themselves. Their formal and informal negotiations over the distribution of benefits and privations address both tangible and intangible resources, and the parties to these negotiations are not necessarily locked into a zero-sum game. The recognition that there exist both homogeneous and heterogeneous interests in a country opens up the possibility of synergistic linkages. The creation and exploitation of such linkages in turn point to prospective evolutions not just in the pertinent political actors' perceptions of their interests but also in their identities, social standing, and political influence.

These changes and adjustments are most likely during critical junctures when a political elite or system is in disequilibrium, transitioning from one regime or type of political economy to another. Naturally, such changes and adjustments are not inevitable or even likely. They will require a conjunction of facilitative timing on both sides of a relationship to achieve a policy breakthrough which may also entail protracted processes to consolidate. Political entrepreneurship as emphasized by the metaphor of two-level games comes into play in engineering synergistic linkages in interstate relations, and the matching and mismatching of domestic incentives and influences on both sides of a relationship set the overall tone and direction of the evolution of these relations.

This evolution has redistributive consequences not just for a country's relationship with another, but also for its own domestic constituents. There are relative winners and losers in the economic and political redistributions in both the international and domestic arenas. A "second face" interpretation of and approach to international relations argues that these relations tend to be motivated by contending domestic interests and competition for influence by their political representatives. The more concentrated interests and powerful groups tend to prevail in these struggles to define the national agenda. Which domestic groups are in ascendance and which vision of national interest is gaining ground are therefore important for understanding the evolution of international relations.

6   Multilateralism in the East and South China Sea disputes

This chapter turns to China's maritime disputes in the East and South China Seas. Before discussing these cases specifically, it would be useful to introduce a broader historical context. A nomothetic interest invites us to consider not only how China has addressed its other cases of contested territory or sovereignty in the past, but also how its behavior compares with that of others such as the US. Such consideration immediately calls into question whether some variables often mentioned to explain current and recent events hold the key to explaining them. Two such variables – Chinese nationalism and China's re-emergence as a major power – are in my view suspect as the primary drivers for its disputes, at least when they are presented in isolation.

Considering China's own past behavior

Nationalism has often been invoked as a reason for China's behavior in the South and East China Sea disputes, and in China's internal and external politics in general (Gries 2004; Wang 2012). If by nationalism one means a people's sense of pride in their country and their overt display of affection for or identification with symbols associated with it (e.g., flag, constitution, founding figures), the Chinese are not obviously more nationalist than other peoples, including Americans (who tend to more often name their schools, streets, national holidays, and landmarks after their political notables). Although observers often point to the prevalence of Chinese narratives of "victimization" and "century of humiliation" as strong motivations in Chinese politics, such collective memories of past traumas are hardly unique to the Chinese (consider the holocaust for Jews, *nakba* or cataclysm for Arabs, the "great patriotic war" for Russians, and "Pearl Harbor" and the 9/11 tragedy for Americans). Historical memories have been subject to efforts by political elites to construct national identities and forge group solidarity the world over. Compared to the behavior of politicians from various countries involved in Asia's maritime disputes (whether they are from Russia, Japan, South

170

Korea, Vietnam, or the Philippines), Chinese leaders have actually been more self-restrained in playing the nationalist card in an effort to boost their domestic popularity (Moss 2012b). They have not, for example, made well-publicized personal visits to the contested islands as their counterparts have done.

Beijing has recognized Mongolia's independence even though it has persisted in its claim of sovereignty over Taiwan. In and of itself, Chinese nationalism cannot account for this difference. Mongolia (or "Outer Mongolia") is bigger than Taiwan, constituting approximately 14% of China's territory. Until the end of World War II and the Kuomintang's 1945 treaty conceding its independence, this country did not enjoy international recognition. As another example, Beijing settled its borders with Russia and the USSR's successor states in Central Asia even though these settlements involved large tracts of land that in its view were lost to the Czarist regime under duress. Whether viewed from a geostrategic perspective of protecting China's national security, a *lebensraum* rationale stemming from "lateral pressure" (Choucri and North 1975; Fravel 2010), or Chinese nationalism motivating irredentism, it is puzzling that China has settled its borders with these countries in general accordance with treaties that it perceives to be unjust while deciding to sustain other disputes – especially those involving uninhabited or uninhabitable rocks in the East and South China Seas.

Moreover, and as documented by Taylor Fravel (2008), Beijing has settled its land borders with most of its neighbors (with India as the major exception) and often on terms more favorable to the latter. Although it has decried past "unequal treaties" that forced China to surrender large areas in the Russian Far East and Central Asia, it has not sought to overturn their ownership. As just mentioned, it has instead settled its contemporary borders with its neighbors largely along demarcations provided by these treaties. Hong Kong and Macao are the only two exceptions where Beijing has recovered territories that were once ceded to foreign powers, Britain and Portugal respectively (Taiwan, of course, was taken over by Japan as a result of the Treaty of Shimonoseki in 1895). Finally, even with respect to the maritime cases, Beijing has made previous concessions – such as when it voluntarily turned over the White Dragon Tail (Bailungwei) Island to North Vietnam in 1957. In and of itself, alleged Chinese nationalism or aggrandizement cannot quite explain these phenomena.

A moment's reflection would also suggest that China's national strength does not correlate well with Beijing's decision to initiate accommodative policy or, conversely, to accept military confrontation. China was relatively speaking at its weakest when it entered the Korean War to resist the US. Its military clashes with the USSR in 1969 and, to a lesser extent, its border war with India in 1962 also came at a time when China was diplomatically isolated and faced internal economic and political challenges. As well, regime similarity or ideological affinity cannot easily account for changes in Beijing's bilateral relations with these counterparts. Both the USSR and Vietnam (Beijing had also fought a border war with the latter in 1979) were fellow communist governments and one-time close allies. Beijing and New Delhi also once had warm relations with the proclamation of *Pan Shilla* and a common anticolonial stance in the 1950s. It would appear that Beijing's relations with these countries are subject to reversal without either party in these disputes changing its official ideology or regime character. Therefore, neither of these latter variables can explain why these countries' relations turned from good to bad, and vice versa.

Moreover, contrary to the view that a rising China poses a greater danger to its neighbors, a weakening China or one that is in distress has resorted to force. Indeed, as mentioned previously, when China has used armed force, it has fought or confronted the strongest opponents bordering it (e.g., the USSR, India, Vietnam, and, in the Korean War and crises across the Taiwan Strait, the US). In contrast, in those cases where it has enjoyed the greatest military advantage (e.g., over Hong Kong and Macao as well as when dealing with weaker neighbors such as Afghanistan, Burma, Mongolia, and Nepal), it has refrained from using force. Thus, when Beijing enjoys a relatively large advantage in a contest, it has not been more inclined to use force, as offensive realists would have predicted.

Although pundits and analysts have focused their attention on recent and prospective power shifts favoring China at the expense of its neighbors, this variable should not in and of itself influence the probability of an armed conflict involving China. When one side of a bilateral relationship gains power and the other loses power, these changes in their respective bargaining position should affect the terms of a possible settlement between them but not the probability of their reaching a settlement. The one gaining power should be able to demand a better deal for itself and the one losing power should be disposed to make more concessions. It is not clear why in and of itself, a shift in relative power should increase the risk of war – unless one introduces additional intervening variables such as by arguing that a trend toward greater power asymmetry encourages one side to become greedier and the other side to become more desperate.

As Bruce Bueno de Mesquita (1981b) has argued, whether greater power balance or greater power imbalance is conducive to peace and stability tends to be conditional on one's view about whether these situations will produce greater certainty or uncertainty for decision makers, and whether this certainty or uncertainty is conducive to peace and stability by affecting the pertinent officials' willingness to pursue risky policies. Traditionally, those who advocate a balance of power see uncertainty (about relative power and hence the outcome of a possible conflict) as inclining leaders to avoid risks and thus to promote peace and stability, whereas others who subscribe to the proposition of hegemonic stability and the danger of power transition tend to reach the opposite conclusion (that decision uncertainty encourages leaders to take risks, such as when a rapidly rising latecomer is poised to overtake an incumbent hegemon).

Finally, geography is in itself a constant factor even though changing technologies affecting transportation and communication have had an impact on physical distance. One cannot easily explain why Beijing has been more inclined to settle most of its land borders in contrast to its ongoing disputes over the control of small islands to its east and south (a description that obviously does not fit Taiwan). If one acknowledges that China has traditionally been a land power and that its ability to project power over water has been severely limited in the past, it would have made more sense for Beijing to drive a harder bargain in negotiations about its land borders where it enjoys greater relative power, and it should be more inclined to make concessions in its maritime disputes. Such an explanation based on relative power – especially from the perspective of offensive realism which stresses the importance of infantry (boots on the ground) and the "stopping power of water" (Mearsheimer 2001) – appears to be contradicted by China's recent behavior.

In the jargon of causal attribution, we run the risk of idiosyncrasy or irrelevance when we invoke reasons such as those mentioned above to explain China's dispute behavior. Idiosyncrasy as a source of mistaken inference happens when the same alleged cause (e.g., Chinese nationalism) can produce different outcomes (e.g., the peaceful settlement of some of China's territorial disputes and the violent escalation of others). Irrelevance presents a problem when the same outcome (e.g., violent territorial clashes) can occur both in the presence and absence of an alleged cause (e.g., whether Beijing shares a similar or dissimilar type of regime with its dispute counterpart). As a matter of empirical record, a focus on *just* China's recent maritime disputes presents a biased sample that omits many occasions when it has come to peaceful terms with its neighbors in the demarcation of their mutual borders.

This practice tends to overemphasize China's assertiveness, and overlooks the need for more probing analysis to explain variations in Beijing's behavior. In the parlance of social science, an exclusive focus on those cases where Beijing continues to contest its neighbors' territorial claims – while disregarding other cases where it has settled its frontiers – is tantamount to "selecting on the dependent variable." Because this selection results in giving attention to only those cases where China has a conflict with its neighbors, it cannot obviously explain variations in China's dispute behavior – that is, this approach to analysis is incapable of differentiating these cases from others where Beijing has cooperated to reach border settlements.

Spatial and temporal dependencies

Beijing's various territorial disputes are not independent cases. They tend to be interdependent. Thus, as discussed previously in the context of a country's reputation, what happens in one case can influence the outcome of another case subsequently. Indeed, Fravel's (2008) prior research has argued that Beijing has sought to communicate its intention to reach an accord with one neighbor by settling its borders with another. For instance, when China reached border agreements with Afghanistan, Burma, Nepal, and Mongolia along existing lines of actual control by the two parties and in general conformity with past treaties involving the British or the Russians, it was openly signaling to India and the USSR its willingness to negotiate accords with them on a similar basis. This observation also indicates that territorial disputes can sometimes be multilateral rather than strictly bilateral affairs. There are other significant parties involved, so that, interestingly, border settlement in one case can provide the impetus and precedent for solving others.

China and Japan are of course the principal contestants over the Senkaku/Diaoyu Islands. However, to a lesser extent Taiwan is also involved and the US, due to its defense treaty with Japan, is also an indirect participant. Washington has declared that it takes no position on the competing sovereignty claims being advanced by Japan and China over these contested rock outcroppings but after the latest escalation stemming from China's declaration of an "air defense identification zone" in late November 2013, it has stated clearly and forcefully that it will intervene to support Japan should there be an armed conflict. The mutual defense treaty between the US and Japan provides the basis for this declared policy, which was repeated by high-ranking US officials (such as Vice President Joe Biden and Defense Secretary Chuck Hagel). These high-profile statements removed any deliberate ambiguity that might have been created about Washington's intentions on previous occasions. Beijing naturally objects to this announced US policy, which appears to be contradictory. It expresses its perplexity about Washington's announced commitment to intervene on Japan's behalf while still professing to maintain a neutral stance regarding the eventual legal status of the disputed islands. As noted previously, the US gained control of these islands after World War II. It turned them over to Japan when in 1971 it agreed to return Okinawa to Japanese sovereignty. Both Beijing and Taipei, however, have claimed that according to the Potsdam Declaration, Japan was obliged to give up all those territories that it had conquered prior to World War II. Tokyo contests this interpretation, arguing that the islands in dispute had not belonged to any country until Japan claimed sovereignty over them.

The disputes in the South China Sea encompass a very large area, with Beijing staking a claim marked by its famous line consisting of nine dashes. The focus of contested sovereignty, however, centers on the Spratly archipelago with overlapping claims that also involve Brunei, Malaysia, the Philippines, Vietnam, and Taiwan. Although Hanoi and Taipei both claim the Paracel archipelago (called Xisha or West Sand Islands by the Chinese), Beijing has established physical control of these islands ever since its forces defeated the South Vietnamese in 1974 and took over the Crescent group of islands in this archipelago (in addition to the eastern or Amphitrite group of islands already under its control at that time). The conflict over the Paracels is basically a bilateral contest between China and Vietnam and unless the latter tries to forcibly evict the Chinese currently in control (an unlikely contingency), there is relatively little risk that this dispute will escalate militarily. The Pratas or Dongsha (meaning, in Chinese, East Sand Islands) are controlled by Taiwan. The jurisdictional dispute over these islands is linked to the status for Taiwan itself, and is qualitatively different from those involving the other states. How relations across the Taiwan Strait will be settled in the future holds the key to resolving the status of the Pratas.

This discussion suggests that the ongoing South China Sea disputes refer mainly to competing claims over the Spratlys or Nansha (South Sand Islands in Chinese). Although these claims are sometimes characterized as pitting China against ASEAN, only some members of the latter organization are involved in these disputes and these countries have also advanced competing claims against each other. This phenomenon in turn signifies that ASEAN does not actually present a united front that puts it in opposition to China, even though Vietnam and the Philippines would naturally be interested in rallying this organization's support and in situating their respective disputes with China, the strongest among the claimant states, in a multilateral context. Many ASEAN members do not have a direct stake in the Spratly disputes, and some of them have views that are more aligned with Beijing's than with those of their fellow ASEAN members.

For example, Cambodia declined to issue a joint communiqué on these disputes following its role as the host of the 2012 meeting of ASEAN leaders, thus aligning itself with Beijing's preference not to "internationalize" its disputes with countries such as the Philippines. Significantly, although its claim covers a large area in the South China Sea, China has the least to contest with Brunei and Malaysia, countries whose claims are more in conflict with the Philippines and Indonesia. Because those portions claimed by Malaysia and Brunei are farthest from the reach of Chinese naval power and because these areas are also the least salient to Beijing, these countries are the most probable candidates to receive Beijing's efforts to reach an accommodation. If, as argued previously, physical distance tends to be inversely correlated with a country's power and its felt stake in a dispute, this variable tends to favor Malaysia and Brunei relative to China with respect to those areas being contested by them.

As Sarah Raine and Christian Le Miere (2013: 121) observe, China does not have a physical presence in areas claimed by Malaysia, and only Vietnam and the Philippines occupy islands that the latter country also claims. As for China and Brunei, they appear to have worked out a tacit understanding for mutual accommodation even in the absence of a formal agreement. China has expressed little opposition to Brunei's oil exploration (with Malaysia) in the disputed area, and Brunei has largely accepted China's preference to keep its South China Sea disputes as bilateral rather than multilateral dialogues (Raine and Le Miere 2013: 122). In addition to those ASEAN countries that do not have a direct stake in the South China Sea disputes and that wish to maintain friendly relations with China (e.g., Thailand, Cambodia, Laos, and Burma), Beijing's concessions to Malaysia and Brunei hold the greatest promise to encourage them to break ranks with the other two ASEAN contenders, Vietnam and the Philippines. This consideration points to the potential for Beijing to "peel off" these countries from a possible united front presented by the ASEAN members against China. This proposition concurs with Chien-peng Chung's (2004: 138) observation that Malaysia and Brunei should be the most likely ones to reach accommodation with China because they had claimed the least number of islets and reefs.

The Philippines is weak militarily and it is also quite vulnerable to economic pressure (as evidenced by its decision to apologize and compensate for the killing of a Taiwanese fisherman in a maritime incident in 2013). At the same time, it has been quite active in contesting China's maritime claims. It objected strongly to China's seizure of Mischief or Meiji Reef in 1994, and it engaged China in a naval standoff at the Scarborough Shoal/Huangyan Island in April 2012. In the latter episode, the Philippines had tried to arrest Chinese fishermen in the disputed area, and this attempt brought about counter-intervention by China's coast guard vessels. As already mentioned, the US was deliberately ambiguous about whether its defense treaty with the Philippines would apply to this situation. Manila's action in this episode failed to receive support from ASEAN and was perceived "in some quarters as recklessly escalatory" (Raine and Le Miere 2013: 70). It also aroused Beijing's ire when in January 2013 the Philippines announced its intention to ask the international Arbitral Tribunal to rule on its maritime claims even though Beijing had specifically opted out of the relevant provision for compulsory dispute settlement (Article 298) when agreeing to the UNCLOS (United Nations Convention on the Law of the Sea). Manila's action was perceived by Beijing as a deliberate effort to challenge the legality of China's nine-dash line. In retaliation, Beijing has tried to isolate Manila diplomatically and to coerce it economically. It has deliberately bypassed Manila in its high-level contacts with various ASEAN capitals, and it has brought economic pressure to bear such as by boycotting bananas from the Philippines and curtailing Chinese tourism to that country (Thayer 2012). It is also perhaps not surprising that the Philippines has pursued a more active and overt opposition to Beijing's claim because it has enjoyed long-standing close ties with Washington because of its colonial legacy. Given Manila's likely expectation of US support, it is also the one most likely to hold out in reaching a deal with Beijing among the various contestants in the South China Sea disputes.

Hanoi had agreed with Beijing's sovereignty claims over the Paracels, Pratas, and Spratlys when both countries were allied in their opposition against the US in the 1950s and 1960s. Since then, however, it has retracted this agreement. The two sides have clashed on several occasions. In their most violent confrontation, in 1988, their armed forces fought a pitched battle around Johnson South Reef or Chigua Jiao, resulting in several dozen fatalities. There have been subsequent incidents such as those involving China's interdiction and seizure of Vietnamese fishing vessels in March 2012. More recently in May 2014, the two countries clashed again when China introduced an oil rig into the disputed waters near the Paracels. Their civilian vessels rammed each other (causing one Vietnamese boat to sink), while their respective navy stood guard at a distance. This confrontation set off anti-Chinese riots in Vietnam which turned violent against those businesses and factories suspected to be owned and operated by Chinese investors, causing widespread property damages and several deaths. Beijing responded by evacuating Chinese nationals, and Hanoi acted quickly to end the anti-Chinese protests. Tension deescalated when Beijing withdrew the oil rig from the contested area in July. This latest episode illustrates efforts by both sides to probe and test the other, but also their attempts to contain their conflict from getting out of control.

Vietnam shares a land border with China and is therefore more subject to the reach of China's military forces should its maritime dispute with Beijing escalate to a larger armed conflict. This country also has very dense commercial ties with China and is therefore also vulnerable to Beijing's application of economic pressure. Being an authoritarian country whose leaders tend to be more politically secure than those in Manila, Hanoi is in a better position to reach an accommodation with Beijing without having as much to fear from a domestic backlash. At the same time, as this country becomes less authoritarian or more pluralistic, its leaders will encounter more popular pressure and elite competition, which are likely to limit their ability to make concessions in their foreign conflict.

Obviously, leaders are more reluctant to reach an interstate deal if they believe that they have more to gain politically, or less to lose, by postponing this deal than by accepting it. One of the reasons for delay is to deflect domestic criticisms and to resort to foreign diversion as a way to boost the incumbent officials' domestic political standing. Being more secure in their office tenure, Hanoi's leaders should have less such incentive to prolong a dispute for reasons of domestic partisanship. As hypothesized previously, facing fewer domestic veto groups, these leaders have potentially a larger win set that should facilitate reaching an accord with Beijing. With more intersecting interests with Beijing, there is also the potential for the two parties to undertake logrolling compromises involving trading off these other interests and making side payments to conclude an agreement on their maritime dispute.

Two inferences drawn from the prior discussion suggest that China's dispute with Japan over the Senkaku/Diaoyu Islands in the East China Sea presents the most difficult case for resolution (Arai et al. 2013). Domestic sentiments on both sides are such that their leaders are likely to feel that they will have more to lose from a nationalist backlash by compromising their differences than by continuing their dispute, albeit keeping it from boiling over. Some politicians on both sides may even be motivated to use this dispute for partisan reasons, such as to embarrass or entrap their domestic opponents (such as when Tokyo Governor Shintaro Ishihara campaigned to purchase the contested islands from their private owners). More than the other maritime disputes, it appears that both the Chinese and Japanese win sets are severely constricted by their respective domestic politics. One may also infer from Beijing's past pattern of behavior that it tends to be more inclined to pursue conciliation and make concessions when negotiating with its smaller and weaker neighbors. That is, when Beijing enjoys a large power asymmetry in its favor, it is more accommodating. It appears to be interested in investing in its reputation for not trying to maximize its power advantage in these cases. Conversely, it appears to care more about its reputation for being resolute and "not allowing itself to be pushed around" against those counterparts that can match or even exceed its capabilities. This greater concern for standing one's ground is likely to be reciprocated by Japan, which has territorial disputes with countries other than China. Thus, Tokyo also has a stake in its reputation since it has contested South Korea and Russia's sovereignty over the Dokdo/Takeshima Island and the Southern Kurils/Northern Territories.

The controversy over the Senkaku/Diaoyu Islands illustrates well the effects of historical memories, domestic partisanship, and difficulty in making credible commitments. Many of the depictions circulating in popular media and even in scholarly discussions reflect the contesting sides' attempts to construct and frame policy discourse and influence public opinion. This controversy is typically portrayed in Japan and the West in the context of "China's rise" and "Japan's decline," and often tied to alleged assertive moves or retaliatory steps taken by Beijing, such as its arrest of several Japanese nationals for taking pictures of a restricted military area in China and the temporary interruption of Chinese exports of rare earth to Japan. Linus Hagstrom (2012) has shown some problematic issues in such popular narratives that dominate outside China, specifically in regard to the incident described in the next paragraph. Similarly, A. Iain Johnston (2013) has discussed pervasive characterization of China's more "assertive" foreign policy in 2010, showing that such attributions tend to be poorly defined and deficient in historical context and descriptive accuracy. They nevertheless affect agenda setting for popular discourse on China prevalent in the West.

Two events have particularly roiled Sino-Japanese relations in the recent past. In September 2010, a Chinese trawler collided with two Japanese coast guard vessels. The Japanese arrested the captain of this Chinese trawler and detained him for over two weeks with the declared intention of prosecuting him for "obstructing the duties of public officials" and "illegal fishing." The Chinese interpreted this action as a violation of a tacit agreement reached previously by the two sides to accept the status quo pending final resolution. On previous occasions of such encounters, the Japanese side had evicted Chinese nationals who had entered the contested area. But in this case, the Chinese side saw an escalation by the Japanese side when the latter arrested, detained, and was preparing to prosecute the Chinese captain under Japanese law. Perhaps, the inexperience of Naota Kan's administration (which had only assumed office three months earlier) and the lack of inter-ministerial and center–local coordination on the Japanese side were reasons for those events interpreted by the Chinese as acts of deliberate provocation, inviting them to escalate in turn.

At the same time, whether Kakuei Tanaka and Chou En-lai (and their respective successors) had ever reached a tacit agreement to set aside this sovereignty dispute – that is, to freeze the status quo – for an indefinite future is itself in dispute (e.g., Yang 2013). Beijing has insisted that there was indeed such an understanding whereas Tokyo has denied it (even though one Japanese official, Takakazu Kuriyama, has acknowledged that "top officials of the two countries had reached a tacit agreement" to shelve the island dispute, according to Weiss 2014: 215). Published reports predating the acrimonies of the past few years showed the Chinese side's belief in the existence of an agreement to set aside the dispute for the time being. Thus, Chi-kin Lo (1989: 171) reported that Deng Xiao-ping stated at a press conference held in Tokyo in October 1978 that "the two governments had agreed to shelve the dispute over the Diaoyudao when they established diplomatic relations in 1972, and had reached the same understanding again when they signed the Peace Treaty [in 1978]." According to the *Peking Review* (November 3, 1978: 16; quoted by Lo 1989: 171–172), Deng said that:

It is true that the two sides maintain different views on this question [competing sovereignty claims over the disputed islands] . . . It does not matter if this question is shelved for some time, say, ten years. Our generation is not wise enough to find common language on this question. Our next generation will certainly be wiser. They will certainly find a solution acceptable to all.

The second incident that further escalated Sino-Japanese tension was the purchase of the disputed islands by Yoshihiko Noda's administration from their private Japanese owners in September 2012. This act was presented by Tokyo as an attempt to head off a more dangerous situation if Tokyo Governor Shintaro Ishihara were to acquire these islands and erect structures on them as he had stated his intentions publicly (a contingency that could further escalate Sino-Japanese tension). The Chinese side was suspicious as to whether this purchase was in fact orchestrated by the Japanese government, and was inclined to downplay the role that Japanese domestic politics had played in the denouement. It has contended that a private Japanese company, instead of the central government, could have just as well made the purchase, thus avoiding the appearance of official ownership of the contested islands and implying a *fait accompli* about their legal status. Michael Swaine (2013: 5) remarks that "From the viewpoint of the Chinese government, the Japanese purchase involved the exercise of 'sovereign rights,' and not a mere transfer of 'property rights' (as Tokyo insisted), thus constituting an adverse change in the status quo and hence a violation of the agreement to shelve the sovereignty issue." Naturally, Beijing's suspicion reflects a basic distrust. In its eyes, what credible commitment has Tokyo undertaken to refrain from undertaking future actions that could further reinforce Japan's claim? Future Japanese prime ministers are not bound to leave the disputed islands uninhabited and undeveloped (and thus not to further secure Japan's physical possession and legal position). Would they even one day order Japanese government personnel to be stationed on these disputed islands (Fujihira 2013)?

The preceding paragraph illustrates two important points. First, the distinction between official and unofficial acts may be quite murky. It is possible for a government to mobilize ostensible private groups as a less confrontational and therefore less risky way to publicize or advance its cause. Thus, Chinese fishing trawlers rather than naval vessels have been deployed in this way to deliberately challenge Japan's sovereignty claim over the Senkaku/Diaoyu Islands. At the same time, Beijing has also suspected that nationalist groups in Japan, such as the *Nihon Seinensha*, might have orchestrated its publicity moves (such as building lighthouses on the disputed islands) with the implicit encouragement and perhaps even explicit collusion of government officials. In this way, actors in the domestic and international arenas (Putnam's so-called Level 1 and Level 2 games) can actually work together to reinforce their mutual agenda (Chung 2004: 36, 58).

Second, the recent Sino-Japanese confrontation over the Senkaku/Diaoyu Islands also highlights the importance of credible commitment. As just mentioned, once Japan's government owns these islands, what credible commitment can it make to Beijing not to further entrench its presence on these islands? Southeast Asian countries involved in the South China Sea disputes with Beijing have a similar concern. Once China has secured a foothold in the Spratly archipelago, it may continue to enlarge its encroachments. A recent example of such action to expand and secure China's foothold has taken the form of land reclamation projects to expand the islands (or islets) under its control (e.g., the Fiery Cross Reef/Yongshu Island, and Johnson South Reef/Chigua Jiao), such as to allegedly build an airstrip on one of them. Its intentions are suspect in the eyes of the other contestants in the absence of any credible commitment by Beijing to restrain itself. As another example, Beijing insisted in its border negotiations with Moscow that the latter must first acknowledge the illegality and injustice of past treaties before the two sides could proceed to settle their boundaries on the basis of these very treaties. Understandably, the USSR was reluctant to accept this proposal because this acceptance would expose it to possible Chinese duplicity (what if Moscow were to carry out the first part of the deal, but Beijing reneged on the second part?). This difficulty faced by Beijing in providing credible commitment impeded a deal until it dropped in 1983 its demand that Moscow must first acknowledge the illegitimacy of past treaties and until Mikhail Gorbachev publicly accepted the *Thalweg* principle to settle the two countries' riparian boundaries (Chung 2004; the *Thalweg* is the line of lowest elevation of a stream or valley, providing the legal convention to demarcate boundaries).

As discussed previously, one can propose two competing though not necessarily mutually exclusive hypotheses on reputation. One of these argues that a country can try to use its settlement of or conciliatory behavior in one territorial dispute to communicate reassurance to its counterpart in another dispute. Thus, for instance, Beijing had previously signaled to India and the USSR its willingness to negotiate border agreements with them following generally the respective countries' actual lines of control and along historical demarcations provided by the pertinent treaties. It did so by concluding treaties with Nepal and Mongolia on this basis, thereby creating precedents for possibly undertaking similar efforts with India and the USSR (Fravel 2008). As another example, it can practice self-restraint in governing Hong Kong and Macao as special administrative areas in order to reassure Taipei that it will receive similar treatment if it accepts reunification.

The second proposition contends that a government wants to invest in a reputation for toughness and resolve when it finds itself possibly in several disputes. By dealing firmly with an initial opponent, it hopes to discourage other subsequent challengers. By refusing to compromise with any and all of its opponents, the Habsburg Empire adopted this approach (Treisman 2004). It thus took on "all comers" (it fought the Dutch, the French, and in Italy) whereas, in contrast, Britain was more disposed to conciliate and even join forces with some of its former competitors (e.g., France, Russia, the US) in order to better focus its resources on its principal adversary (Germany). London apparently did not think its accommodation of US regional hegemony in the Western Hemisphere would hurt its reputation for resolve elsewhere, and thus imply its lack of determination to oppose Germany's ambitions.

As already noted, those involved in maritime disputes with China also have disputes with other countries. Do they want to pursue all their disputes concurrently or would they rather make compromises in some of these disputes so that they can better concentrate on a particular one? Disputes that are farther away are less salient. Thus, China's disputes with Brunei and Malaysia are much more amenable to a negotiated settlement than its dispute with Japan over the Senkaku/Diaoyu Islands. From the perspective of at least some of the countries caught up in the maritime disputes in the South China Sea, their own closer neighbors present a more relevant security concern than China, which is farther away. It was not so long ago at the end of the Vietnam War that the threat coming from Hanoi was presented as the public rationale for organizing ASEAN (especially on the part of Vietnam's continental neighbors such as Thailand, Cambodia, and Laos). To the extent that leaders in Kuala Lumpur and Manila perceive themselves to be more immediate rivals, there is likely to be a greater incentive on their part to be the first one to settle with Beijing rather than joining collective action against the latter. The first one to settle is likely to get more favorable terms than the last holdout. One implication of this hypothesis is that there can be a protracted period of negotiation stalemate but this impasse can be followed by a sudden and rapid succession of deals to settle the disputes.

There is in any situation of collective action the temptation to free ride (Olson 1965). The contestant taking on China in the most visible adversarial role will likely focus Beijing's resentment and hostility on itself, while conferring upon the other claimant countries any favorable consequences that are produced by its actions. Thus, Manila's recent actions might have antagonized Beijing to such an extent as to invite Chinese retribution against it while at the same time encouraging Chinese reassurances to the other claimant states. That is, they might have had the effect of getting Beijing to invest in a reputation for being both tougher against it and softer toward others. By similar logic, Beijing's tougher stance against Tokyo may rebound to Russia and South Korea's benefit as the latter two countries also have their own island disputes with Japan. This would be the case if Tokyo decides to accommodate these two other countries in order to better focus its efforts on its dispute with Beijing. Because the countries involved have multilateral disputes, actions taken in one area can affect other relations.

China's past behavior shows that it is quite capable of compromising when it comes to territorial settlements. In general, its approach to the East and South China Sea disputes is reminiscent of its past conduct in managing its other territorial conflicts. "Reactive assertiveness" has been used to characterize its general posture. Trevor Moss (2012a) sums up this disposition in these words, "China doesn't pick fights, but ... if someone picks a fight with China it will offer a forceful response." Echoing a similar view, Michael Swaine and Taylor Fravel (2011: 11) conclude, "As in its approach to the South China Sea, Beijing has not altered its existing strategy in the East China Sea arena, choosing instead to defer settlement and engage in political and diplomatic negotiation while defending its existing claims to disputed territory."

Although Beijing is certainly capable of initiating offensive moves (e.g., by attacking the South Vietnamese in the Paracels in 1974), the characterization of reactive assertiveness argues that it more often escalates a dispute in reaction to what it perceives to be aggressive moves made by its counterparts. It sees itself as a latecomer in the "scramble for the Spratlys," while others have already made first moves to occupy various maritime features and build structures on them. From its perspective, Manila's deployment of its largest naval vessel to arrest Chinese fishermen in the Scarborough Shoal/Huangyan Island incident was a provocation. It also saw the detention of the Chinese trawler captain and the purchase of the Senkaku/Diaoyu Islands by the Japanese government as unilateral changes to the status quo in violation of a prior tacit agreement. Instead of making this purchase itself, Chinese officials have questioned whether the Japanese national government could have acted in a less prejudicial manner such as by encouraging a private corporation (e.g., Toyota, Mitsubishi) to undertake this transaction. Naturally, Beijing's interpretations and perceptions are not generally shared in the Western media where, for example, its declaration of an "air defense identification zone" in November 2013 was presented almost universally as a unilateral action to change the status quo. This impression was created even though Washington, Tokyo, and Seoul had all instituted their own zones previously and by unilateral declaration (US policy, however, does not require foreign aircraft to identify themselves if they do not have a US destination).

With respect to Beijing's declaration of the above-mentioned air defense identification zone, Washington had deliberately shown its objection by flying two unarmed B-52 bombers over this area without announcing their flight to the Chinese authorities. It underscored its point by publicizing this action to the mass media. The propagation of this information is significant in light of my earlier discussion of "tying hands." Even though the Chinese can be expected to have noticed the presence of these US aircraft in the zone and in fact Beijing said that its personnel had monitored their flight, this information would not have the same significance if it were kept a secret among the relevant officials on both sides. Making it publicly available and circulating it widely gives credibility to the US intention to support Japan. Therefore, Washington wanted not only to inform Beijing, but its message was also very much intended to reassure Tokyo and signal to the other Asian capitals. To reinforce this message, several high-ranking US officials stated publicly that the US–Japan defense treaty would come into effect should there be a Sino-Japanese military conflict over the Senkaku/Diaoyu Islands. If Beijing had intended to test the US alliance commitment to Japan, Washington's response in this episode has provided a clear answer.

It is, however, interesting to note that the US has nevertheless asked its civilian aircraft to notify the Chinese authorities when entering the air defense identification zone announced by Beijing, professing travelers' safety to be its paramount concern. Australia, Singapore, Thailand, and Taiwan have also given similar instructions to their airlines, whereas Japan and South Korea have told their airlines to disregard the Chinese request for voluntary identification when their aircraft enter this zone. Whether or not intended by Beijing as an information-seeking probe, its announcement of this zone has forced the other countries to clarify their intentions. Their responses in this episode can provide meaningful indications of how they are likely to act in a possible future Sino-Japanese showdown. Therefore, the actual military significance of China's declared zone is probably far less important than the relevant states' communication of their current stance and perhaps even their likely future alignment in the larger regional picture.

To characterize China's posture as reactive assertiveness is to in effect acknowledge that China does not always control the initiative. After all, it takes at least two sides to have a dispute. Both participants must feel strongly about their respective cause, suggesting that neither has a mono-poly on nationalism. For obvious reasons, the weaker side has a greater incentive to escalate a dispute in order to publicize its plight, focus international attention, and recruit foreign help. It behaves in this way in order to escape from a highly lopsided match. This tendency seems quite natural. Thus, China's dispute counterparts do not always act with only Beijing in mind. Their conduct may be aimed at seeking to engage the US, and to test, probe, and secure Washington's commitment. In turn, the US is clearly aware of the competing concerns of supporting its allies in Manila, Taipei, and Tokyo on the one hand, and the danger of entrapment by them for these allies' own agenda on the other hand (Snyder 1997).

Even a brief survey of East Asia's various maritime disputes calls attention to the fact that they involve both democratic and authoritarian regimes, and also countries that have made gains in their international stature and capabilities in recent years and others that have suffered relative decline. Certainly, many of the participants in these disputes have economies that are highly interdependent. Although the pertinent maritime disputes are obviously too small in number for statistical analy-sis, it is apparent that democratization, bilateral power asymmetry, and economic interdependence have not prevented their occurrence.

Beyond reactive assertiveness

Whether one agrees or not with the characterization of Beijing's approach to its maritime disputes thus far as reactive assertiveness, there is a larger and more elusive theoretical and policy question that looms. What will be China's intentions when it gains even more power – perhaps to the point when it can act unilaterally and decisively to impose settlements on its weaker neighbors? It is one thing for Chinese leaders to assume a low and even essentially defensive profile and to bide their time when they still lack the requisite capabilities to throw their weight around. It is a different matter after they actually come to possess these capabilities. Discourse on "China's threat" and on the power-transition theory more generally of course attends to future Chinese behavior when other countries may be in a much weaker position to check Chinese power (e.g., Fogel 2010; Friedberg 2011).

How Beijing has handled its territorial disputes in the past may provide outside analysts a window to gauge its general disposition in conducting China's foreign relations. There are, however, important differences among these disputes that bear on this attempt to infer Chinese intentions and motivations. Taiwan is in a category of its own as the contest over this island's sovereignty has been presented by Beijing as a matter of China's internal affairs – and this contest has been largely recognized by the international community, including the US, as such. Whether one labels this contest as an unfinished civil war, "homeland defense," or a "core interest" of China's, Beijing's conduct in this case may be perceived by most other countries as not indicative of its foreign policy intentions or motivations in general (Kang 2007). That is to say, most other countries may very well be inclined to see the Taiwan case as distinct and therefore not necessarily useful for making predictions about Beijing's behavior elsewhere.

Whereas China's dispute with Taiwan may be accorded this unique status by many other countries, this is not true of its other maritime disputes. Both by Beijing's own account and in the perceptions of other countries, these other disputes involve interstate disagreements. That is, the legal status of the disputing parties as sovereign political entities is not in question. This fact is significant in that it implies that Beijing faces a higher standard of scrutiny for its conduct in these other cases. If it were to resort to force in these latter cases, this behavior would be more likely to be construed as a generalizable indication of its aggressive disposition, whereas international opinion may be more permissive when it comes to Beijing's use of force against Taiwan to the extent that the latter contest is accepted to fall within China's domestic jurisdiction.

The logic of this reasoning in turn introduces two implications. First, precisely because Beijing may be given greater benefit of the doubt in its conduct in the Taiwan dispute, its self-restraint in this case will be more remarkable. *Ceteris paribus*, if China refrains from using force in dealing with Taiwan even when it is likely to suffer less severe reputation repercussions, this behavior is informative about its character. This disclosure gains more credibility if Beijing's self-restraint continues in the face of its accumulating coercive capabilities. That is, if Beijing continues to eschew the use of force even after gaining an increasingly large military advantage over Taipei, this self-restraint will be even more remarkable with the passage of time. There will of course always be uncertainties in making such inferences about a powerful country's intentions and motivations in its relations with a recalcitrant, even sometimes hostile, neighbor. It would be useful to consider historical and geostrategic parallels to introduce some benchmark to assess and compare Beijing's conduct. How has the US behaved toward Cuba, and Turkey toward Cyprus? There has been far more accommodation and rapprochement across the Taiwan Strait than in the latter two cases.

Second and as explained already, the reputation cost to Beijing will be higher if it uses force in its interstate disagreements. In such an event other countries will have greater misgivings about its general intentions and motivations, especially if this force is directed against the smaller and weaker contestants. Even when a tense situation fails to reach the actual use of armed forces, the identity of the other party engulfed in a confrontation with China is an important consideration. One may reach different inferences about Beijing's intentions and motivations, depending on whether it picks a confrontation with Brunei, Malaysia, the Philippines, or even Vietnam – as opposed to, say, Japan. Relative size, historical experience, and physical distance would all suggest that China has little to fear from the former countries. It would be far more of a stretch for Beijing to claim that its vital security interests are threatened in disputes with these countries than in its contest with Japan.

Therefore, if Beijing were to escalate militarily its disputes with the Southeast Asian countries, this behavior would be a more ominous harbinger of its aggressive agenda than if its opposite number were Japan. Put differently, one could more plausibly argue that Washington was interested in defending its national security when it blockaded Cuba for the announced purpose of evicting the Soviet missiles there in 1962. Washington's agenda could not be as easily justified when the US invaded small, weak neighbors such as Grenada, Panama, and the Dominican Republic – countries that cannot plausibly be argued to threaten its national security. In short, how a powerful country deals with a vulnerable, even defenseless, neighbor can be highly informative of its intentions and motivations. How does it act when it does not have to worry about other countries pushing back? One's character is more likely to be revealed when one can act with relative impunity. When a country is truly powerful, even peerless, others are less able to restrain it. It will have to restrain itself – and this restraint is most likely to be shown in how it deals with its weak but unfriendly neighbors.

In contrast to China's other maritime disputes, Taiwan obviously presents a much larger piece of real estate. This island has a large resident population and a quite consequential and vibrant economy on the world stage. These factors naturally complicate Beijing's efforts to seek reunification. As already mentioned, it has to try hard to reassure the people on Taiwan and win their hearts and minds. From the perspective of China's other neighbors, the prospective reunification of Taiwan with China raises the specter of adding to the latter's already substantial power base – or as a traditional Chinese saying would put it, giving wings to a tiger. From Beijing's perspective, this concern has evidently motivated foreign support for Taiwan's *de facto* independence among those who want to check China's ascent. This interpretation suggests that compared to Beijing's other maritime disputes, Taiwan is more important to China for a host of reasons, both tangible and intangible ones. This importance stems from this island's geostrategic location, its political symbolism, and its power gains to scale for China. Precisely for these reasons, there is also a stronger impulse for some countries to frustrate and resist Beijing's efforts to absorb Taiwan.

In contrast to Taiwan, the atolls involved in China's other maritime disputes are largely uninhabited and even uninhabitable. These land features are less valuable than the seas surrounding them both in terms of the security of international navigation and the promise of ocean resources such as fish stocks and mineral deposits. As mentioned earlier, disputes about tangible resources should be easier to resolve than disputes involving intangible values. Negotiations to provide equal access to and equitable distribution of tangible resources should be easier to undertake, and the terms of a settlement should be easier to monitor and enforce. This observation in turn implies that the South China Sea disputes should be more amenable to an amicable and equitable compromise resolution. That such resolution has not yet been achieved obviously means that the parties cannot yet agree on the terms of a settlement. China is evidently not the only one to accept "wait and see," as the other contestants appear also to be inclined to hold out for a better deal in the future.

Naturally, the contestants cannot all be correct in their expectation of improving their relative bargaining strength in the future. So what is likely to dispose some of them to wait rather than to make a deal now? One plausible reason is that they lack confidence in the enforceability of a deal. Another plausible reason is that the domestic costs of accepting a deal now outweigh those of waiting. Paradoxically, precisely because the relevant capitals do not see their disputes to be fraught with the danger of unwanted and unexpected escalation, they lack a sense of urgency to address the issues. This lack of urgency makes putting up with the costs of a deadlock more acceptable. Naturally, such an attitude may be based on complacency and false confidence, as attested by British views prior to the Falklands/Malvinas war.

When Beijing asserted its claim over the South China Sea by drawing a line of nine dashes over a large expanse of this area, this claim aroused consternation in other capitals and engendered concerns about its intentions. Beijing's claim has been kept deliberately vague as there are questions about whether it applies only to the waters surrounding the land features being claimed or whether it covers the entire ocean area encompassed by the nine-dash line. The southern tip of this line lies far away from China's coastline; it comes near the coastal waters of Indonesia and Brunei. As just implied, however, China's demarcation may just represent an initial move staking out a maximalist position that is subject to adjustment in subsequent negotiations. Beijing's claim (represented by the nine-dash line) was presented officially to the international community in response to a joint submission by Vietnam and Malaysia to the United Nations that staked out these countries' respective claims.

To the extent that Beijing's past approach to negotiating its boundaries provides a guide for predicting its future behavior, the prospects for it to compromise in the South China Sea are substantial. Indeed, there are already precedents for it to agree to joint undertakings with other countries to survey and explore the ocean's resources. Beijing's past practice in settling its land borders has been generally accommodative when dealing with its smaller and weaker neighbors, and it has typically taken a tougher stance when dealing with its bigger and stronger counterparts. If this pattern continues, we can expect Beijing to be more inclined to settle its South China Sea disputes on an equitable basis and even on terms more favorable to the other claimant states. In contrast, the contested status of the Senkaku/Diaoyu Islands will be more intractable and difficult to resolve. Beijing is likely to be more adamant and less yielding in its relations with Tokyo. This latter dispute is more likely to be "put on hold."

As already mentioned, with the significant exception of Taiwan, the islands (or islets) being contested by China are less important than the seas surrounding them. Even the ocean's resources, such as its rumored mineral and hydrocarbon deposits, seem less important than the safety of shipping access, or China's Sea Lines of Communication. The Chinese economy is heavily dependent on foreign commerce and an overwhelming portion of its imports and exports travel by the shipping lanes of the South and East China Seas. Although it is quite literally unthinkable that any country would contemplate launching an invasion of the Chinese mainland (to in effect repeat Japan's disastrous experience in the decades before 1945), one can more easily imagine China being subjected to naval interdiction and an economic blockade. Worries about being denied their overseas markets and supplies of foodstuffs and strategic materials were very much on the minds of German and Japanese leaders in their fateful decision processes leading to World War I and II, respectively.

The US and its allies are in control of the world's strategic points of seaborne traffic, including the Panama and Suez Canals, the Straits of Dardanelles, Hormuz, Gibraltar, and Magellan, and, for China, especially the Straits of Malacca and Tsushima. The latter two straits are dominated by preponderant US air and naval capabilities in addition to the military assets of US allies. Their narrow passages are obvious choke points that could threaten an overwhelming amount of the shipping destined for or departing from China. From Beijing's perspective, they represent the two anchors of a formidable ocean barrier, one that is further buttressed by Taiwan in the middle. China is hemmed in by a string of naval and air forces deployed by the US and its formal or informal allies in forward positions that follow the entire length of China's coastline and often within close distance of it.

Chinese analysts have pointed to two such island chains, with the first formed by the Kurils, the Japanese archipelago, the Ryukyus (including Okinawa and the Senkaku/Diaoyu Islands), Taiwan, the Philippines, and Borneo, and the second one extending farther to the east from Japan, connecting it with the Bonins, Marianas, Carolines, and Indonesia. To the extent that Vietnam has made competing claims for the Paracels and Spratlys, China faces a further constraint in the Gulf of Tonkin and the South China Sea more generally.

Aaron Friedberg (2011: 228) has described China's security predicament in these words:

In the event of a crisis or war, the United States and its partners could seize or sink Chinese commercial vessels at critical chokepoints or on the high seas, and there would be very little that Beijing could do about it. Because of its rapidly growing need for imported oil and other raw materials, the great bulk of which reach it by water, China is already vulnerable to the effects of a naval blockade, and it will become even more so as its economy grows.

Friedberg goes on to remind his readers the experience of Germany during World War I, when its economy was hobbled by the British navy. Washington has often indicated that the US has a paramount interest in maintaining free, unhindered shipping, including the passage of naval vessels, in international waters. In light of this discussion, Beijing should have no less a concern for the freedom of navigation, as the danger that its access to foreign markets and its import of vital resources could be subjected to naval interdiction is a far more palpable threat to its national security than any possibility of a direct physical assault on the Chinese homeland. At the same time, it understands that Washington's support for unhindered shipping, including the passage of naval vessels, is not absolute and unqualified – as attested by US actions to blockade Cuba in 1962 and to "neutralize" the Taiwan Strait in 1951. China's maritime claims should thus be seen in this broader security context of Beijing seeking to break out of a seaward confinement.

Concluding comments

One major and clear conclusion from Fravel's (2008) study of China's past behavior in its border disputes (involving both maritime as well as land frontiers) is that Beijing has shown a strong disposition to delay and postpone a definitive resolution rather than seeking to impose a settlement by resort to arms. It has certainly used armed forces in some of these disputes, such as those involving India, the USSR, and Vietnam. But as Fravel has shown persuasively, Beijing's resort to force has usually been a response to other countries' assertive moves intended to change the status quo. Moreover, this decision to use force has typically reflected a perception that China's bargaining position in a conflict has eroded, that is, it has corresponded with Beijing's self-perception of increased weakness and vulnerability rather than improved strength. With respect to its contested sovereignty in the maritime domain, Beijing has moved to forestall or redress what it perceives to be the other claimant states' earlier attempts to alter a situation, such as the scramble by Vietnam and the Philippines to seize various features in the Spratly archipelago, Japan's arrest and detention of the captain of a Chinese trawler and its purchase of the Senkaku/Diaoyu Islands from their private owners, and Taiwan's gradual and repeated moves toward *de jure* independence (especially during Chen Shui-bian's administration). Although one may question the validity of these Chinese perceptions, that these views are held by Beijing's officials will naturally influence their policy conduct.

Beijing's general inclination toward a defensive and reactive posture corresponds to the fact that it has in the past lacked the requisite capabilities to enforce its maritime claims. Whether this inclination is due to this lack of capabilities or due to its inherent disposition will become clearer as China acquires a stronger military (especially naval forces). The latter development will give China the wherewithal to challenge and even evict the other contestants from the disputed islands and areas surrounding them. If Beijing continues to refrain from a temptation to impose a unilateral settlement by force even after it has gained much greater relative capabilities, this tendency will strengthen the argument that its prior restraint is more a reflection of its modest intention than of its weak capabilities. As such, this pattern will contradict the proposition of offensive realism, which claims that all states will be motivated by greed and seek to aggrandize when given the wherewithal. One hint pointing to whether Beijing belongs to the revisionist (or greedy) type of states or to the status-quo type comes from its past behavior: it has generally refrained from engaging in opportunistic behavior such as trying to maximize its territorial gains when its opponents in these disputes have been weakened on the battlefield or besieged by domestic problems (again Beijing's 1974 campaign to seize the western Paracels from Saigon provides an instance contradicting this generalization).

One implication follows from this line of interpretation: contrary to conventional renditions that cast Beijing in the role of a challenger, China has often been engaging in its own deterrence against attempts by rival claimants perceived by it to be altering the status quo unilaterally. In undertaking this policy, Beijing has usually been the defender, and has been generally disposed to put aside these disputes in conducting its relations with the other claimant states rather than seeking confrontations with them. To the extent that its policy is successful, these various disputes (as well as the one over China's land border with India) should resemble the dynamics of punctuated equilibrium.

This process is characterized by a prolonged period of seeming stasis that consists of only very slow and small changes. These minor incremental changes can, however, accumulate over time and when a catalyst presents itself, there can be a sudden major transformation of the situation. Past research on enduring rivalries, for example, shows that these conflict relations can last a long time until they are altered by a dramatic event such as a defeat in foreign war and/or a domestic regime change. A breakthrough, such as agreeing to a peace accord or border settlement, is more likely to follow in the wake of a major war or domestic regime change (such as with the resolution of controversies over the Svalbard archipelago and the Beagle Channel islands). For now, Beijing is willing to bide its time and "play nice" (Fravel 2012). Seen from a slightly different angle, one can ask what events would likely alter Beijing's heretofore basic strategy of wait and see, which inclines it to put off the resolution of its maritime disputes for the time being. What events could incline Beijing's leaders to abandon this strategy in favor of a more confrontational approach seeking to break the current impasse even at the risk of a military clash?

China has been more inclined to adopt a confrontational posture involving the use of force when it finds itself in a weakened or more vulnerable position. In the parlance of prospect theory (Kahneman and Tversky 1979, 2000), Chinese leaders are more likely to use force when they perceive themselves in the domain of an actual or impending loss. A preventive motivation, stemming from an urgent sense of desperation to arrest an unfavorable trend, inclined German and Japanese leaders to gamble on initiating two world wars (e.g., Copeland 1996, 2000).

Because it is unlikely that any Asian country will be able to militarily outmuscle China in its maritime disputes, the impetus for a revision in China's traditional policy posture is likely to originate from two other sources. First, because the US is the only country that currently enjoys a military superiority over China (an advantage that is likely to last for at least the next two decades), the extent of and manner in which the US may become involved in China's maritime disputes are pertinent to this line of inquiry. US involvement in the defense of an ally in such a dispute could put China in a domain of loss. Second, China's own domestic developments could create a crisis that inclines its leaders to become more desperate and consequently more risk acceptant. Mass disaffection due to economic distress or official corruption could put incumbent officials in such a domain of loss, and thus dispose them to initiate or accept a foreign confrontation for diversionary reasons. More intense competition among elite factions, making incumbent officials more politically insecure, could also precipitate a reanalysis of China's heretofore policy of biding time and putting off a definitive resolution of its maritime disputes.

The politics of democratization, as discussed earlier, can have the general effect of increasing elite competition and causing officials to align their policies more in line with mass attitudes, which tend to be more nationalistic and bellicose than elite views. By definition, democratization constrains the discretion of officials and increases the number of veto groups whose consent, or at least acquiescence, would be needed to reach foreign accords. Naturally, democratization and intra-elite competition can also affect politics inside the other contesting countries, such as by encouraging popular sentiments favoring independence on Taiwan or giving greater voice to nationalist groups in Japan, Vietnam, and the Philippines. The potential for such cross-border interactive effects argues that the escalation or settlement of disputes is hardly a unilateral matter within the exclusive control of either Chinese leaders or the leaders of their foreign counterparts. As discussed previously, the alignment or misalignment of domestic conditions on both sides of a dispute influences the confluence of events that can serve as the background variables for an outbreak of hostilities, or a window of opportunity to reach a peaceful settlement. As was also mentioned previously, politically secure leaders can generally be expected to have an easier time overcoming domestic opposition and reaching out to their foreign counterparts, making bold concessions in order to enhance the prospect of an accord. Conversely, politically insecure leaders are more likely to engage in diversionary attempts to exploit foreign confrontations for the sake of bolstering their domestic popularity.

7   Conclusion

When the invading troops landed, they declared their mission to be the liberation of the islanders. After their victory, however, this declared intention was reversed. The invading troops were American rather than Chinese, and the islands in question were Cuba and the Philippines. After evicting the Spaniards, the victorious Americans restricted the former's sovereignty severely (including claiming Guantanamo, which continues to this day to be US territory) and waged an anti-insurgency campaign that conquered the latter as an outright colony.

In 1895, Washington successfully coerced London to accept the Monroe Doctrine and to submit the boundary dispute between British Guiana and Venezuela to international arbitration. As a result of the Spanish-American War three years later (1898), the US also acquired Puerto Rico and Guam in addition to the Philippines. These events were preceded in 1893 by the overthrow of Queen Liliuokalani by American plantation owners in the Hawaiian archipelago, which was also annexed by the US in 1898. In 1903 the US navy intervened to support Panamanian rebels wishing to secede from Colombia, and this secession in turn enabled Washington to gain the right to build the Panama Canal. A zone bordering this canal became sovereign US territory. Occurring at a time when the US was a rising power, these events provide a historical context and benchmark for assessing China's conduct today. They suggest a far greater revisionist impulse and expansionist agenda than one may infer from China's conduct thus far. The pattern of US behavior indicates more clearly offensive or acquisitive intentions than China's behavior, for which strong defensive reasons are likely motivations as well.

The geostrategic position faced by the US in the late 1800s and early 1900s was far more benign than the security environment China faces today. With the defeat of the Spaniards and the decision by the British to retrench, the Americans were able to achieve regional hegemony in the Western Hemisphere. They were able to dominate the Caribbean and the Gulf of Mexico, and both US coasts, facing the Atlantic and the Pacific respectively, were not in any danger of being blockaded by a hostile navy.

195

As described in the last chapter, China confronts a more challenging maritime environment. It is hemmed in by island chains controlled by the US and its allies, often within close physical proximity to its coastline. The geography of China's maritime environment is such that any attempt by Beijing to break out of this confinement will impinge on the interests of others and will encounter objections from one or more of its neighbors, as shown by the protests against its intention to institute an air defense identification zone in the East China Sea in late November 2013. This move was criticized by not only the US and Japan (even though they had also instituted these zones), but also South Korea, Taiwan, Australia, and the Southeast Asian states. The habitual reference by international relations scholars to the security dilemma – that one country's attempt to enhance its security necessarily causes another to become less secure – is especially pertinent in this situation. This observation in turn suggests that the US and other countries can with a reasonable degree of confidence count on China's various maritime neighbors to mobilize of their own accord to oppose any perceived unilateral attempt by this country to alter the status quo. As a corollary, China will have to try harder to reassure its neighbors of its peaceful intentions simply because of its geostrategic circumstances.

Although it is almost universally agreed that China's capabilities have grown in the past decades, there is no such consensus that its goals have expanded. One can argue that Beijing's articulation of its objectives in its territorial or sovereignty disputes has been remarkably consistent over time. These objectives, such as with respect to Taiwan and the East and South China Sea islands, have not changed – but China now has more ability to back up its claims whereas it lacked such ability previously (indeed, the nine-dash line outlining China's claim in the South China Sea was first introduced by the Kuomintang in 1947 when it still ruled the mainland). Does this situation make China revisionist (Odgaard 2013)? It shouldn't if this term (revisionism) is used to describe a situation whereby a country expands its goals as it gains more power. Beijing's sovereignty claims in the East and South China Sea disputes have remained remarkably consistent over time (e.g., Lo 1989). Moreover, Chinese foreign policy in recent years has generally shown continuity with the past rather than breaking with tradition in a more assertive direction (e.g., Johnston 2013).

Revisionism, however, may be appropriately applied if this term is meant to suggest that Beijing aspires to recover from China's historical humiliations and restore its standing as a great power. Such an aspiration would necessarily suggest questioning and even seeking to alter the status quo. As a latecomer that has been presented a series of historical *faits accomplis*, Beijing is naturally disinclined to endorse the sanctity of the status quo. In its eyes, the maintenance of stability – advocated as a priority by countries such as the US – should not necessarily trump other values such as its perceptions of justice and equity. In efforts to frame public discourse, Beijing feels aggrieved because the status quo often freezes it out of a situation and its counterparts often decline to negotiate with it. For instance, Tokyo refuses to even acknowledge that there is a dispute over the Senkaku/Diaoyu Islands, and Taiwan has been reluctant to enter into political negotiations with China. When Beijing takes actions to force the other side to pay attention to its claims, these actions are often seen as threatening and unilateral moves to change the status quo. Yet putting up with the status quo would be from Beijing's perspective tantamount to accepting the other side's position. This predicament is reminiscent of the situation facing the Argentines when they dealt with the British over the status of the Falklands/Malvinas. When things were quiet, London and the Kelpers saw no reason to make concessions, but when Buenos Aires turned up the heat, the other parties objected to negotiating under pressure.

Beijing has sometimes clearly gone on the offensive, so that the generalization of reactive assertiveness does not always apply. For instance, it acted opportunistically when it evicted the South Vietnamese from the Paracels (thus, China is also quite capable of creating a *fait accompli*). When it finds itself in an advantageous position, Beijing can also reject a request from the other side to open a negotiation to alter the existing situation. This said, Beijing has also acted in the opposite way, when it turned over the Bailungwei Island to the North Vietnamese in 1957. Naturally, just labeling a country as being revisionist or status-quo oriented is too simplistic as all countries are quite capable of playing both offense and defense, and sometimes both simultaneously, as they seek to adapt to their strategic circumstances. Their behavior can be highly dependent on the issue area, that is, on whether they command large advantages in the existing institutions or have to pay high adjustment costs to alter the current way of conducting affairs. This behavior can be highly varied and evolve over time for countries such as China and the US concerning issues such as the use of force in interstate relations, nuclear non-proliferation, climate change, and financial regulation (Foot and Walter 2011). A country can therefore be revisionist in some issue areas and status-quo oriented in others.

It is also almost a truism to say that a country's future intentions will be shaped by its circumstances – including how others have acted toward it. This line of reasoning in turn raises the question of why China and its counterparts in their maritime disputes appear willing to accept an impasse rather than seeking an early deal. Why would both sides feel that it would be more advantageous or at least less costly to delay rather than settle now?

It is possible, for example, that a settlement has thus far eluded the disputing countries because their leaders have discrepant expectations about how their bargaining position will change in the future. Both sides to a dispute may expect ongoing power shifts will enable them to gain more favorable settlement terms in the future. Even when they expect China's relative power to grow, China's counterparts can still hold the view that the US will continue to maintain its power edge and to offset China's growing capabilities by tilting in their favor. It is also possible to imagine that even if China's capabilities continue to grow, Beijing's disposition to use them may continue to be constrained, including by its own calculations of the benefits of self-restraint.

To the extent that the future is inherently difficult to predict, the respective leaders' time horizon and risk propensity present pertinent considerations. Leaders with a long time horizon are likely to be patient and inclined to hold out for better terms in the distant future, whereas those who are disposed to discount future returns in favor of current returns will act in the opposite way. One may hypothesize that regular electoral cycles and term limitations tend to induce a shorter time horizon for leaders in democracies compared to their authoritarian peers. As for risk propensity, leaders who find themselves in the domain of gain are more likely to act cautiously and even conservatively, whereas those who are in the domain of loss are more likely to gamble in the hope of recovering their losses (Kahneman and Tversky 1979, 2000). This generalization implies that politically insecure leaders and those whose administration or country is facing a serious setback are more disposed to pursue risky policies. Conversely, leaders of a country that is making relative power gains are more inclined to eschew such policies. This proposition in turn means that a declining China and one whose leaders are besieged by domestic crises is more likely to escalate foreign conflicts than a China that is growing in power and one whose leaders are self-confident and have a strong grip on power.

China's counterparts may also be of the mind that any deal struck will be difficult to enforce. This concern about defection can stand in the way of an agreement being reached in the first place. Thus, until they can be more confident about China's commitment they will be reluctant to commit themselves. Democratic regimes have more transparent political processes than authoritarian regimes, and this transparency discloses useful information to foreigners about the democracies' intentions and hence the credibility of their policy commitments (Fearon 1994a; Kydd

2005). Moreover, political opposition groups and independent observers in democracies serve as important watchdogs that increase the political costs for those leaders who fail to honor their promises (Schultz 2001). These features enhance democratic leaders' ability to reassure foreigners about their sincerity – that is, for democratic leaders to demonstrate the credibility of their announced commitments. This is so because democratic leaders are more likely to be sanctioned by their own public or their political opposition if they renege on their announced policies. Authoritarian leaders' announced policies are in contrast less credible because they are less likely to be held accountable by powerful domestic groups (even though policy failures can also be very costly for these leaders as they can also be censured by their powerful domestic stakeholders).

These features should contribute to dispute settlement to the extent that China becomes more democratic in the future. At the same time and as mentioned previously, political decentralization and the introduction of a larger number of heterogeneous groups imply that the democratization process may produce a smaller win set for reaching agreements with foreigners. After all, those groups that can challenge a dictator's negotiation with foreigners are fewer and possibly weaker in autocracies, and a dictator thus has less to worry about domestic opposition to ratification.

Finally, other countries may be reluctant to settle their respective disputes with China if they believe that the prospective domestic costs for gaining acceptance of such a deal will become lower in the future. The principal–agent problem suggests that even though it may be in the interest of a country to settle its dispute, the incumbent leaders may be reluctant to do so because this dispute creates a partisan advantage. Thus, for reasons of domestic politics, incumbent officials may decide that it is more advantageous to keep a dispute alive rather than burying it. Until recently, the protracted US-Cuban feud may be an example of such incentives at work on both sides. The same dynamic helps to explain that leaders sometimes postpone terminating foreign disputes until they become insulated from a domestic backlash, such as when a US president is in his second term of office. For risk-averse leaders, the prospective costs of trying to conciliate with a foreign adversary and then encountering a failure by this adversary to reciprocate their overture can be very costly politically (Colaresi 2004). If leaders on both sides avoid undertaking such overtures, then a conflict can drag on for a long time.

The various hypotheses presented above are of course not mutually exclusive. Moreover, there is no reason to expect that they should be equally applicable to all the parties involved in China's maritime disputes. For instance, prospective domestic ratification costs are likely to be a more pertinent consideration for a democracy with competitive politics than for an authoritarian leader with a strong grip on power. Similarly, expectations about the effects of China's power and the offsetting influence of US capabilities will presumably differ according to a country's physical distance from and economic dependency on China and its historical ties with the US (such as Vietnam and Taiwan compared to Japan and the Philippines). Naturally, timing and sequence can matter, in the sense that the one to first settle with China will be least able to draw on precedents to judge Beijing's negotiation approach but is most likely to gain more favorable terms because of the advertisement value that its settlement promises to Beijing. Conversely, the last holdout will have most information about Beijing's capabilities and intentions (including its prior record of honoring its commitments), but it will presumably be most likely left to negotiate with China in a bilateral context without the support of others who would have already settled their disputes with Beijing. This holdout's claims may be also compromised by these prior settlements to the extent that China is not the only country involved in their territorial disputes; it thus runs the risk of being cut out of a deal now that the other contestants have come to an agreement without its participation.

I have hypothesized earlier that Beijing's prior behavior implies that it is more likely to settle disputes with the smaller, weaker, and more distant counterparts than others that are bigger, stronger, and nearby. Thus, the probability of Beijing settling its maritime disputes with Brunei and Malaysia should be higher than with Japan, and the former countries are more likely to receive favorable terms in a negotiated settlement. One may also infer from Fravel's (2008) research that Beijing will attach a higher priority to addressing its domestic challenges (whether economic or political) than to settling its border disputes at the cost of escalating international tension. It may be more forthcoming to settle these disputes when it has to attend to pressing domestic problems. Chinese leaders have historically emphasized responding to internal disorder (*neiluan*) before dealing with external disaster (*waihuo*). Thus, one may expect these moments to create a window of opportunity for China's counterparts to reach an agreement with Beijing. This said, Chinese leaders may also be acutely sensitive to attempts by their counterparts, especially the bigger and stronger ones, to exploit their country's insecurity during its times of distress. Such perceived attempts to take advantage of Chinese vulnerability are likely to motivate Beijing to adopt a more adamant stance and to push back harder if it feels challenged. Beijing's reactive assertiveness fits this motivation. Consequently, periods of domestic uncertainties and difficulties are likely to be occasions for Beijing to undertake conciliatory moves to settle its border disputes or, alternatively, for it to engage in forceful deterrence against others trying to change the status quo.

Naturally, the very ideas of reactive assertiveness and military deterrence imply that China does not have unilateral control over the timing or probability of détente or escalation. The other party in a relationship also has a say in this matter. Paul Schroeder (1994) has studied how the smaller or weaker European states responded to Napoleon's policies. He shows that their responses were heterogeneous and did not always follow the realist dictum of balancing against a rising and expansionist power. Some of France's neighbors sought to bandwagon with it, others accommodated it, and still others sought to "hide" from or "transcend" their security challenges. Balancing against France was but one of their responses and it did not come about until relatively late, after Napoleon's incessant aggression left his neighbors little choice but to fight back. His overreaching played a large role in motivating the victims of his aggression to finally form a countervailing coalition against him. These remarks argue that how China's neighbors respond to China's rise will also depend on how China acts toward them. Their response is not preordained.

Acknowledging that China's neighbors, including those involved in border disputes with it, can respond to its rise in a variety of ways, rather than similarly as predicted by balance of power theory, does not imply that analysts are bereft of predictive generalizations. From research by scholars such as Huth and Allee (2002), one may hypothesize that politically secure leaders are in a better position to make peace overtures to their foreign counterparts and to gain ratification for deals that they have negotiated with the latter. A corollary of this hypothesis is that politically insecure (or unpopular) leaders are more inclined to resort to foreign confrontation in order to divert domestic attention (such as in the case of the Argentine junta in the Falklands/Malvinas War). This diversionary motivation may be especially powerful for politicians in democracies when they are competing for public support in closely contested elections. If so, these are also the most likely occasions for Beijing's reactive assertiveness. Conversely, a breakthrough to gain a negotiated settlement is more likely shortly after there has been a leadership succession, especially a landslide electoral victory, in China's counterpart country. A recently elected leader will enjoy a honeymoon period and perhaps a strong popular mandate from a decisive electoral victory, especially if this successful candidate is ineligible to seek political office again. This person would be in a better position to reach out to his/her foreign counterparts and offer terms that would be acceptable to the latter.

Also, he/she will have an easier time gaining domestic support for the ratification of any negotiated deal.

These hypotheses suggest that détente and escalation are likely to reflect how the domestic politics of both sides of a dispute may be aligned or misaligned, which in turn suggests that the timing for such détente and escalation should not be randomly distributed. To the extent that Beijing's behavior in one dispute may reassure or alarm third parties involved in its other disputes, there may be serial dependency. For instance, if Beijing offers persuasive evidence showing its benign intentions in negotiating a particular settlement and its commitment to honor this settlement, its behavior could encourage others to also settle their border disputes with it – thus creating a positive chain reaction. Conversely, if Beijing's behavior in one dispute alarms its other neighbors, one would expect to see their negotiations stalled and settlements delayed – thus perpetuating an impasse in these other disputes. This view inclines one to hypothesize that either all of China's current maritime disputes will linger in a state of deadlock for a long time or, if they should be resolved, these resolutions will come in quick succession in a relatively short period of time.

As just emphasized, the occurrence and subsequent escalation of militarized interstate disputes has to be understood in a context of bilateral and even multilateral interactions. This is another way of saying that it would be analytically unrewarding and politically imprudent to study China's current maritime disputes from the perspective of just one party, such as that of Beijing's policy agenda. When a country is already involved in a territorial contest with another country, one would expect its leaders to be more reluctant to initiate another confrontation with a third country. That is, *ceteris paribus,* leaders should be wary of starting another militarized dispute when it is already in one. Significantly, if these leaders are already participating in multiple concurrent disputes, there is a greater danger that they will decide to escalate. Only highly resolved leaders will involve their country in a second or third dispute after they have already become involved in the first one. Less resolved leaders would not have taken on multiple opponents concurrently. This being the case, the implied higher resolve of leaders involved in multiple disputes tends to be manifested in a greater tendency for them to escalate their disputes. Moreover, behavioral patterns from past interstate conflicts suggest that the closer the site of a contest is located to a country, the more likely it is to be resolved to fight for it (Huth *et al.* 1993). These cross-national empirical regularities are obviously pertinent to developing a more refined understanding of China's maritime disputes, identifying those situations that have a high risk of escalation.

Some other commonly cited variables, however, are pertinent in ways that are more nuanced than typically suggested. For instance, power shifts among the contesting countries, and especially between China and the US, matter, but not in the manner in which national strength is typically assessed in aggregate terms. Whether or not an attempt at deterrence is likely to succeed depends more on the distribution of forces deployed in the immediate vicinity of a potential conflict and the prospects of turning back a military challenge in the early stages of this conflict (Holmes and Yoshihara 2010; Huth and Russett 1993). Moreover, static indicators of military balance are not as predictive of conflict occurrence and escalation as dynamic ones pointing to the rates of armament buildup and changes in relative capabilities. These results from past quantitative research in international relations steer discussions about ongoing power shifts in the Asia Pacific in more specific directions. This research also suggests that alliances – such as the one between the US and Japan, and the one between the US and the Philippines – may discourage China from initiating a challenge in the first place. However, if China has already initiated such a challenge, the existence of such an alliance actually predicts a greater Chinese willingness to escalate this dispute. These alliances must have been discounted by Beijing when it decided to initiate its challenge. Knowing the existence of such an alliance, a less resolved China would not have initiated a challenge in the first place. Thus, the existence of an alliance between the US and another country involved in a dispute with China actually suggests a more resolved China should Beijing decide to initiate a militarized dispute. Finally, if cross-national patterns have a predictive value for Chinese dispositions, the leaders in Beijing are not likely to challenge their foreign counterparts when the latter are in domestic trouble. They will not act opportunistically to exploit this situation as some analysts may expect, because their insecure foreign counterparts are instead likely to stand firm and even push back.

If one accepts the characterization of Beijing's current policy posture as reactive assertiveness and the attribution of a general disposition for it to shelve disputes until an indefinite future time, two implications follow from this premise. First, if there should be a general and steady rise in tension involving China's maritime disputes, this evidence would imply that the contesting countries do not value their economic relationships as much as I have suggested in this analysis. Should this situation arise, all participants would appear to be willing to pursue their maritime claims even if their actions would roil their economic relationships. Such behavior would suggest that they are the "politics first" rather than "economics first" type. This development would augur a basic transformation of regional relations and reverse the process of rising economic interdependence that has been unfolding in recent decades.

Second, should the other claimant states challenge China's maritime claims more actively to the point of taking more confrontational and provocative steps, this behavior would suggest that they have more confidence in being supported by the US. As mentioned earlier, being weaker than China, all these claimant states except perhaps Japan would not want to take on China in a strictly bilateral contest. Internationalizing their bilateral conflicts would be an obvious strategy for these weaker states to overcome their relatively weak bargaining position. The logic of selection – suggesting that officials would not want to get themselves into a situation unless they have considered others' likely reaction to their behavior (in this case, especially that of the US) – motivates this hypothesis. According to this reasoning, escalation of tension involving China's maritime disputes implies a vote of confidence by China's counterparts in the US coming to their aid. Thus, their behavior is indicative of not only perceptions of Beijing's capabilities and intentions, but also those of the US. By the way, the characterization of Beijing's basic posture as reactive assertiveness also argues that the initiative to escalate is likely to come from China's counterparts.

These remarks in turn draw attention to several enduring elements in Beijing's strategic culture, general dispositions that have tended to characterize its management of past conflict situations. One such element in Beijing's approach to diagnosing and addressing a particular problem or situation is for its leaders to first identify the "main contradiction," in communist ideological parlance – that is, to recognize and pivot on the principal antagonistic relationship that holds the key to understanding and deciding the secondary ones. This injunction means that one should always be mindful of the "big picture" – *daju* in Chinese – so that if necessary, one seeks compromise, makes concessions, or sets aside a disagreement in order to more effectively advance one's cause in coping with the principal adversary. Thus, for example, China was quite willing to postpone a confrontation over the Senkaku/Diaoyu Islands when Deng Xiao-ping was eager to recruit Japan to join an anti-Soviet coalition. By analogous logic and as discussed in the previous paragraph, Beijing is likely to analyze its current maritime disputes through the prism of Sino-American relations. China's maritime disputes are likely to be seen as derivative of the overall relationship between Beijing and Washington, and will be subordinated to considerations concerning this relationship. At the same time, Washington's actions and intentions are likely to be taken as the key factor determining how these disputes will evolve. If true, this attribution in turn implies that Beijing's actions and inaction in these disputes are not just aimed at its neighbors involved in disputes with it. Its behavior may very well be intended with Washington in mind, seeking to probe and test US intentions and capabilities. Beijing's declaration of an air defense identification zone in late 2013 and its missile tests in Taiwan's vicinity in 1995–96 are certainly compatible with this proposition, even if these actions might also have other intended purposes. Whether warranted or not, Beijing's predilection for focusing on the main contradiction argues that it will be unlikely to see its maritime disputes as just bilateral conflicts, and that it will assign a principal role and an enormous amount of influence to Washington in shaping future events.

A posture of reactive assertiveness also implies a second element in Chinese strategic thinking, one that emphasizes patience, perseverance, a determination to outwait one's opponent, and a disposition against taking rash action before circumstances mature. The Chinese fable of "the foolish old man who removed mountains" exalted these virtues, which were further propagated in a famous speech by Mao Tse-tung in 1945. This fable told of a stubborn old man who was determined to dig up two mountains by dint of his own and his descendants' labor, and promoted the idea of overcoming long odds by hard work and a commitment to the long haul. Accepting an extended horizon also implies a strategic confidence or optimism that things will work out in one's favor in the long run, despite the possibility of temporary setbacks and reversals in the short run. If true, this tendency implies a belief that time is on China's side and that as such serves to dampen the incentive to launch a preventive attack (to strike an opponent before it becomes stronger). This attribution casts China in a generally defensive rather than offensive role. It tends to contradict the popular depiction of a late rising power offered by the power-transition theory, one that is impulsive and impatient to displace a declining hegemon in order to assume the mantle of global leadership.

The adjective "reactive" in the description of Chinese policy of reactive assertiveness does not imply passivity. As should have been clear from the previous discussion, Beijing is quite capable of resorting to arms. Yet, contrary to the characterizations offered by the power-transition theory and the theory of offensive realism, this analysis argues that any Chinese resort to arms is more likely to be motivated by defensive concerns and out of a sense of insecurity and vulnerability rather than an agenda of aggrandizement. As emphasized already, Beijing is especially likely to react strongly when its leaders perceive that others are trying to exploit its ongoing difficulties and coerce their country under duress. This tendency is likely to be more pronounced in China's dealings with those adversaries that are stronger than it or are at least roughly comparable to it. As explained previously, Beijing appears to be especially adamant in showing that it cannot be cowed or intimidated by such adversaries (e.g., the US, the USSR, Japan, and India). Conversely, it tends to be more conciliatory and even accommodating when dealing with counterparts that are clearly in a much weaker bargaining position. Indeed, when Beijing is able to gain these counterparts' agreement on matters of principle (such as an acknowledgment by them that China's territorial losses in the past were a result of unjust treaties imposed by the imperialists), it is quite willing to make practical concessions in order to reach a settlement. These tendencies in turn imply that Beijing is interested in investing in its general reputation, suggesting that it believes its conduct in one case or situation can have salutary effects in another one. The general reputation that it wishes to cultivate is of course that it can stand up to the strong and even push back, and that it can be reasonable and even nice to those that are weak. This motivation can be pursued in a circuitous manner, such as when China focuses its pressure on a weak link among its opponents in order to demonstrate the adverse consequences of confronting China. The Philippines, a traditional US ally, seems to fit this role in China's multiple maritime disputes in the South China Sea. Beijing can single out such a target in order to discourage other potential opponents. At the same time, it can deliberately pursue conciliatory policies toward other claimants in these disputes, such as Brunei, in order to show the gains to be made through friendly relations with China. As a result of such policies, Beijing is less likely to be confronted by a united front formed by these other claimants.

Taking a general view of the overall situation pertaining to China's maritime disputes, one may encounter long periods of seeming stasis that are interrupted by bursts of activities. This expectation follows from the process of punctuated equilibrium, a process that was originally applied by paleontologists to describe evolutionary history as shown by the available evidence from fossil records (Eldredge and Gould 1972; Gould 2002). These records indicate protracted periods of stability when plant and animal species appeared to show only minor changes. These periods of gradualism and even seeming stagnation can then be followed by abrupt and sharp changes. Thus, species have not apparently evolved in a smooth incremental manner; their transformation has instead appeared as sudden breakthroughs. Political scientists have used punctuated equilibrium to describe the life cycles of political institutions, public policies, enduring rivalries, and international legal systems (Baumgartner and Jones 1993; Diehl and Goertz 2000; Diehl and Ku 2010) as well as the evolution of relations across the Taiwan Strait (Hu 2012). All these accounts seek to explain the dynamics of stasis and change created by the balance of forces between those sustaining inertia and others promoting adjustment and adaptation. The former forces typically manage to maintain the status quo during long periods of gestation, during which the latter forces gradually gain strength. This situation is sustained until the balance of forces tips in favor of change that suddenly introduces a burst of massive transformation.

Ongoing macro trends can thus build up pressure to adjust relations between China and its neighbors, and the cumulative influence of these trends may not become entirely visible until these relations are transformed in major ways and for many countries concurrently. The end of the Cold War and the concomitant phenomenon of falling dominoes that brought about the sudden and unexpected demise of communist regimes all over Eastern and Central Europe provides but one recent dramatic example. China's maritime disputes are both the symptoms and products of the current status of its relations with its neighbors. Specific factors pertinent to the individual disputes aside, Asia Pacific relations are subject to the general macro trends pointing to increasing economic interdependence, declining ideological alignment, rising democratization, and the inexorable pace of generational change for the politically relevant public (Chan 2013). States are developing denser economic ties, turning to omni-directional diplomacy (instead of the Cold War pattern of exclusive alliances), greater openness and sensitivity to popular sentiments, and the replacement of older age cohorts by younger ones. The phenomenon of generational change suggests changing mass values and attitudes, so that nationalist sentiments and historical memories will ebb and materialist concerns will be overtaken by expressive values as a country modernizes (Inglehart 1977, 1990, 1997). Taking a long-term view, recent power shifts favoring China will inevitably decelerate and even reverse over time, so that other latecomers such as India and Indonesia will rise and gain relative power at China's expense.

Most of the processes just mentioned should have a general effect that contributes to easing tension and promotes the resolution of territorial disputes. Although the idea of punctuated equilibrium suggests that it may take a significant amount of time for states' relations to reach a new plateau, the ongoing processes point in a favorable direction for dampening conflict and settling disputes. Not only is this direction for change favorable, but the pace of change appears to be accelerating with respect to ongoing processes promoting economic interdependence, political democracy, and the adoption of more cosmopolitan (and less ethnocentric) values by the mass public. Forgetting and forgiving will over time erase memories of past wrongs (whether actual or perceived), and erode the potency of nationalism. This optimism of course does not deny the possibility of interruptions and even reversals during a period of protracted transition (e.g., newly democratizing countries or ones beset by domestic challenges can experience backsliding).

This said, the ongoing macro processes' collective and cumulative effects over time will be more powerful than the preferences and intentions of individual politicians. For these politicians and the states that they represent, it will always be more rewarding to have the macro trends just mentioned as tailwinds pushing at their back than as headwinds blowing in their face. This is another way of saying that Chinese leaders' future intentions do not take shape in a vacuum. Even when their country becomes more powerful, their intentions to use this power will be influenced by those macro forces just mentioned. Although China's capabilities have grown and may continue to grow in the foreseeable future, its stakes in the existing international order have also grown. Thus, although Beijing has acquired more power to shape this order, its motivations to challenge and destabilize it have concomitantly diminished because it now has a larger stake in it. The historical pattern of its foreign conduct suggests that it has become less bellicose and more moderate as its international position has strengthened over time.

References

Abdelal, Rawi and Jonathan Kirshner. 1999–2000. "Strategy, Economic Relations, and the Definition of National Interests." *Security Studies* 9(1–2), 119–156.

Achen, Christopher and Duncan Snidal. 1989. "Rational Deterrence Theory and Comparative Case Studies." *World Politics* 41(2), 143–169.

Allison, Graham T. and Phillip D. Zelikow. 1999. *Essence of Decision: Explaining the Cuban Missile Crisis*. 2nd edn. New York: Longman.

Anand, Priya. 2011. "Former Professor Dies of Stroke at 86." www.gwchat.com/2011/09/15/former-professor-dies-of-stroke-at-86/ (accessed on February 2, 2013).

Arai, Tatsushi, Shihoko Goto, and Zheng Wang (eds.). 2013. *Clash of National Identities: China, Japan, and the East China Sea Territorial Disputes*. Washington, DC: Wilson Center. www.wilsoncenter.org/sies/default/files/asia_china_seas_web.pdf (accessed on December 12, 2013).

Axelrod, Robert. 1984. *The Evolution of Cooperation*. New York: Basic Books.

Barnhart, Michael A. 1987. *Japan Prepares for Total War: The Search for Economic Security, 1919–1945*. Ithaca, NY: Cornell University Press.

Baumgartner, Frank R. and Bryan D. Jones. 1993. *Agendas and Instability in American Politics*. Chicago: University of Chicago Press.

Benson, Brett V. and Emerson M.S. Niou. 2007. "Economic Interdependence and Peace: A Game-Theoretic Analysis." *Journal of East Asian Studies* 7(1), 35–59.

Berger, Thomas U. 1998. *Cultures of Antimilitarism: National Security in Germany and Japan*. Baltimore: Johns Hopkins University.

Betts, Richard K. 2012. *American Force: Dangers, Delusions, and Dilemmas in National Security*. New York: Columbia University Press.

Blainey, Geoffrey. 1973. *The Causes of War*. New York: Free Press.

Blanchard, Jean-Marc F. 2000. "The U.S. Role in the Sino-Japanese Dispute over the Diaoyu (Senkaku) Islands 1945–1971." *China Quarterly* 161, 95–123.

Boulding, Kenneth. 1962. *Conflict and Defense: A General Theory*. New York: Harper & Row.

Brooks, Stephen G. 1997. "Dueling Realisms." *International Organizations* 51(3), 445–477.

Brooks, Stephen G. and William Wohlforth. 2008. *World out of Balance: International Relations and the Challenge of American Primacy*. Princeton, NJ: Princeton University Press.

Bueno de Mesquita, Bruce. 1981a. *The War Trap*. New Haven, CT: Yale University Press.

Bueno de Mesquita, Bruce. 1981b. "Risk, Power Distributions, and the Likelihood of War." *International Studies Quarterly* 25(4), 541–568.

Bueno de Mesquita, Bruce, Alastair Smith, Randolph M. Siverson, and James D. Morrow. 2003. *The Logic of Political Survival*. Cambridge, MA: MIT Press.

Bush, Richard C. 2005. *Untying the Knot: Making Peace in the Taiwan Strait*. Washington, DC: Brookings Institution Press.

Bush, Richard C. 2013. *Uncharted Strait: The Future of China-Taiwan Relations*. Washington, DC: Brookings Institution Press.

Cha, Victor D. 1999. *Alignment despite Antagonism: The United States-Korea-Japan Security Triangle*. Stanford, CA: Stanford University Press.

Chan, Steve. 2004. "Can't Get No Satisfaction? The Recognition of Revisionist States." *International Relations of the Asia-Pacific* 4(2), 207–238.

Chan, Steve. 2006. "The Politics of Economic Exchange: Carrots and Sticks in Taiwan, China and U.S. Relations." *Issues & Studies* 42(2), 1–22.

Chan, Steve. 2008. *China, the U.S., and the Power-Transition Theory: A Critique*. London: Routledge.

Chan, Steve. 2009a. "Commerce between Rivals: Realism, Liberalism, and Credible Communication across the Taiwan Strait." *International Relations of the Asia-Pacific* 9(3), 435–467.

Chan, Steve. 2009b. "Strategic Anticipation and Adjustment: Ex Ante and Ex Post Information in Explaining Sanction Outcomes." *International Political Science Review* 30(3), 319–338.

Chan, Steve. 2010. "The Taiwan Relations Act Considered from Alternative Perspectives." *Issues & Studies* 46(3), 1–27.

Chan, Steve. 2012a. *Looking for Balance: China, the United States, and Power Balancing in East Asia*. Stanford, CA: Stanford University Press.

Chan, Steve. 2012b. "Loss Aversion and Strategic Opportunism: Third-Party Intervention's Role in War Instigation by the Weak." *Peace & Change* 37(2), 171–194.

Chan, Steve. 2012c. "Programmatic Research on Democratic Peace." *In*: Paul Diehl, Sara McLaughlin Mitchell, and James Morrow (eds.) *A Guide to the Scientific Study of International Processes*. New York: Wiley-Blackwell, 151–169.

Chan, Steve. 2012d. "Money Talks: International Credit/Debt as Credible Commitment." *Journal of East Asian Affairs* 26(1), 77–103.

Chan, Steve. 2013. *Enduring Rivalries in the Asia-Pacific*. Cambridge: Cambridge University Press.

Chan, Steve and William Safran. 2006. "Public Opinion as a Constraint against War: Democracies' Responses to Operation Iraqi Freedom." *Foreign Policy Analysis* 2, 137–156.

Chang, Gordon H. and Di He. 1993. "The Absence of War in the U.S.-China Confrontation over Quemoy and Matsu." *American Historical Review* 98(5), 1500–1524.

Chen, Jian. 1994. *China's Road to the Korean War: The Making of the Sino-American Confrontation*. New York: Columbia University Press.

Chicago Council of Global Affairs. 2010. *Global Views 2010: Constrained Internationalism – Adapting to New Realities; Results of a 2010 National Survey of Public Opinion*. Chicago: Chicago Council of Global Affairs. http://www.thechicagocouncil.org/sites/default/files/Global%20Views%202010.pdf

Choucri, Nazli and Robert C. North. 1975. *Nations in Conflict*. San Francisco: Freeman.

Christensen, Thomas J. 1996. *Useful Adversaries: Grand Strategy, Domestic Mobilization, and Sino-American Conflict, 1947–1958*. Princeton, NJ: Princeton University Press.

Christensen, Thomas J. 2001. "Posing Problems without Catching Up: China's Rise and Challenges for U.S. Security Policy." *International Security* 25(4), 5–40.

Christensen, Thomas J. 2011. "The Advantages of an Assertive China: Responding to Beijing's Abrasive Diplomacy." *Foreign Affairs* 90(2), 54–67.

Christensen, Thomas J. and Jack Snyder. 1990. "Chain Gangs and Passed Bucks: Predicting Alliance Patterns in Multipolarity." *International Organization* 44(2), 137–168.

Chung, Chien-peng. 2004. *Domestic Politics, International Bargaining and China's Territorial Disputes*. London: Routledge.

Ciorciari, John D. 2010. *The Limits of Alignment: Southeast Asia and the Great Powers since 1975*. Washington, DC: Georgetown University Press.

Colaresi, Michael. 2004. "When Doves Cry: International Rivalry, Unreciprocated Cooperation, and Leadership Turnover." *American Journal of Political Science* 48(3), 555–570.

Copeland, Dale C. 1996. "Economic Interdependence and War: A Theory of Trade Expectations." *International Security* 20(4), 5–41.

Copeland, Dale C. 2000. *The Origins of Major War*. Ithaca, NY: Cornell University Press.

Copeland, Dale C. 2007. "Do Reputations Matter?" *Security Studies* 7(1), 33–71.

Crawford, Timothy W. 2003. *Pivotal Deterrence: Third-Party Statecraft and the Pursuit of Peace*. Ithaca, NY: Cornell University Press.

Cunningham, David E. 2011. *Barriers to Peace in Civil War*. Cambridge: Cambridge University Press.

Cunningham, David E., Kristian S. Gleditsch, and Idean Salehyan. 2009. "It Takes Two: A Dyadic Analysis of Civil War Duration and Outcome." *Journal of Conflict Resolution* 53(4), 570–597.

Danilovic, Vesna. 2001a. "Conceptual and Selection Bias Issues in Deterrence." *Journal of Conflict Resolution* 45(1), 97–125.

Danilovic, Vesna. 2001b. "The Sources of Threat Credibility in Extended Deterrence." *Journal of Conflict Resolution* 45(3), 341–369.

Davis Jr., James W. 2000. *Threats and Promises: The Pursuit of International Influence*. Baltimore: Johns Hopkins University Press.

De Castro, Renato Cruz. 2013. "Territorial Disputes, Realpolitik, and Alliance Transformation: The Case of Twenty-first Century Philippine-U.S. Security Relations." *Issues & Studies* 49(1), 141–177.

DeLisle, Jacques. 2012. "Troubled Waters: China's Claims and the South China Sea." *Orbis* 56(4), 608–642.

Deutsch, Karl W., Sidney A. Burrell, Robert A. Kann, Maurice Lee, Jr., Martin Lichtenman, Raymond E. Lindgren, Francis L. Loewenheim, and Richard W. Van Wagenen. 1957. *Political Community and the North Atlantic Area: International Organization in the Light of Historical Experience*. New York: Greenwood.

Deutsch, Karl W. and J. David Singer. 1969. "Multipolar Power Systems and International Stability." *In*: James N. Rosenau (ed.) *International Politics and Foreign Policy: A Reader in Research and Theory*. New York: Free Press, 315–324.

Diehl, Paul F. and Gary Goertz. 2000. *War and Peace in International Rivalry*. Ann Arbor: University of Michigan Press.

Diehl, Paul F. and Charlotte Ku. 2010. *The Dynamics of International Law*. Cambridge: Cambridge University Press.

Downs, Anthony. 1957. *An Economic Theory of Democracy*. New York: Harper and Row.

Downs, Gregory W. 1989. "The Rational Deterrence Debate." *World Politics* 41(20), 225–237.

Drezner, Daniel W. 1999. *The Sanctions Paradox: Economic Statecraft and International Relations*. New York: Cambridge University Press.

Drezner, Daniel W. 2009. "Bad Debts: Assessing China's Financial Influence in Great Power Politics." *International Security* 34(2), 7–45.

Eldredge, Niles and S.J. Gould. 1972. "Punctuated Equilibria: An Alternative to Phyletic Gradualism." *In*: Thomas J.M. Schopf (ed.) *Models of Paleobiology*. San Francisco: Freeman, Cooper, 82–115.

Ellyatt, Holly. 2013. "Falkland Votes With $167 Billion in Oil Revenue at Stake." www.cnbc.com/id/100537413 (accessed March 9, 2013).

Elman, Colin. 2003. "Introduction: Appraising Balance of Power Theory." *In*: John A. Vasquez and Colin Elman (eds.) *Realism and the Balancing of Power: A New Debate*. Upper Saddle River, NJ: Prentice-Hall, 1–22.

Evans, Peter B., Harold K. Jacobson, and Robert Putnam (eds.). 1993. *Double-Edged Diplomacy: International Bargaining and Domestic Politics*. Berkeley: University of California Press.

Farber, Henry S. and Joanne Gowa. 1997. "Common Interests or Common Politics?" *Journal of Politics* 59(2), 393–417.

Fearon, James D. 1994a. "Domestic Political Audiences and the Escalation of International Disputes." *American Political Science Review* 88(3), 577–592.

Fearon, James D. 1994b. "Signaling versus the Balance of Power and Interests: An Empirical Test of a Crisis Bargaining Model." *Journal of Conflict Resolution* 38(2), 236–269.

Fearon, James D. 1995. "Rationalist Explanations for War." *International Organization* 49(3), 379–414.

Fearon, James D. 1997. "Signaling Foreign Policy Interests: Tying Hands versus Sinking Costs." *Journal of Conflict Resolution* 41(1), 68–90.

Finne, Geir. 1977. "*Svalbard: A Soviet/Norwegian Interest Conflict*." M.A. Thesis. University of Colorado, Boulder.

Fischhoff, Baruch and Ruth Beyth. 1975. "'I Knew It Would Happen:' Remembered Probabilities of Once-Future Events." *Organizational Behavior & Human Performance* 13(1), 1–16.

Fogel, Robert. 2010. "$123,000,000,000,000, China's Estimated Economy by the Year 2040. Be Warned." *Foreign Policy* 177(January/February), 1–1.1. http://foreignpolicy.com/articles/2010/01/04/123000000000000 (accessed on December 11, 2013).

Foot, Rosemary and Andrew Walter. 2011. *China, the United States, and Global Order*. Cambridge: Cambridge University Press.

Fortna, Virginia P. 2004. *Peace Time: Cease-Fire Agreements and the Durability of Peace*. Princeton, NJ: Princeton University Press.

Fravel, M. Taylor. 2007a. "Power Shifts and Escalation: Explaining China's Use of Force in Territorial Disputes." *International Security* 32(2), 44–83.

Fravel, M. Taylor. 2007b. "Securing Borders: China's Doctrine and Force Structure for Frontier Defense." *Journal of Strategic Studies* 30(4–5), 705–737.

Fravel, M. Taylor. 2008. *Strong Border, Secure Nation: Cooperation and Order in China's Territorial Disputes*. Princeton, NJ: Princeton University Press.

Fravel, M. Taylor. 2010. "International Relations Theory and China's Rise: Assessing China's Potential for Territorial Expansion." *International Studies Review* 12(4), 505–532.

Fravel, M. Taylor. 2011. "China's Strategy in the South China Sea." *Contemporary Southeast Asia* 33(3), 292–319.

Fravel, M. Taylor. 2012. "All Quiet in the South China Sea: Why China Is Playing Nice (For Now)." *Foreign Affairs*. https://www.foreignaffairs.com/articles/china/2012-03-22/all-quiet-south-china-sea (accessed on August 7, 2015).

Freedman, Lawrence. 1988. *Britain and the Falklands War*. Oxford: Blackwell.

Freedman, Lawrence and Virginia Gamba-Stonehouse. 1991. *Signals of War: The Falklands Conflict of 1982*. Princeton, NJ: Princeton University Press.

Friedberg, Aaron L. 1988. *The Weary Titan: Britain and the Experience of Relative Decline, 1895–1905*. Princeton, NJ: Princeton University Press.

Friedberg, Aaron L. 1993/94. "Ripe for Rivalry: Prospects for Peace in Multipolar Asia." *International Security* 18(1), 5–33.

Friedberg, Aaron L. 2011. *A Contest for Supremacy: China, America, and the Struggle for Mastery in Asia*. New York: Norton.

Frieden, Jeffrey A. 1991. "Invested Interests: The Politics of National Economic Policies in a World of Global Finance." *International Organization* 45(4), 425–452.

Fujihira, Shinju. 2013. "Can Japanese Democracy Cope with China's Rise?" *In*: Tatsushi Arai, Shihoko Goto, and Zheng Wang (eds.) *Clash of National Identities: China, Japan, and the East China Sea Territorial Disputes*. Washington, DC: Wilson Center, 37–45. www.wilsoncenter.org/sies/default/files/asia_china_seas_web.pdf (accessed on December 12, 2013).

Gamba, Virginia. 1987. *The Falklands/Malvinas War: A Model for North-South Crisis Prevention*. London: Allen & Unwin.

Gartner, Scott S. and Randolph M. Siverson. 1996. "War Expansion and War Outcomes." *Journal of Conflict Resolution* 40(1), 4–15.

Gartzke, Erik. 1999. "War Is in the Error Term." *International Organization* 53(3), 567–587.

Gartzke, Erik. 2007. "The Capitalist Peace." *American Journal of Political Science* 51(1), 166–191.

Gartzke, Erik and Quan Li. 2003a. "War, Peace, and the Invisible Hand: Positive Political Externalities of Economic Globalization." *International Studies Quarterly* 47(4), 561–586.

Gartzke, Erik and Quan Li. 2003b. "How Globalization Can Reduce International Conflict." *In:* Gerald Schneider, Kathleen Barbieri and Nils P. Gleditsch (eds.) *Globalization and Conflict.* Boulder, CO: Rowman & Littlefield, 123–140.

Gartzke, Erik, Quan Li, and Charles Boehmer. 2001. "Investing in the Peace: Economic Interdependence and International Conflict." *International Organization* 55(2), 391–438.

Gartzke, Erik and Alex Weisiger. 2014. "Under Construction: Development, Democracy, and Difference as Determinants of Systemic Liberal Peace." *International Studies Quarterly* 58(1), 130–145.

Garver, John W. 1997. *Face Off: China, the United States, and Taiwan's Democratization.* Seattle: University of Washington Press.

George, Alexander L. and Richard Smoke. 1974. *Deterrence in American Foreign Policy.* New York: Columbia University Press.

Gibler, Douglas M. 2007. "Bordering on Peace: Democracy, Territorial Issues, and Conflict." *International Studies Quarterly* 51(3), 509–532.

Gibler, Douglas M. 2014. "Contiguous States, Stable Borders, and the Peace between Democracies." *International Studies Quarterly* 58(1), 126–129.

Gibler, Douglas M. and Jaroslav Tir. 2010. "Settled Borders and Regime Type: Democratic Transitions as Consequences of Peaceful Territorial Transfers." *American Journal of Political Science* 54(4), 951–958.

Gilley, Bruce. 2010. "Not So Dire Straits." *Foreign Affairs* 89(1), 44–56, 58–60.

Glaser, Charles. 2011. "Will China's Rise Lead to War? Why Realism Does Not Mean Pessimism." *Foreign Affairs* 90(2), 80–91.

Goddard, Stacie. 2006. "Uncommon Ground: Indivisible Territory and the Politics of Legitimacy." *International Organization* 60(1), 35–68.

Goh, Evelyn. 2007/08. "Great Powers and Hierarchical Order in Southeast Asia: Analyzing Regional Security Strategies." *International Security* 32(3), 113–157.

Goldstein, Avery. 2013. "First Things First: The Pressing Danger of Crisis Instability in U.S.-China Relations." *International Security* 37(4), 49–89.

Gould, Stephen J. 2002. *The Structure of Evolutionary Theory.* Cambridge, MA: Harvard University Press.

Gowa, Joanne. 1994. *Allies, Adversaries, and International Trade.* Princeton, NJ: Princeton University Press.

Green, Michael J. 2001. *Japan's Reluctant Realism: Foreign Policy Challenges in an Era of Uncertain Power.* New York: Palgrave.

Grieco, Joseph M. 1988. "Anarchy and the Limits of Cooperation: A Realist Critique of the Newest Liberal Institutionalism." *International Organization* 42(3), 485–507.

Gries, H. Peter. 2004. *China's New Nationalism: Pride, Politics and Diplomacy.* Berkeley: University of California Press.

Haas, Ernst B. 1958. *The Uniting of Europe*. Stanford, CA: Stanford University Press.

Hagstrom, Linus. 2012. "'Power Shift' in East Asia? A Critical Reappraisal of Narratives in the Diaoyu/Senkaku Islands Incident in 2010." *Chinese Journal of International Relations* 5, 267–297.

Hayton, Bill. 2014. *The South China Sea: The Struggle for Power in Asia*. New Haven, CT: Yale University Press.

He, Yinan. 2009. *The Search for Reconciliation: Sino-Japanese and German-Polish Relations since World War II*. New York: Cambridge University Press.

Heginbotham, Eric and Richard J. Samuels. 1999. "Mercantile Realism and Japanese Foreign Policy." *In*: Ethan B. Kapstein and Michael Mastanduno (eds.) *Unipolar Politics: Realism and State Strategies after the Cold War*. New York: Columbia University Press, 183–217.

Hemmer, Christopher and Peter J. Katzenstein. 2002. "Why Is There No NATO in Asia? Collective Identity, Regionalism, and the Origins of Multilateralism." *International Organization* 56(3), 575–607.

Hensel, Paul R. 1994. "One Thing Leads to Another: Recurrent Militarized Disputes in Latin America, 1816–1986." *Journal of Peace Research* 31(3), 281–297.

Hensel, Paul R. 1998. "Interstate Rivalry and the Study of Militarized Conflict." *In*: Frank P. Harvey and Ben D. More (eds.) *Conflict in World Politics: Advances in the Study of Crises, War and Peace*. London: Macmillan, 162–204.

Heraclides, Alexis. 1990. "Secessionist Minorities and External Involvement." *International Organization* 44(3), 341–378.

Hermann, Charles F. 1969. "International Crisis as a Situational Variable." *In*: James N. Rosenau (ed.) *International Politics and Foreign Policy: A Reader in Research and Theory*. New York: Free Press, 409–421.

Hirschman, Albert O. 1945. *National Power and the Structure of Foreign Trade*. Berkeley: University of California Press.

Holmes, James R. and Toshi Yoshihara. 2010. "When Comparing Navies, Measure Strength, Not Size." *Global Asia* 5(4), 26–31.

Howell, William G. and Jon C. Pevehouse. 2007. *While Dangers Gather: Congressional Check on Presidential War Powers*. Princeton, NJ: Princeton University Press.

Hsieh, John F.S. and Emerson M.S. Niou. 2005. "Measuring Taiwan Public Opinion on Taiwanese Independence." *China Quarterly* 181(1), 158–168.

Hu, Weixing. 2012. "Explaining Change and Stability in Cross-Strait Relations: A Punctuated Equilibrium Model." *Journal of Contemporary China* 21(78), 933–953.

Huang, Annie. 2012. "China Uses Trade to Influence Taiwan Election." January 9. http://news.yahoo.com/china-uses-trade-influence-taiwan-election-0817 15266.html;_ylt=A0LEV7u9weJUCjwA.4YnnIlQ;_ylu=X3oDMTEzbn M3aWYwBHNlYwNzcgRwb3MDMDQRjb2xvA2JmMQR2dGlkA1lIUzAw M18x (accessed on February 16, 2015).

Hufbauer, Gary C., Jeffrey J. Schott, and Kimberly A. Elliott. 1990. *Economic Sanctions Reconsidered.* 2nd edn. Washington, DC: Institute for International Economics.

Huth, Paul K. 1988a. *Extended Deterrence and the Prevention of War.* New Haven, CT: Yale University Press.

Huth, Paul K. 1988b. "Extended Deterrence and the Outbreak of War." *American Political Science Review* 82(2), 423–444.

Huth, Paul K. 1996. *Standing Your Ground: Territorial Disputes and International Conflict.* Ann Arbor: University of Michigan Press.

Huth, Paul K. 2007. "Reputations and Deterrence: A Theoretical and Empirical Assessment." *Security Studies* 7(1), 72–99.

Huth, Paul K. and Todd L. Allee. 2002. *The Democratic Peace and Territorial Conflict in the Twentieth Century.* New York: Cambridge University Press.

Huth, Paul K., Christopher Gelpi, and D. Scott Bennett. 1993. "The Escalation of Great Power Militarized Disputes: Testing Rational Deterrence Theory and Structural Realism." *American Political Science Review* 87(3), 609–623.

Huth, Paul K. and Bruce Russett. 1984. "What Makes Deterrence Work? Cases from 1900 to 1980." *World Politics* 36(4), 496–525.

Huth, Paul K. and Bruce Russett. 1988. "Deterrence Failure and Crisis Escalation." *International Studies Quarterly* 32(1), 29–46.

Huth, Paul K. and Bruce Russett. 1990. "Testing Deterrence Theory: Rigor Makes a Difference." *World Politics* 42(4), 466–501.

Huth, Paul K. and Bruce Russett. 1993. "General Deterrence between Enduring Rivals: Testing Three Competing Models." *American Political Science Review* 87(1), 61–73.

Huth, Paul K., D. Scott Bennett, and Christopher Gelpi. 1992. "System Uncertainty, Risk Propensity, and International Conflict among the Great Powers." *Journal of Conflict Resolution* 36(3), 478–517.

Inglehart, Ronald. 1977. *The Silent Revolution.* Princeton, NJ: Princeton University Press.

Inglehart, Ronald. 1990. *Culture Shift in Advanced Industrial Countries.* Princeton, NJ: Princeton University Press.

Inglehart, Ronald. 1997. *Modernization and Postmodernization: Cultural, Economic, and Political Change in 43 Societies.* Princeton, NJ: Princeton University Press.

International Crisis Group. 2013 "Dangerous Waters: China-Japan Relations on the Rocks." Asia Report No 245, April 8.

James, Scott C. and David A. Lake. 1989. "The Second Face of Hegemony: Britain's Repeal of the Corn Laws and the American Walker Tariff of 1846." *International Organization* 43(1), 1–29.

Janis, Irving L. 1982. *Groupthink: Psychological Studies of Foreign-Policy Decisions and Fiascoes.* Boston: Houghton Mifflin.

Jerden, Bjorn and Linus Hagstrom. 2012. "Rethinking Japan's China Policy: Japan as an Accommodator in the Rise of China, 1978–2011." *Journal of East Asian Studies* 12(2), 215–250.

Jervis, Robert. 1989. "Rational Deterrence: Theory and Evidence." *World Politics* 41(2), 183–207.

Jervis, Robert, R. Ned Lebow, and Janice G. Stein (eds.). 1985. *Psychology and Deterrence*. Baltimore: Johns Hopkins University Press.

Johnston, Alastair I. 2003. "Is China a Status Quo Power?" *International Security* 7(4), 5–56.

Johnston, Alastair I. 2013. "How New and Assertive Is China's New Assertiveness?" *International Security* 37(4), 7–48.

Kahneman, Daniel, Paul Slovic, and Amos Tversky (eds.). 1982. *Judgments Under Uncertainty: Heuristics and Biases*. Cambridge: Cambridge University Press.

Kahneman, Daniel and Amos Tversky. 1979. "Prospect Theory: An Analysis of Decision under Risk." *Econometrica* 47(2), 263–291.

Kahneman, Daniel and Amos Tversky (eds.). 2000. *Choices, Values and Frames*. Cambridge: Cambridge University Press.

Kang, David C. 2007. *China Rising: Peace, Power, and Order in East Asia*. New York: Columbia University Press.

Karabell, Zachary. 2009. *Superfusion: How China and America Became One Economy and Why the World's Prosperity Depends on It*. New York: Simon & Schuster.

Kastner, Scott L. 2006. "Does Economic Integration across the Taiwan Strait Make Military Conflict Less Likely?" *Journal of East Asian Studies* 6(3), 319–346.

Kastner, Scott L. 2007. "When Do Conflicting Political Relations Affect International Trade?" *Journal of Conflict Resolution* 51(4), 664–688.

Kastner, Scott L. 2009. *Political Conflict and Economic Interdependence across the Taiwan Strait*. Stanford, CA: Stanford University Press.

Kastner, Scott L. and Phillip C. Saunders. 2012. "Is China a Status Quo or Revisionist State? Leadership Travel as an Empirical Indicator of Foreign Policy Priorities." *International Studies Quarterly* 56(1), 163–177.

Kaufman, Chaim. 2004. "Threat Inflation and the Failure of the Marketplace of Ideas: The Selling of the Iraq War." *International Security* 29(1), 5–48.

Kaufman, Chaim. 2005. "Selling the Market Short: The Marketplace of Ideas and the Iraq War." *International Security* 29(4), 196–207.

Kaufman, William. 1956. "The Requirements of Deterrence." *In:* William Kaufman (ed.) *Military Policy and National Security*. Princeton, NJ: Princeton University Press, 12–38.

Kegley Jr., Charles W. and Margaret Hermann. 1995. "Military Intervention and the Democratic Peace." *International Interactions* 21(1), 1–21.

Kegley Jr., Charles W. and Margaret Hermann. 1996. "How Democracies Use Intervention: A Neglected Dimension in Studies of the Democratic Peace." *Journal of Peace Research* 33(3), 309–322.

Keohane, Robert O. and Joseph S. Nye. 1977. *Power and Interdependence: World Politics in Transition*. Boston: Little, Brown.

Khanna, Parag and John Gilman. 2012. "Does Norway Hold Key to Solving China Sea Dispute?" www.cnn.com/2012/11/13/opinion/khanna-south-china-sea-dispute/index.html (accessed on January 22, 2013).

Khong, Yuen Fong. 1992. *Analogies at War: Korea, Munich, Dien Bien Phu, and the Vietnam Decisions of 1965*. Princeton, NJ: Princeton University Press.

Kinney, Douglas. 1989. *National Interest/National Honor: The Diplomacy of the Falklands Crisis*. New York: Praeger.

Kirshner, Jonathan. 2000. "Rationalist Explanations of War?" *Security Studies* 10(1), 143–150.

Kirshner, Jonathan. 2014. *American Power after the Financial Crisis*. Ithaca, NY: Cornell University Press.

Kissinger, Henry. 1994. *Diplomacy*. New York: Simon & Schuster.

Koo, Min Gyo. 2009. *Island Disputes and Maritime Regime Building in East Asia: Between a Rock and a Hard Place*. New York: Springer.

Kuomintang. 2013. "Opinion Poll on Taiwan People's National Identity." www .kmt.org.tw/english/page.aspx?type=article&mnum=112&anum=1262, (accessed on March 1, 2013).

Kydd, Andrew H. 1997. "Sheep in Sheep's Clothing: Why Security-Seekers Do Not Fight Each Other." *Security Studies* 7(1), 114–154.

Kydd, Andrew H. 2005. *Trust and Mistrust in International Relations*. Princeton, NJ: Princeton University Press.

Lasswell, Harold D. 1941. "The Garrison State." *American Journal of Sociology* 46 (4), 455–468.

Lebow, R. Ned. 1981. *Between Peace and War: The Nature of International Crisis*. Baltimore: Johns Hopkins University Press.

Lebow, R. Ned. 1985. "Miscalculation in the South Atlantic: The Origins of the Falklands War." *In*: Robert Jervis, R. Ned Lebow, and Janice G. Stein (eds.) *Psychology and Deterrence*. Baltimore: Johns Hopkins University Press, 85–124.

Lebow, R. Ned. 2010. *Forbidden Fruit: Counterfactuals and International Relations*. Princeton, NJ: Princeton University Press.

Lebow, R. Ned and Janice G. Stein. 1989. "Rational Deterrence Theory: I Think, Therefore I Deter." *World Politics* 4(2), 208–224.

Lebow, R. Ned and Janice G. Stein. 1990. "Deterrence: The Elusive Dependent Variable." *World Politics* 42(3), 336–369.

Lemke, Douglas and William Reed. 2001. "War and Rivalry among Great Powers." *American Journal of Political Science* 45(2), 457–469.

Leng, Tse-kang. 1996. *The Taiwan-China Connection: Democracy and Development Across the Taiwan Straits*. Boulder, CO: Westview.

Levy, Jack S. 1981. "Alliance Formation and War Behavior: An Analysis of the Great Powers, 1495–1975." *Journal of Conflict Resolution* 25(4), 581–614.

Levy, Jack S. 1987. "Declining Power and the Preventive Motivation for War." *World Politics* 60(1), 82–107.

Levy, Jack S. 2008. "Preventive War and Democratic Politics." *International Studies Quarterly* 52(1), 1–24.

Levy, Jack S. and William R. Thompson. 2005. "Hegemonic Threats and Great-Power Balancing in Europe, 1495–1999." *Security Studies* 14(1), 1–33.

Levy, Jack S. and William R. Thompson. 2010. "Balancing on Land and at Sea: Do States Ally Against the Leading Global Power?" *International Security* 35(1), 7–43.

Li, Mingjiang. 2011. "China's New Security Posture: Non-Confrontational Assertiveness." *East Asia Forum*, June 4, www.eastasiaforum.org/2011/06/

04/china-s-new-security-posture-non-confrontational-assertiveness (accessed on January 30, 2015).

Li, Mingjiang. 2012. "China's Non-Confrontational Assertiveness in the South China Sea." East Asia Forum, Jun 14, www.eastasiaforum.org/2013/06/14/china-s-non-confronational-assertiveness-in-the-south-china-sea (accessed on January 30, 2015).

Liberman, Peter. 1996. "Trading with the Enemy: Security and Relative Economic Gains." *International Security* 21(1), 147–175.

Lieberthal, Kenneth. 2005. "Preventing a War over Taiwan." *Foreign Affairs* 84(2), 53–63.

Lippincot, Don and Gregory F. Treverton, 1988. "Negotiations Concerning the Falklands/Malvinas Dispute; Part A: Breakdown of Negotiations and Part B: The Haig Mediation Effort." Pew Case Studies 406. Washington, DC: Georgetown University Institute for the Study of Diplomacy.

Liu, Xiaoyuan. 2006. *Reins of Liberation: An Entangled History of Mongolian Independence, Chinese Territoriality, and Great Power Hegemony, 1911–1950.* Washington, DC: Woodrow Wilson Center Press.

Lo, Chi-kin. 1989. *China's Policy towards Territorial Disputes: The Case of the South China Sea Islands.* London: Routledge.

Lobell, Steven E. 2007. "The Second Face of Security: Britain's 'Smart' Appeasement Policy towards Japan and Germany." *International Relations of the Asia-Pacific* 7(1), 73–98.

Long, William J. 1996. *Economic Incentives and Bilateral Cooperation.* Ann Arbor: University of Michigan Press

Little, Richard. 2007. "British Neutrality versus Offshore Balancing in the American Civil War: The English School Strikes Back." *Security Studies* 16(1), 68–95.

Mani, Kristina. 2011. *Democratization and Military Transformation in Argentina and Chile: Rethinking Rivalry.* Boulder, CO: FirstForumPress.

Mansfield, Edward D. and Jack Snyder. 2005. *Electing to Fight: Why Emerging Democracies Go to War.* Cambridge, MA: The MIT Press.

Mason, T. David, Mehmet Gurses, Patrick T. Brandt, and Jason Michael Quinn. 2011. "Why Civil Wars Recur: Conditions for Durable Peace after Civil War." *International Studies Perspectives* 12(2), 171–189.

Mastanduno, Michael. 1992. *Economic Containment: CoCom and the Politics of East-West Trade.* Ithaca, NY: Cornell University Press.

May, Ernest R. 1973. *'Lessons' of the Past: The Use and Misuse of History in American Foreign Policy.* New York: Oxford University Press.

McDonald, Patrick J. 2009. *The Invisible Hand of Peace: Capitalism, the War Machine, and International Relations Theory.* New York: Cambridge University Press.

Mearsheimer, John J. 2001. *The Tragedy of Great Power Politics.* New York: Norton.

Mearsheimer, John J. 2006. "China's Unpeaceful Rise." *Current History* 105 (690), 160–162.

Mearsheimer, John J. and Stephen M. Walt. 2003. "An Unnecessary War." *Foreign Policy* (January–February), 50–59.

Mercer, Jonathan. 1996. *Reputation and International Politics*. Ithaca, NY: Cornell University Press.

Mercer, Jonathan. 2007. "Reputation and Rational Deterrence Theory." *Security Studies* 7(1), 100–113.

Mercer, Jonathan. 2013. "Emotion and Strategy in the Korean War." *International Organization* 67(2), 221–252.

Meernik, J. 1996. "U.S. Military Interventions and the Promotion of Democracy." *Journal of Peace Research* 33(4), 391–402.

Merritt, Richard. 1966. *Symbols of American Community*. New Haven, CT: Yale University Press.

Mitchell, Sara McLaughlin and Brandon C. Prins. 1999. "Beyond Territorial Contiguity: Issues at Stake in Democratic Militarized Interstate Disputes." *International Studies Quarterly* 43(1), 169–183.

Mitrany, David. 1966. *A Working Peace System*. Chicago: Quadrangle Books

Morgan, Patrick M. 1977. *Deterrence: A Conceptual Analysis*. Beverly Hills, CA: Sage.

Morrow, James D. 1989. "Capabilities, Uncertainty, and Resolve: A Limited Information Model of Crisis Bargaining." *American Journal of Political Science* 33(4), 941–972.

Morrow, James D. 1997. "When Do 'Relative Gains' Impede Trade?" *Journal of Conflict Resolution* 41(1), 12–37.

Morrow, James D. 2003. "Assessing the Role of Trade as a Source of Costly Signals." *In*: Edward D. Mansfield and Brian Pollins (eds.) *Economic Interdependence and International Conflict*. Ann Arbor: University of Michigan Press, 89–95.

Moss, Trevor. 2012a. "China's Not-So-Hard-Power Strategy." http://thediplomat.com/2012/06/28/chinas-not-so-hard-power-strategy.

Moss, Trevor. 2012b. "China's Restrained Nationalism." http://thediplomat.com/flashpoints-blog/2012/08/28/china-restrained-natinalism/comment-page-1/.

Most, Benjamin A. and Harvey Starr. 1989. *Inquiry, Logic and International Politics*. Columbia: University of South Carolina Press.

Natebuff, Barry. 1989. "Rational Deterrence in an Imperfect World." *World Politics* 43(3), 313–335.

Nincic, Miroslav. 2011. *The Logic of Positive Engagement*. Ithaca, NY: Cornell University Press.

Odgaard, Liselott. 2013. "Coexistence and Nationalism in China's Maritime Disputes in the East and South China Sea." Presented at the European Union Academic Programme Annual Conference in Hong Kong, Security Communities and Security Risk Management in Europe and East Asia, University of Hong Kong, November 28.

Olson, Mancur, Jr. 1965. *The Logic of Collective Action: Public Goods and the Theory of Groups*. Cambridge, MA: Harvard University Press.

Olson, Mancur, Jr. 1982. *The Rise and Decline of Nations: Economic Growth, Stagflation, and Social Rigidities*. New Haven, CT: Yale University Press.

Organski, A.F.K. 1958. *World Politics*. New York: Knopf.

Organski, A.F.K. and Jacek Kugler. 1980. *The War Ledger*. Chicago: University of Chicago Press.

Owen, John. M. 1997. *Liberal Peace, Liberal War: American Politics and International Security*. Ithaca, NY: Cornell University Press.

Papayoanou, Paul A. 1999. *Power Ties: Economic Interdependence, Balancing, and War*. Ann Arbor: University of Michigan Press.

Papayoanou, Paul A. and Scott L. Kastner. 1999. "Sleeping with the (Potential) Enemy: Assessing the U.S. Policy of Engagement with China." *Security Studies* 9(1/2), 157–187.

Pape, Robert A. 1997. "Economic Sanctions Do Not Work." *International Security* 22(2), 90–136.

Park, Johann and Michael Colaresi. 2014. "Safe Across the Border: The Continued Significance of the Democratic Peace When Controlling for Stable Borders." *International Studies Quarterly* 58(1), 118–125.

Pastor, Robert A. 1993. "The United States and Central America: Interlocking Debates." *In*: Peter B. Evans, Harold K. Jacobson, and Robert D. Putnam (eds.) *Double-Edged Diplomacy: International Bargaining and Domestic Politics*. Berkeley: University of California Press, 303–329.

Peceny, Mark. 1999. *Democracy at the Point of Bayonets*. University Park: Pennsylvania State University.

Peceny, Mark, Caroline Beer, and Shannon Sanchez-Terry. 2002. "Dictatorial Peace?" *American Political Science Review* 96(1), 15–26.

Przeworski, Adam and Henry Teune. 1970. *The Logic of Comparative Social Inquiry*. New York: Wiley.

Putnam, Robert D. 1988. "Diplomacy and Domestic Politics: The Logic of Two-Level Games." *International Organization* 42(3), 427–460.

Purser, Ben. 2013. *"What Explains Why Some Maritime Disputes Are Settled While Others Remain Contested?"* M.A. Qualifying Paper. University of Colorado, Boulder.

Raine, Sarah and Christian Le Miere. 2013. *Regional Disorder: The South China Sea Disputes*. London: Routledge.

Ray, James Lee and Bruce Russett. 1996. "The Future as Arbiter of Theoretical Controversies: Predictions, Explanations and the End of the Cold War." *British Journal of Political Science* 26(4), 441–470.

Reiter, Dan and Eric R. Tillman. 2002. "Public, Legislative, and Executive Constraints on the Democratic Initiation of Conflict." *Journal of Politics* 64(3), 810–826.

Resnick, Evan. 2013. "The Perils of Containing China." RSIS Commentary 069/2013 distributed electronically by getresponse@getresponse.com on behalf of RSIS Publications [rsispublication@ntu.edu.sg], Nanyang Technological University, Singapore.

Rigger, Shelley. 2001. *From Opposition to Power: Taiwan's Democratic Progressive Party*. Boulder, CO: Lynne Rienner.

Rigger, Shelley. 2006. *Taiwan's Rising Rationalism: Generations, Politics, and "Taiwanese Nationalism."* Washington, DC: East-West Center Policy Studies.

Rigger, Shelley. 2011. "Why Giving Up Taiwan Will Not Help US with China." AEI Asian Outlook, www.aei.org/article/foreign-and-defense-policy/regional/asia/why-giving-up-tiwan-will-not-help-us-with-china (accessed on July 2, 2013).

Ripsman, Norrin M. and Jack S. Levy. 2007. "The Preventive War that Never Happened: Britain, France, and the Rise of Germany in the 1930s." *Security Studies* 16(1), 32–67.

Rosato, Sebatian. 2003. "The Flawed Logic of Democratic Peace Theory." *American Political Science Review* 97(4), 585–602.

Rosenau, James N. 1969. *Linkage Politics: Essays on the Convergence of National and International Systems*. New York: Free Press.

Ross, Robert S. 1999. "The Geography of Peace: East Asia in the Twenty-first Century." *International Security* 23(4), 81–118.

Ross, Robert S. 2004. "Bipolarity and Balancing in East Asia." *In*: T.V. Paul, James J. Wirtz, and Michel Fortmann (eds.) *Balance of Power: Theory and Practice in the 21st Century*. Stanford, CA: Stanford University Press, 267–304.

Russett, Bruce M. 1969. "Refining Deterrence Theory: The Japanese Attack on Pearl Harbor." *In*: Dean G. Pruitt and Richard C. Snyder (eds.) *Theory and Research on the Causes of War*. Englewood Cliffs, NJ: Prentice Hall, 127–135.

Russett, Bruce M. and John R. Oneal. 2001. *Triangulating Peace: Democracy, Interdependence and International Organizations*. New York: Norton.

Samaniego, Catherine. 2012. "The Scarborough Shoal Dispute in America's Asia-Pacific Pivot." RSIS Commentary 090/2012 distributed electronically by getresponse@getresponse.com on behalf of RSIS Publications [rsispublication@ntu.edu.sg], Nanyang Technological University, Singapore.

Sambanis, Nicholas. 2000. "Partition as a Solution to Ethnic War: An Empirical Critique of the Theoretical Literature." *World Politics* 52(4), 37–83.

Sanders, Alan J.K. 1987. *Mongolia: Politics, Economics and Society*. Boulder, CO: Lynne Rienner.

Sartori, Anne E. 2002. "The Might of the Pen: A Reputational Theory of Communication in International Disputes." *International Organization* 56(1), 121–149.

Sartori, Anne E. 2005. *Deterrence by Diplomacy*. Princeton, NJ: Princeton University Press.

Saunders, Phillip C. and Scott L. Kastner. 2009. "Bridge over Troubled Waters: Envisioning a China-Taiwan Peace Agreement." *International Security* 33(4), 87–114.

Schelling, Thomas C. 1966. *Arms and Influence*. New Haven, CT: Yale University Press.

Schoppa, Leonard J. 1993. "Two-Level Games and Bargaining Outcomes: Why Gaiatsu Succeeds in Japan in Some Cases but Not Others." *International Organization* 47(3), 353–386.

Schroeder, Paul W. 1976. "Alliances, 1815–1945: Weapons of Power and Tools of Management." *In*: Klaus Knorr (ed.) *Historical Dimensions of National Security Problems*. Lawrence: University Press of Kansas, 227–262.

Schroeder, Paul W. 1994. "Historical Reality vs. Neo-realist Theory." *International Security* 19(1), 108–138.

Schultz, Kenneth A. 2001. *Democracy and Coercive Diplomacy*. Cambridge: Cambridge University Press.

Schweller, Randall L. 2006. *Unanswered Threats: Political Constraints on the Balance of Power*. Princeton, NJ: Princeton University Press.

Senese, Paul D. and John A. Vasquez. 2008. *The Steps to War: An Empirical Study*. Princeton, NJ: Princeton University Press.

Shambaugh, David. 2004/05. "China Engages Asia: Reshaping the Regional Order." *International Security* 29(3), 64–99.

Shen, Zhihua and Danhui Li. 2011. *After Leaning to One Side: China and Its Allies in the Cold War*. Stanford, CA: Stanford University Press.

Simmons, Beth A. 1994. *Who Adjusts? Domestic Sources of Foreign Economic Policy during the Interwar Years*. Princeton, NJ: Princeton University.

Simmons, Beth A. 2002. "Capacity, Commitment, and Compliance: International Institutions and Territorial Disputes." *Journal of Conflict Resolution* 46(6), 823–856.

Simon, Sheldon W. 2012. "Conflict and Diplomacy in the South China Sea: The View from Washington." *Asian Survey* 52(6), 995–1018.

Singer, J. David and Melvin Small. 1968. "Alliance Aggregation and the Onset of War, 1815–1945." *In*: J. David Singer (ed.) *Quantitative International Politics: Insights and Evidence*. New York: Free Press, 247–286.

Singh, Ellen C. 1980. *The Spitsbergen (Svalbard) Question: United States Foreign Policy, 1907–1935*. Oslo: Universitetsforlaget.

Siverson, Randolph M. and Michael R. Tennefoss. 1984. "Power, Alliance, and the Escalation of International Conflict, 1815–1965." *American Political Science Review* 78(4), 1057–1069.

Slantchev, Branislav. 2010. "Feigning Weakness." *International Organization* 634 (3), 357–388.

Smith, Alastair. 1998. "Extended Deterrence and Alliance Formation." *International Interactions* 24 (4), 315–343.

Snyder, Glenn H. 1997. *Alliance Politics*. Ithaca, NY: Cornell University Press.

Snyder, Jack. 1993. "East-West Bargaining Over Germany: The Search for Synergy in a Two-Level Game." *In*: Peter B. Evans, Harold K. Jacobson, and Robert D. Putnam (eds.) *Double-Edged Diplomacy: International Bargaining and Domestic Politics*. Berkeley: University of California Press, 104–127.

Snyder, Jack and Erica D. Borghard. 2011. "The Cost of Empty Threats: A Penny, Not a Pound." *American Political Science Review* 105(3), 437–456.

Solingen, Etel. 2007. "Pax Asiatica versus Belli Levantina: The Foundations of War and Peace in East Asia and the Middle East." *American Political Science Review* 101(4), 757–780.

Starr, Harvey and Benjamin A. Most. 1976. "The Substance and Study of Borders in International Relations Research." *International Studies Quarterly* 20(4), 581–620.

Starr, Harvey and Benjamin A. Most. 1978. "A Return Journey: Richardson, 'Frontiers,' and Wars in the 1946–1965 Era." *Journal of Conflict Resolution* 22(3), 441–467.

Stein, Janice G. 1993. "The Political Economy of Security Agreements: The Linked Costs of Failure at Camp David." *In*: Peter B. Evans, Harold K. Jacobson, and Robert D. Putnam (eds.) *Double-Edged Diplomacy: International Bargaining and Domestic Politics*. Berkeley: University of California Press, 77–103.

Stent, Angela E. 1999. *Russia and Germany Reborn: Unification, the Soviet Collapse, and the New Europe*. Princeton, NJ: Princeton University Press.

Swaine, Michael. 2013. "Chinese Views Regarding the Senkaku/Diaoyu Islands Dispute," *China Leadership Monitor*, 41. http://carnegieendowment.org/files/CLM41MS.pdf.

Swaine, Michael D. and M. Taylor Fravel. 2011. "China's Assertive Behavior, Part Two: The Maritime Periphery." *China Leadership Monitor*, 35. http://media.hoover.org/sites/default/files/documents/CLM35M5.pdf.

Tharoor, Ishaan. 2013. "A Sea of Troubles: Asia Today Compared to Europe before World War I." world.time.com/2013/02/01/a-sea-of-troubles-asia-to day-compared-to-europe-before-world-war-i/ (accessed on February 10, 2013).

Thayer, Carlyle A. 2012. "Standoff in the South China Sea: Scarborough Shoal Standoff Reveals Blunt Edge of China's Peaceful Rise." *Yale Global Online*. http:/yalegobal.yale.edu/content/standoff-south-china-sea (accessed on January 12, 2014)

Thompson, William R. 2003. "A Streetcar Named Sarajevo: Catalysts, Multiple Causation Chains, and Rivalry Structures." *International Studies Quarterly* 47(3), 453–474.

Tillema, Herbert K. and John R. Van Wingen. 1982. "Law and Power in Military Intervention by Major Powers after WWII." *International Studies Quarterly* 26(2), 220–250.

Tir, Jaroslav. 2003. "Averting Armed International Conflicts Through State-to-State Territorial Transfers." *Journal of Politics* 65(4), 1235–1257.

Tir, Jaroslav. 2005a. "Keeping the Peace after Secessions: Territorial Conflicts between Rump and Secessionist States." *Journal of Conflict Resolution* 49(5), 713–741.

Tir, Jaroslav. 2005b. "Dividing Countries to Promote Peace: Prospects for Long-Term Success in Partitions." *Journal of Peace Research* 42(5), 545–562.

Tir, Jaroslav. 2010. "Territorial Diversion: Diversionary Theory of War and Territorial Conflict." *Journal of Politics* 72(2), 413–425.

Tir, Jaroslav and Paul F. Diehl. 2002. "Geographic Dimensions of Enduring Rivalries." *Political Geography* 21(2), 262–286.

Tonnesson, Stein. 2013. "Steps Forward for China to Resolve its Disputes in the South China Sea." *Global Asia* 8(2), 92–100.

Trachtenberg, Marc. 2012. "Audience Costs: An Historical Analysis." *Security Studies* 21, 3–42.

Treisman, Daniel S. 2004. "Rational Appeasement." *International Organization* 58(2), 345–373.

Tsebelis, George. 2002. *Veto Players: How Political Institutions Work*. Princeton, NJ: Princeton University Press.

Tucker, Nancy Bernkopf (ed.). 2005. *Dangerous Strait: The U.S.-Taiwan-China Crisis*. New York: Columbia University Press.

Tucker, Nancy Bernkopf and Bonnie Glaser. 2011. "Should the United States Abandon Taiwan?" *Washington Quarterly* 34(4), 23–37.

Tversky, Amos and Daniel Kahneman. 1974. "Judgment under Uncertainty: Heuristics and Biases." *Science* 185(4157), 1124–1131.

Tyler, Patrick. 1999. *A Great Wall, Six Presidents and China: An Investigative History*. New York: Perseus.

Valencia, Mark J. and Hong Nong. 2013. "Joint Development Possibilities: What, Where, Who and How?" *Global Asia* 8(2), 102–109.

Vasquez, John A. 1993. *The War Puzzle*. New York: Cambridge University Press.

Vasquez, John A. 2009. *The War Puzzle Revisited*. New York: Cambridge University Press.

Vasquez, John A. and Marie T. Henehan. 2010. *Territory, War, and Peace*. London: Routledge.

Vasquez, John A. and Christopher S. Leskiw. 2001. "The Origins and War Proneness of Interstate Rivalries." *Annual Review of Political Science* 4, 295–316.

Wachman, Alan M. 2007. *Why Taiwan?: Geostrategic Rationales for China's Territorial Integrity*. Stanford, CA: Stanford University Press.

Wagner, R. Harrison. 1988. "Economic Interdependence, Bargaining Power, and Political Influence." *International Organization* 42(3), 461–483.

Wagner, R. Harrison. 2000. "Bargaining and War." *American Journal of Political Science* 44 (3), 469–484.

Walt, Stephen M. 1987. *The Origins of Alliances*. Ithaca, NY: Cornell University Press.

Walter, Barbara F. 2002. *Committing to Peace: The Successful Settlement of Civil Wars*. Princeton, NJ: Princeton University Press.

Walter, Barbara F. 2003. "Explaining the Intractability of Territorial Conflict." *International Studies Review* 5(4), 137–153.

Walter, Barbara F. 2006. "Building Reputation: Why Governments Fight Some Separatists but Not Others." *American Journal of Political Science* 50(2), 313–330.

Waltz, Kenneth N. 1979. *Theory of International Politics*. Reading, MA: Addison-Wesley.

Wang, Yuan-kang. 2002. "Preserving Peace in the Taiwan Strait." *Chinese Political Science Review* 33, 149–174.

Wang, Yuan-kang. 2011. *Harmony and War: Confucian Culture and Chinese Power Politics*. New York: Columbia University Press.

Wang, Yuan-kang. 2013. "Taiwan Public Opinion on Cross-Strait Security Issues: Implications for US Foreign Policy." *Strategic Studies Quarterly* 7(2), 93–113.

Wang, Zheng. 2012. *Never Forget National Humiliation: Historical Memory in Chinese Politics and Foreign Relations*. New York: Columbia University Press.

Weeks, Jessica. 2008. "Autocratic Audience Costs: Regime Type and Signaling Resolve." *International Organization* 62(1), 35–64.

Weeks, Jessica. 2012. "Strongmen and Straw Men: Authoritarian Regimes and the Initiation of Interstate Conflict." *American Political Science Review* 106(2), 326–347.

Weiss, Jessica Chen. 2012. "Authoritarian Signalling, Mass Audiences, and Nationalist Protest in China." *International Organization* 67(1), 1–35.

Weiss, Jessica Chen. 2014. *Powerful Patriots: Nationalist Protest in China's Foreign Relations*. Oxford: Oxford University Press.

Werner, Suzanne and Amy Yuen. 2005. "Making and Keeping Peace." *International Organization* 59(2), 261–292.

Whiteman, Hilary. 2013. "How a Remote Rock Split China and Japan." www .cnn.com/2012/09/17/world/asia/china-japan-islands-dispute-explained (accessed on February 6, 2013).

Whiting, Allen S. 1960. *China Crosses the Yalu: The Decision to Enter the Korean War*, New York: Macmillian, 1960.

Wohlforth, William C. (ed.) 2003. *Cold War Endgame: Oral History, Analysis, and Debates*. University Park: Pennsylvania State University Press.

Wolford, Scott. 2007. "The Turnover Trap: New Leaders, Reputation, and International Conflict." *American Journal of Political Science* 51(4), 772–788.

Womack, Brantly. 2011. "The Spratlys: From Dangerous Ground to Apple of Discord." *Contemporary Southeast Asia* 33(3), 370–387.

Wu, Samuel G. 1990. "To Attack or Not to Attack: A Theory and Empirical Assessment of Extended Immediate Deterrence." *Journal of Conflict Resolution* 34(3), 531–552

Yang, Daqing. 2013. "History: From Dispute to Dialogue." *In*: Tatsushi Arai, Shihoko Goto, and Zheng Wang (eds.) *Clash of National Identities: China, Japan, and the East China Sea Territorial Disputes*. Washington, DC: Wilson Center, 19–28. www.wilsoncenter.org/sies/default/files/asia_china_seas_ web.pdf (accessed on December 12, 2013).

Yarbrough, Beth V. and Robert M. Yarbrough. 1986. "Reciprocity, Bilateralism, and Economic 'Hostage': Self-enforcing Agreements in International Trade." *International Studies Quarterly* 30(1), 7–21.

Young, Robert A. 1997. "How do Peaceful Secessions Happen?" *In*: David Carment and Patrick James (eds.) *International Politics of Ethnic Conflict*. Pittsburgh: University of Pittsburgh Press, 45–60.

Yuan, Elizabeth. 2013. "Former Japanese Prime Minister Slammed as 'Traitor' at Home." www.cnn.com/2013/01/18/world/asia/japan-hatoyama-china/in dex.html (accessed on February 2, 2013).

Zhang, Shu Guang. 1998. *Deterrence and Strategic Culture: Chinese-American Confrontations, 1949–1958*. Ithaca, NY: Cornell University Press.

Name Index

Subject Index

231